D0087807

The Origins of the Present Troubles in Northern Ireland

John Whyte

10 June 1997

Belfast, N. I.

ORIGINS OF MODERN WARS
General editor: *Harry Hearder*

The Origins of the Present Troubles in Northern Ireland

CAROLINE KENNEDY-PIPE

LONGMAN
London and New York

Addison Wesley Longman Limited
Edinburgh Gate
Harlow
Essex CM20 2JE
United Kingdom
and Associated Companies throughout the world

*Published in the United States of America
by Addison Wesley Longman Inc., New York*

© Addison Wesley Longman Limited 1997

The right of Caroline Kennedy-Pipe to be identified
as author of this Work has been asserted by
her in accordance with the Copyright,
Designs and Patents Act 1988.

All rights reserved; no part of this publication may be
reproduced, stored in a retrieval system, or transmitted
in any form or by any means, electronic, mechanical,
photocopying, recording, or otherwise without either
the prior written permission of the Publishers or a
licence permitting restricted copying in the United
Kingdom issued by the Copyright Licensing Agency
Ltd., 90 Tottenham Court Road, London W1P 9HE.

First published 1997

ISBN 0 582 21712 1 CSD
ISBN 0 582 10073 9 PPR

British Library Cataloguing-in-Publication Data

A catalogue record for this book is available
from the British Library

Library of Congress Cataloging-in-Publication Data

Kennedy-Pipe, Caroline, 1961-
    The origins of the present troubles in Northern Ireland / Caroline
Kennedy-Pipe.
        p.   cm. — (Origins of modern wars)
    Includes bibliographical references (p.   ) and index.
    ISBN 0-582-21712-1. — ISBN 0-582-10073-9 (pbk.)
        1. Northern Ireland—History—1969-1994.   2. Political violence-
-Northern Ireland—History—20th century.   3. Nationalism—Northern
Ireland—History—20th century.   4. Northern Ireland—History,
Military.   5. Irish unification question.   I. Title.   II. Series.
DA990.U46K464   1997
941.60824—dc20   96-21149
                                                                          CIP

Set by 7 in 10/12 New Baskerville
Produced by Longman Singapore Publishers (Pte) Ltd.
Printed in Singapore

Contents

List of Maps

Editor's Foreword

To give a fair account and show a deep understanding of the Troubles in Northern Ireland and their origins requires historical interpretation and imagination of a high order. Dr Kennedy-Pipe has shown precisely that kind of interpretation and imagination in the writing of this book. She has managed to expound the ideas and the motives of the various parties involved in the dispute, and to show how these have changed with changing circumstances.

The book is the sixteenth in the series, and marks a departure in that it is concerned with neither an international, nor – in the strict sense – a civil war. To include it in a series of volumes on the origins of wars may be considered to make a statement of a political nature. Only the IRA and one small extreme section of the Loyalists would claim that the Troubles constitute 'a war'. In International Law we are certainly not dealing with 'a war', and the editor, by including the volume in the series, equally certainly does not wish to make a statement of a political nature. The Troubles have been 'a war' only in the general sense, as one might speak of 'a war against the drug traffic', or 'a war to defend the environment'. Yet some of the characteristics of a war have been present, even if two organized armies have not been consistently facing each other, as in the case of the American Civil War or the Spanish Civil War. Recently, for example, the term 'cease-fire' has been used. The term has in the past been used mainly with reference to international war. A cease-fire is followed by an armistice and, ultimately, by a peace treaty. It is unusual – perhaps unique – for two forces like those facing each other in Northern Ireland to be asked to grant a 'cease-fire', as though they both had armies permanently visible in the field.

If the scale of the conflict is to be considered an element in deciding whether we are dealing with a war or not, some statistics provided by Dr Kennedy-Pipe are relevant. From 1969 to 1972 the percentage of the population of Northern Ireland killed in the Troubles was twice that of Britain during the Boer War, and twice that of the USA in either Korea or Vietnam. For so small a country as Northern Ireland this was, indeed, a war. The argument was not purely an academic one; it had practical consequences. If it was 'a war' paramilitary prisoners would be treated as 'prisoners of war', rather than common criminals, though, of course, they would not be protected by the Geneva Convention, which relates only to international war. But even if it was not 'a war', paramilitary prisoners could be treated as 'political offenders', rather than common criminals. In the nineteenth century political offenders were usually treated better than ordinary criminals, not only in Britain, but, for example, in the Habsburg Monarchy and united Italy. But Dr Kennedy-Pipe reminds us that the Gardiner Committee reported, in 1975, that the distinction was a misapplied one in Northern Ireland, since it gave a certain prestige to Republican prisoners.

The general point emerging from Caroline Kennedy-Pipe's book is the immense complexity of the whole Irish question and the conflict in Northern Ireland in particular. For example, a point which may well be unfamiliar to English readers concerns Sinn Fein's attitude to the Republic, which it regarded as an illegal institution until the 1980s, but which it then decided to recognize, so that its members could stand for elections to the Irish Parliament. On the other hand, if Dr Kennedy-Pipe shows great familiarity with the history of Ireland as a whole, she is especially enlightening on the changing role of the British Army in Northern Ireland.

The scholarship behind this book makes it a safe guide to the tragic history of the Troubles of Northern Ireland and their origins.

HARRY HEARDER

Acknowledgements

To write a textbook on the history and politics of Northern Ireland is a controversial and difficult task. The story of the Province is one told in different forms and with competing voices. To attempt any judgements about the causes and longevity of the Irish 'troubles' is inevitably to question received wisdoms and undermine 'accepted' truths. A 'neutral' history of the Province may not be entirely possible but different interpretations are. This work attempts to understand the current 'troubles' through looking at how the British became and remained involved in the conflict between two Irish communities. In this endeavour I have many people to thank. Harry Hearder has always, as a teacher and friend been willing to ponder the nature of human conflict and the seeming inability of government to reconcile warring communities. Likewise Ken Booth as a teacher and friend has stressed the need to understand the causes of civil conflict. Colin McInnes has been generous in providing expertise and information on British strategy. My colleagues in the Institute for International Studies have provided great friendship during the writing of this book; Clive Jones in particular has proved an invaluable source of information on military behaviour in the Province. Both he and Lindsey Tams have been a great source of support. Finally, the team at Addison Wesley Longman have been professional and generous with their time and advice. To all the above I remain grateful. Any faults or biases in the text are of course mine.

Abbreviations

HC	House of Commons Debate
INLA	Irish National Liberation Army
IRA	Irish Republican Army
IRIS	Irish Republican Information Service
NICRA	Northern Ireland Civil Rights Association
NIO	Northern Ireland Office
PIRA	Provisional Irish Republican Army
PRONI	Public Record Office of Northern Ireland
PSF	Provisional Sinn Fein
RUC	Royal Ulster Constabulary
SAS	Special Air Service
SDLP	Social Democratic and Labour Party
SPG	Special Patrol Group
UDA	Ulster Defence Association
UDR	Ulster Defence Regiment
UFF	Ulster Freedom Fighters
UVF	Ulster Volunteer Force

In affectionate memory of
Harry Hearder
8 June 1996

Introduction: The British Army in Northern Ireland

Even as this work is completed, the British Army is still involved in fighting a conflict in Northern Ireland nearly three decades after the initial and 'temporary' deployment of troops in August 1969. This makes it one of the longest-running conflicts in twentieth-century European history and the longest counter-insurgency operation carried out by British troops. This book looks at the origins of this conflict through an examination of the British military role in Ireland. This is not a military history,[1] but an attempt to evaluate the strategies of the British Government in subduing violence against the state. Its central theme is that British military policies have altered the original parameters of the conflict, have prolonged and escalated violence, yet have also provided a necessary peacekeeping element in the turbulent affairs of Northern Ireland. There are many academic works on the problems of Ireland[2] but few that examine the role of the Army in its broad military-political context. This book therefore provides a new interpretation of the origins and evolution of the contemporary conflict in Ireland.

The British military involvement did not actually begin in 1969. It is often said by those involved in studying the politics and history of Ireland that one cannot understand the contemporary situation without understanding what has proceeded it, particularly the legacy of the Anglo-Irish relationship.[3] Chapter One outlines

1 For military histories of the conflict, see David Barzilay, *The British Army in Ulster*, vol. 1. (Belfast: Century Books, 1973, reprinted 1978) and Desmond Hamill, *Pig in the Middle: The Army in Northern Ireland 1969–1984* (London: Methuen, 1985).

2 One of the best works on Ireland is R.F. Foster, *Modern Ireland 1600–1972* (London: Penguin, 1988).

3 See Nicholas Mansergh, *The Irish Question 1840–1921*; a commentary on Anglo-Irish relations and on social and political forces in Ireland in the age of reform and revolution (Third edition, London: Allen and Unwin, 1975), pp. 20–4.

some of the major developments in Irish history prior to the events of 1969 and describes the antecedents to the modern conflict. From the sixteenth century onwards, the British Government were engaged in the subjugation of the island and the imposition of an alien ruling class on the native Catholic peoples. In particular, large numbers of Scottish Protestants emigrated to Ireland in the so-called 'plantation' of Ulster to uphold British rule on the island. The rise in the eighteenth century of Irish nationalism, embedding a violent opposition to British rule, undercut British hegemony and, following the strains of World War I, by 1919 the British Government were prepared to withdraw from Ireland. The Irish Protestant ruling classes opposed such a move, seeking to keep Ireland within the United Kingdom. The subsequent division of Ireland was therefore designed to satisfy these two aspirations. The British Government withdrew its military forces from the southern part of Ireland, but only after a series of bitter and bloody military battles with Republican paramilitaries. The state of Northern Ireland was established, carving out a Loyalist Protestant enclave within a predominantly Catholic Ireland. A small military garrison was maintained by the British Government in the North, underwriting at least symbolically, the tie to the mainland.

Chapter One demonstrates that the division of the territory was a highly contested issue. In the south, the Irish Republican Army opposed the establishment of the new southern Irish Government, regarding it as illegitimate and falling a long way short of its ideal of a united Ireland. The Government in Dublin invoked repressive legislation against its opponents, using censorship and internment whenever necessary to subdue the IRA, yet the administration too supported the ideal of a nationalist republican Ireland.[4] This support for unification caused tension with the state in the North, leading to friction throughout the inter-war period. In the North itself, the Protestants, through the institutions of the Province, not least through the police force, established dominance over the Catholic minority, establishing a sectarian state. Despite the nature of the Northern regime, until the 1960s the two states in Ireland co-existed, allowing the British Government on the mainland to believe that the 'problem' of Ireland had been finally resolved. The emergence of a Civil Rights movement within the Catholic community in 1968 posed the first real threat to the stability of the

---

4 Charles Townshend, *Political Violence in Ireland: Government and Resistance since 1848* (Oxford: Oxford University Press, 1983), p. 373.

Irish settlement since partition. As Chapter Two illustrates, the Civil Rights protesters publicly exposed the sectarian nature of the Northern Irish regime. The abuse of power highlighted by Catholic demands for equality in employment, housing and education provided an impetus for reform of the Province.[5] The subsequent bloody conflict between the Catholic and Protestant communities on the streets of Northern Ireland over these demands for political reconstruction threw the Irish question back on to the agenda of the British Government. In the first instance, it was this antagonism between two opposed communities that sparked conflict in 1969. The inability of the indigenous police force to control the violence meant that British troops were placed in Ireland to act as peacekeepers.

Chapter Three of the book analyses how, within a year of the deployment of British troops, the parameters of the conflict changed. In the first instance, British troops 'policed' the separation of the warring communities, controlling riots and defending Catholic communities against the attacks of their Protestant neighbours. The troops built so-called 'peace walls' between districts and replaced the police force as the enforcers of law and order. Not least, British troops attempted to control riots and demonstrations.[6] These troops did not expect to be in Ireland longer than the few months it would take for the politicians on the mainland to hammer out some reforms of the Northern Irish institutions and so rectify the abuse of the minority population. The chapter argues that all of this changed with both the failure of the politicians to act rapidly to invoke reform and the emergence of the Provisional IRA (PIRA). The Provisionals, operating behind the façade of the Civil Rights movement, reignited the battle between the forces of Irish Republicanism and Britain. The PIRA presented itself as the true defender of the Catholic communities and began a campaign to drive the British influence out of Northern Ireland once and for all. The British Army became the target of paramilitary attacks. This in turn meant that British soldiers changed function from peacekeepers to a force engaged in counter-insurgency against the PIRA. In one twist

---

5 On this issue, see Rosemary Harris, *Prejudice and Tolerance in Northern Ireland: A Study of Neighbours and 'Strangers' in a Border Community* (Manchester: Manchester University Press, 1972) and R. Rose, *Governing Without Consensus: An Irish Perspective* (London: Beacon Press, 1971).

6 For a description of the initial duties of British soldiers, see 'Report on the Study Period by the GOC Northern Ireland, HQNI, Held by the Tactical Doctrine Retrieval Cell'.

of history, the British Army were turned from protectors of the Catholic communities into its enemy. This transformation of the conflict in 1970–71 is shown to have hinged around the question of the military response to that of the paramilitaries. The use of methods such as internment against the Catholic community meant an upsurge in support for the PIRA. The Irish conflict therefore became, for the British Government in the early 1970s, a question of subduing and eradicating the threat from the PIRA. This in turn raised a whole host of questions (examined in the chapter) about how democratic states should respond to the threat of political violence. From 1970–75 the British Government invoked a panoply of repressive legislation and military tactics, many derived from the experience in the colonies, to try to achieve a 'victory' over the paramilitaries. By 1975, the British military had, with the deployment of 22,000 troops, managed to contain the situation and, if not eradicate the PIRA, then at least drive them out of the cities of Northern Ireland. Yet, for the Army and indeed a wider audience, all of this begged the question of what the wider British political objective was in Northern Ireland. Would or should the British Army be deployed indefinitely to contain a small number of Republican paramilitaries? In lieu of any political solutions in the early 1970s, this appeared to be inevitable. British attempts to find political solutions to satisfy both communities in Northern Ireland had failed miserably. In 1974, for example, the British administration tried to impose a powersharing arrangement on Northern Ireland, through which the Catholics would have representation on the political institutions of the Province. The Sunningdale Agreement was, however, destroyed by the Protestant community, who organized a Province-wide strike against this new regime. In this, they had the acquiescence of the British military, who, during 1974, refused to break the strike. The episode demonstrated the key role of the British military in dictating the terms of the conflict. Their actions, or lack of actions, directly undermined this political initiative and raised the possibility of the military directing the future of the Province. Overall, Chapter Three looks at how and why the British Army became tied into Northern Ireland in the early 1970s and its critical role in redefining the terms of the conflict.

By 1975 the British Government was determined to redesign the security arrangements in the Province. This meant, at least in theory, a reduction of the British military role and a relative down-grading of British involvement. Hence, Chapter Four examines the policies of Ulsterization and criminalization, which were designed to allow withdrawal of some British troops and designate the conflict as a local one, which indigenous forces could control. Ulsterization and criminalization (also known as normalization) were attempts to depict the conflict as one in which the PIRA were merely violent criminals, who could be dealt with by the police. The Royal Ulster Constabulary (RUC) were brought into a central role *vis-à-vis* the security of the Province and the Army handed over its leading role. Yet, these strategies were, as the chapter describes, deeply contradictory. At the same time as the PIRA were designated criminals, a whole host of 'emergency' and 'special' legislation was put in place to control them. The chapter analyses whether this approach was successful or if the incarceration of powerful members of the PIRA allowed Republicans to regroup, reorganize their strategy and enter the political arena. Indeed, the chapter also describes one of the central paradoxes of security policy in the period which was that alongside Ulsterization, the Army was involved in a counter-insurgency campaign of some ferocity. Running parallel to the increased activity of the RUC in policing the Province, the British Army was actually engaged in a 'secret war' on the border with the PIRA. British special forces were deployed to fight a rural guerrilla campaign in the Irish countryside. This was not 'normal'. Indeed, the rural 'conflict' presented the British military with a series of challenges which broadened the conflict once again. How could the British troops deal with an organization whose members could not only seek 'refuge' in the south, but actually launch attacks on British military personnel from this refuge. As Chapter Four discusses, the rural campaign made it inevitable that the British military embark on concerted joint operations with the southern Irish. This meant the entry of the Dublin Government into formal discussion of the conflict.[7]

Chapter Five looks at the conflict in Ireland during the 1980s. It describes the way in which the British Government under Prime Minister Thatcher slowly recognized the importance of the southern Irish Government in underwriting any future peace settlement. It also raises the possibility, ignored in much of the literature, that the British Government was interested at this stage in a military withdrawal from Ireland. This, of course, had been part of the intention behind the Ulsterization process, but Chapter

7 For a discussion of the position of the Dublin Government at this stage, see Padraig O'Malley, *The Uncivil Wars, Ireland Today* (Belfast: Blackstaff Press, 1983).

Five argues that the Government became more seriously engaged in pursuing some form of Irish settlement in the early 1980s for a number of reasons. The first was what might be termed the 'internationalization' of the conflict. After the deaths of several hunger strikers in Northern Irish prisons in 1981, international pressure, not least from North America, began to build for the British Government to end the conflict.[8] Simultaneously, the evolution of the judicial institutions of the European Community provided a forum for open criticism of British behaviour in Ireland.[9] The second imperative for change was that the PIRA was beginning to enter 'normal' politics through contesting elections. If they succeeded, the British Government feared a radical and hard-line Republican lobby could veto future political develop-ments. Chapter Five argues that these considerations led Mrs Thatcher to sign the Hillsborough Agreement in 1985, allowing the southern Irish a formal voice in the affairs of Northern Ireland and thus, the chapter argues, paving the way for an eventual dilution of British influence. Throughout this political activity, the Army underwent perhaps its most controversial phase in Ireland, when the security forces were accused of operating a 'shoot to kill' campaign in the Province. The damage to the reputation of the RUC that inquiries into these allegations raised, meant that despite high-level discussions on a way to redesign the security arrangements and withdraw troops, the British Army was regarded as key to maintaining stability in an era of political transformation.

Not least, the British military had to bear the brunt of Protestant anger as the reality of the Hillsborough Agreement became clear. While British soldiers had always had to be prepared to face Protestant paramilitary forces, the activities of these groups became more marked towards the end of the decade. This theme of Protestant paramilitary violence is analysed in Chapter Six. Indeed, in many ways the British Government, through the Anglo-Irish Agreement, fuelled the extremists in both communities in Northern Ireland. While the Protestants objected to Hillsborough as a 'sell out' of British sovereignty, the Republicans claimed it represented an unacceptable Unionist veto over the future of Ireland and escalated activities. The continuing ability of the PIRA

8 See S. Cronin, *Washington's Irish Policy 1916–1986. Independence; Partition; Neutrality* (Dublin: Anvil, 1987) and Jack Holland, *The American Connection: US Guns, Money and Influence in Northern Ireland* (New York: Poolbeg, 1987).

9 See Gerard Hogan and Clive Walker, *Political Violence and the Law in Ireland* (Manchester: Manchester University Press, 1989).

to operate, supported by external funding, not least through the Libyan connection, forms the core analysis of Chapter Six. British troop numbers in the Province were once again increased and, despite attempts by Tom King, the British Secretary of State for Northern Ireland, to have 'talks on talks' with all parties involved in Northern Ireland, a violent stalemate was reached in the affairs of the Province.

The attempts to break out of this institutionalization of violence in Northern Ireland forms the basis for discussion in Chapter Seven. Throughout the 1990s, politicians in the United Kingdom and Ireland grew increasingly anxious to reach a settlement for the Province. Closer relations between the Governments on the mainland and in Dublin marked a determination to lower levels of violence and agree the future. In particular, the chapter looks at the new attempts to decrease British troop levels in the Province and reassert the authority of the RUC. It also looks at the attempts to decommission paramilitary arms within the Province. Overall, it points to the beginning of an endpoint in which the British Army presence *will* be decreased but soldiers not fully withdrawn.

Finally, Chapter Eight sums up the experience of the British Army in Northern Ireland. It discusses the difficulties encountered by a military force in first policing a 'local conflict' and then in trying to defeat an indefatigable paramilitary opponent. In particular, it outlines the constraints faced by British soldiers in trying to operate within a democracy and critically evaluates the strategies employed by the British Army, which, it is argued, in many ways strengthened the appeal of the paramilitaries. Yet, the chapter points out, more than anything else, that the British Army was fatally weakened by the lack of direction in British policy *vis-à-vis* Ireland in the early 1970s. The processes of Ulsterization and criminalization at least made it apparent that the Army would not be at the forefront of the conflict forever. Yet, until the 1990s, as the book demonstrates, the attempts to redraw the security equation in Northern Ireland to allow a permanent reduction of troops always failed. The tensions between the two communities, the strength of the rival paramilitary groupings and the inability of the RUC to combat the PIRA in the countryside meant that only the Army could perform multifaceted security duties in this complex environment. This meant that at times when political initiatives were invoked, the role of the Army was central to the success or failure of such endeavours. The British Army was and remains a key to any settlement of the conflict in Ireland.

CHAPTER ONE

The Background to 1969:
Political Violence, Rebellion and
Nationalisms in Ireland

Political and military violence in Ireland is not a phenomenon of
the last twenty-five years. Ireland's history over the last 300 years is
one of a protracted struggle for land and power between groups
with competing interests and religions. In particular, the modern
conflict hinged upon the battle between those who sought to rid
Ireland of its English connection and those who wished to
maintain the link with the Protestant mainland. This division
between so-called Unionists and nationalists can be traced back to
the seventeenth-century Protestant 'plantation of Ireland', when
the British Crown sponsored English and Scottish Protestants to
settle in the north-eastern part of the colony. The 'plantation' of
Ulster, as it became known, opened a period in which the
Protestant English gentry confiscated land and oversaw a massive
influx of Scottish settlers. They took into Ireland a different
religion and culture from that of the indigenous peoples. These
settlers and their descendants formed a Loyalist base and firmly
implanted a connection with the mainland. Violence was endemic
between the Anglo-Scottish settlers and the native Irish inhabitants
as disputes over land ownership broke out.[1] These struggles
foreshadowed the development of what might be termed two
nationalisms in Ireland over the next 200 years. The two
nationalisms or identities are best described as that of a 'Catholic
Irishness' and a 'Protestant Irishness', which established distinct
identities and interests aligned to geographic locations; the
Catholics in the south and the Protestants in the north of the
island. The later British problem in Ireland was shaped in this
period. The English supported the Protestants in securing their

1 Robert Kee, *The Most Distressful Country.* Vol. one of *The Green Flag* (London:
Quartet Books, 1976).

position in the island, but were unable fully to subdue the
Catholics into acceptance of the arrangement.

From 1649 onwards, Oliver Cromwell, who had just won the
English Civil War, turned his attention to Ireland and attempted
to subdue the rebellious Catholic Irish. Such was his success that
by 1655, four-fifths of the land in Ireland had been taken by the
English. It is in this period that contemporary Irish Protestant
rituals and myths can be located. In 1688, when the Catholic
monarch James II was displaced, he fled to Ireland and claimed
authority there. The Protestant communities in the northern
towns of Derry and Enniskillen rose against him, in support of his
son-in-law, William of Orange, who had succeeded to the British
throne. In May 1689, when the Protestant garrison in Derry was
besieged by an Irish Army, the apprentice boys locked the town's
gates and withstood the attacks until they were relieved by one of
William's armies, over three months later. During the next two
years, the forces of King William defeated the Jacobite armies in
Ireland. He scored two notable victories at the Battle of the Boyne
in 1690 and the Battle of Aughrin in 1691. These victories became
enshrined in Protestant mythology.

The Protestant community, which was primarily located in the
North-east, became identified as the holders of wealth, power and
land shored up by the English. Throughout the following years,
the hegemony of the Protestant community was upheld by the use
of violence and intimidation. Organizations such as the Orange
Lodges and the Peep O'Day Boys were formed to maintain a hold
on the land. These groups continually clashed with the secret
societies formed by the Irish natives, such as the Defenders and
the Ribbonmen, which were dedicated to the overthrow of English
Protestant power.[2] In 1798, the Irishman Wolfe Tone, aided by the
French, attempted to overthrow English power. He led a rebellion
in Co. Mayo, but was defeated by Crown forces at the Battle of
Vinegar Hill. As a result of this rebellion, the English Parliament
passed the Act of Union in 1801, declaring the integration of
Ireland with England and Scotland, thus ending one part of Irish
history. In part, the Act of Union arose from fears that Napoleon
Bonaparte might have taken advantage of rebellious Ireland to
launch an attack on the mainland as had been feared in 1798. The
British took the view that Ireland must be subdued and secured
through military force if necessary.

2 Ibid.

The period before the Act of Union clearly revealed the different dimensions of the conflict in Ireland: military force was used by the English to subdue the rebellious Irish; political violence was also a feature of the conflict between the native Irish and the settlers; while the competing interests of the landed classes during the English Civil War sparked bloodshed. The use of foreign armies in these conflicts formed part of the Irish historical landscape. From the Act of Union, however, the primary struggle in Ireland took place between the nationalists and the English, backed by the Protestant Unionists who wanted to maintain the connection with England. This axis was reinforced by formidable military power. Throughout the nineteenth century, the British military establishment in Ireland varied between 15,000 and 30,000 troops with battalions rotated in and out of the country on a three-year basis. Lord Redesale, who was sent to Ireland as Lord Chancellor in 1802, neatly summed up the twinning of British and Irish Protestant interests when he said: 'I have said this country must be kept for some time as a garrisoned county. I meant a Protestant garrison.'[3] This assumption was underwritten by successive British Governments.

The estrangement between the Unionist and nationalist communities in Ireland was further sharpened in the nineteenth century as two trends developed. The first was the growth of a dynamic nationalist consciousness in Ireland among the Catholic communities that culminated in the Home Rule Campaign of the 1880s. The second trend was the rise of a distinct Protestant identity in Ulster, which arose partly as a response to nationalist demands. Unionists believed that Home Rule would threaten their economic and religious interests. This fear led to the grouping together of Unionist interests, premised on the need to maintain their power base through the connection with Britain.

By the 1880s therefore two distinct communities were in place. The two were distinguished by religion, culture and the vexed question of the connection with Britain. The North wanted to maintain its special relationship with the mainland, while the southern nationalists were determined to sever the connection with Westminster. It was this issue of the relationship with Britain that, more than any other, began to mark the struggle between

---

3 R. Barry O'Brien, *Dublin Castle and the Irish People* (London: Kegan Paul, Trench, Treubner and Co. 1909), p. 43, quoted in Elizabeth A. Muenger, *The British Military Dilemma in Ireland Occupation Politics, 1886–1914* (Kansas/Dublin: University Press of Kansas/Gill and Macmillan, 1991), p. 3.

the two at the end of the nineteenth century. The century had, on the whole, been marked by an uneasy co-existence, but the nationalist campaign for Home Rule exposed the cleavages between the two. For example, in 1885 Ulster had not been completely opposed to Home Rule – of the thirty-three seats in Ulster, seventeen of them were actually won by the Home Rule Party – but over the next twenty years, the picture was transformed and resistance to Home Rule in the Irish North-east grew. The opposition of the Unionists to an independent Ireland arose from a diversity of sources.

The first was that the Protestants in the North-east regarded themselves as different from the Catholic occupants of the island, in the simple terms they were Unionists first and foremost. They saw a division of Ireland lying between the Catholic Irish and the rest of Britain. The geographical separation of Ireland from the mainland was not, to Unionist minds, the important boundary. As descendants of British settlers they believed that they had carved out and constructed an enclave that was superior economically, culturally and socially to that of the native Irish peoples. This enclave had to be protected against absorption into an Irish Catholic state.[4]

Cultural and historical factors which prohibited Protestant Ulster's acceptance of Irish Republicanism were underwritten by powerful economic rationales. Unionists believed that the relative economic prosperity of the business centres in the North would be threatened by southern rule. Business interests in Belfast did not believe that a nationalist government in Dublin would maintain the necessary economic links with the mainland. In addition, many in the North feared the nature and political immaturity of any future government in the south. By the beginning of the twentieth century, Unionists saw themselves as inhabiting a flourishing region that needed to maintain the industrial link with imperial Britain, not be tied to the agrarian south.[5]

Opposition also centred on the issue of the church and the state. The Protestant North was deeply distrustful of any regime which would be dominated by a Catholic majority. Many Protestants equated rule from Dublin with 'Rome Rule'. This distrust of Catholicism ran deep. In Ulster itself, Catholic communities had long suffered discrimination. The Catholics, on

4 For an explanation of the Unionist mentality, see A.T.Q. Stewart, *The Narrow Ground: Aspects of Ulster 1609–1969* (London: Faber & Faber, 1977).

5 J.C. Whyte, *Interpreting Northern Ireland* (Oxford: Clarendon Press, 1990), p. 159.

the whole, underwent relative economic deprivation in comparison with their Protestant counterparts. The nature of the Catholic communities, with their devotion to the church in Rome, helped set them apart from the majority in the North.[6] The Unionists had no desire to cede control of the region to a government in the south which they believed would not only side with the Catholics but actively oppose Protestant religious beliefs. Yet at the end of the nineteenth century most of the British establishment had accepted that some measure of self-government for Ireland was both necessary and appropriate; it was a question of how much. Much of the debate on the British mainland over Ireland was over exactly what constitutional solutions would be acceptable to the Unionists yet would also stem the rising tide of nationalism.

In their opposition to Home Rule, the Unionists felt confident that they could count upon the support of at least part of the British establishment. The Conservative Party had, at the end of the nineteenth century, openly sided with the Unionists. While this support was motivated by pure political opportunism as much as anything else, it provided a powerful filip to the Unionist cause. In 1886, for example, the Conservatives under Randolph Churchill had used the issue of Home Rule to break the Liberal Government of Gladstone. Lord Randolph Churchill declared that the Orange card was the card to play. Churchill decided that if Gladstone opted for Home Rule, the Conservatives would oppose it. He declared: 'Ulster will fight and Ulster will be right.' There was at this point, however, no need for Ulster to fight as the bill for Home Rule was defeated in Parliament. In Belfast the Unionists were triumphant and during the ensuing 'celebrations', several Catholics were killed. The British Parliament was subsequently dissolved and the Conservatives were returned to office under Salisbury. The battle over Home Rule was not yet over and in 1882 Gladstone was returned, and with the support of the Irish representatives in the House carried a Second Home Rule bill in 1893. This time it was defeated by the House of Lords and it appeared as if Home Rule was indeed a lost cause. Yet outside the British Parliament, the forces of Irish nationalism continued to grow. In 1893, the Gaelic League was founded. This movement was dedicated to the revival of Irishness in a non-sectarian fashion and attempted to foster the Irish language and Irish literature.

6 See A.C. Hepburn (ed.), *Minorities in History* (London: Edward Arnold, 1978), p. 85.

Around this group, Irish nationalist political aims developed and, as the century drew to a close, the nationalist aim became an Irish republic divorced from the mainland.

By the beginning of the twentieth century the triangular shape of the violent struggle in Ireland had been set. The nationalists were intent on independence from Britain, antagonizing the Protestants in the North who sought and gained a commitment to the Union from the Conservative Party in Westminster. This in turn provoked bloody sectarian violence between the two communities in the North.

The decade between 1910 and 1920 was one of particular turmoil. In 1912, under the Liberal Government of Asquith, the Third Home Rule bill passed through the British Parliament. This was made possible not only by the genuine commitment of the Liberal Party to the cause of Home Rule, but also by the rise of the Irish Parliamentary Party. The votes of the eighty-four Irish nationalist seats were critical to the life of the Asquith regime. This combination of Irish nationalism and Liberal commitment forced the success of the bill. The Home Rule Act was placed on the statute books in 1914 but remained dormant. The Ulster Unionists were determined that it should not be implemented and half a million Protestants, under the leadership of Sir Edward Carson, signed a covenant to defeat Home Rule. Conservative politicians once again pledged their support to the Unionist cause. In Ulster the Ulster Volunteer Force (UVF) was founded with a membership of 100,000 and the aim of defeating Home Rule through military means if necessary, and then to form a provisional government if required. Some of the British military garrison in Ireland announced that they would not fight against the UVF.[7]

The militant resistance of the Loyalists in the North, meant that by 1914, a devolved system of government for the south was unlikely to be initiated for the whole of Ireland. Loyalist resistance and the delay of the passage of the Home Rule bill in Westminster had immediate and violent repercussions in the south. The Irish volunteers (otherwise known as the IRA) was formed in 1913 and dedicated itself to the achievement of political reform by violent means. The Irish Republican Brotherhood, who since the 1850s had been the driving force behind nationalist violence, joined the organization.[8] After almost three decades of attempts to find a

7 Muenger, op. cit., p. 3.
8 See Michael Hopkinson, *Green Against Green: The Irish Civil War* (Dublin: Gill and Macmillan, 1988), p. 2.

constitutional solution to the question of Ireland, the island appeared ready to lurch back into violence, with the British military garrisons embroiled between Northern and southern factions. By 1913, the British Government had become alarmed over the loyalty of Crown forces in Ireland. Many in the Army had sympathy with the position of the Protestant Unionists and were clearly worried at the prospect of having to underwrite any banishment from Britain of Protestants.[9] In addition, the formation of rival paramilitary organizations in both North and south had greatly increased the prospect of armed conflict. Civil war between North and south appeared to be inevitable, but was tempered by the outbreak of World War I. Recruiting, conscription and the general question of what level of support the Irish should provide for the war had replaced Home Rule as the central question for debate in the south. At first, recruitment to the British cause in the larger towns reached reasonable levels.[10] The southern Irish were, broadly, in favour of the British position but with one important caveat. This was that Irish support would be rewarded by a Home Rule settlement for all of Ireland. The IRA itself split over the war with a majority supporting the British position but a significant minority opposing.

Irish nationalism became more militant during the war years.[11] In particular, the military committee of the IRA planned to take advantage of the struggle with Britain whose forces from 1914 onwards were bogged down on the battlefields of France. The IRA was dedicated to the establishment of a thirty-two-county republic and was the spearhead of the Anglo-Irish war of 1916, This began with the Easter rising of 1916, which took the British garrison by surprise. Military reinforcements were rushed from the mainland to impose martial law.[12] The uprising failed, not least because the IRA was badly organized and uncontrolled.[13] The nationalist position however flourished, partly because of the brutality of British actions in subduing the rebellion. A panoply of repressive measures were taken, including execution and internment.[14] The

---

9 Ibid., p. 2.

10 See *An tÓglach* (the new volunteer journal), October 1918, quoted in Charles Townshend, *Political Violence in Ireland: Government and Resistance Since 1948* (Oxford: Clarendon Press, 1983), p. 320.

11 Robert Moss, *Urban Guerillas* (London: Temple Smith, 1972), p. 91.

12 See House of Commons Debate (hereafter HC), vol. 82, cols 935–70, 3 May–1 June 1916.

13 Hopkinson, op. cit., pp. 10–11.

14 HC, vol. 82, cols 935–47, 11 May 1916.

nationalist position was particularly strengthened by the birth of new Sinn Fein as a political party. Sinn Fein (ourselves alone) had been founded as a political party by a Dublin journalist – Arthur Griffith – in 1905. Its original goal had been the imposition of a dual monarchy for Britain and Ireland and a policy of complete Irish withdrawal from British institutions. This policy was never really taken seriously. Sinn Fein was not part of the Easter rising, but benefited from the emotional atmosphere after the 1916 failure. The convention to promote Sinn Fein met on 25 October 1917 and formulated a position explicitly designed to appeal to the various strands of nationalist sentiment. In particular, it adopted a policy of abstentionism from Westminster and a programme for a republic which succeeded in rallying the various groups to the leadership of Sinn Fein.[15] The appointment of Eamon De Valera, who had been in charge of the Easter uprising, brought along a substantial number of Irishmen committed to the cause of a republic. The continuing British failure to establish a Home Rule settlement during negotiations in late 1916–17 and indeed, the prolonged debate over the partition of Ireland, hardened nationalist sentiment in the south and support for Sinn Fein. As a consequence, Sinn Fein made significant victories in the elections of 1917.[16]

Nationalist grievances were further compounded in April 1918, when the British Government passed the Military Service bill, which provided authority to impose conscription in Ireland by an order in council. This meant that there need be no further debate on the issue. By April 1919, Sinn Fein, in pursuit of its abstentionist policies, had refused to take seats in the House of Commons, established the Dail, declared independence and provisionally constituted a republic.[17] In addition, in an attempt to override the British Government, they made a direct plea to the Paris Peace Conference to try to find an international solution to the problems of British rule in Ireland. This however came to nothing, and Ireland was left caught between the somewhat incoherent rule of the Dail[18] and the military conflict with the British Government. This confrontation is known variously as either the Anglo-Irish war or the Irish war of Independence. (Some analysts dislike the latter term, as Ireland did achieve full independence.)

15 *Contemporary Review* CXIII (June 1918), p. 606, quoted in A.C. Hepburn, *The Conflict of Nationalities in Modern Ireland* (London: Edward Arnold, 1980), pp. 108–9.
16 Ibid., pp. 108–9.
17 See *An tÓglach*, quoted in Townshend, op. cit., pp. 324–5.
18 See Hopkinson, op. cit., p. 7.

The most important figure in the military conflict on the Irish side was Michael Collins. He was Director of Organization and Intelligence in the Volunteers, but he was also Minister of Finance in the Dail. This combination of functions summed up the dualistic nature of politics and the military in Ireland at this time. It was Collins who was responsible for the conduct of the war, but also the operation of government. De Valera, the President of the Dail, was, in this period, either in jail in Lincoln or later, with the help of Collins, was smuggled to the United States. Between 1918 and 1921 the IRA under Collins waged a struggle designed to break the British will to stay in Ireland. The IRA strategy was to fight a guerrilla war consisting of hit-and-run attacks on military garrisons, political assassinations and kidnapping. A great deal of romanticism still attaches itself to many assessments of the Anglo-Irish war, yet historians, while acknowledging the superficial attractiveness of the notion of gallant Irishmen taking on the might of the British military, also point to the part-time and episodic nature of the military confrontation.[19] In particular, it has been argued that the military efforts made by the IRA remained concentrated in few areas and were always dictated by a shortage of arms and, in some places, by the lack of volunteers. Despite this, in the course of the conflict, the IRA achieved success, managing to tie down 43,000 British troops, police and auxiliaries.

The British Cabinet had vacillated during the course of the conflict about how it should respond both politically and militarily to the Irish challenge. Specifically, the British Government did not want to acknowledge the struggle as a war, because it was believed that this would confer legitimacy upon the IRA.[20] As in the modern conflict after 1969, the British Government preferred to describe the IRA as a group of criminals engaged in a conspiracy against the Crown. However, despite British protestations that this was a rebellion, not a war, there were substantial casualties. During the period 1920–21, Crown forces suffered losses of 525 killed, while 707 civilians died. The British Government banned the Dail, proscribed nationalist organizations, reinforced the garrisons in Ireland and, from the beginning of 1920, began to recruit in

19 Ibid., pp. 108–9. See also Charles Townshend, *The British Campaign in Ireland 1919–21: The Development of Political and Military Policies* (Oxford: Clarendon Press, 1975).

20 Keith Jeffrey, 'British Security Policy in Ireland 1919–1921' in Peter Collins (ed.), *Nationalism and Unionism: Conflict in Ireland, 1885–1921* (Belfast: Queens University Belfast, Institute for Irish Studies, 1994), p. 172.

England for auxiliary 'forces' which could be sent to Ireland. The result was the so-called 'Black and Tans'. These volunteers were recruited from former servicemen, criminals and mercenaries, and by May over 1,000 had arrived in Ireland. The brutality of their behaviour, as they raced around the countryside in armoured cars engaging in what was essentially a policy of counter-terror, became infamous. In particular, they undertook a strategy of reprisals, that is attacking the property or families of those connected to Sinn Fein, that merely hardened nationalist resistance and escalated the use of violence. Michael Collins, in particular, led some spectacular and bloody assaults against the British forces. On the morning of 21 November 1920, Collins engineered the simultaneous shooting of over a dozen British intelligence officers. This became the first of many Sundays in Ireland which would be remembered for their bloodshed. At the end of 1920, the Cabinet was driven into a declaration of martial law in south-west Ireland. (The remit of martial law eventually covered the counties of Cork, Kerry, Tipperary, Limerick, Clare, Kilkeny, Waterford and Wexford.)[21]

Despite the 'reinforcement' of British forces and tactics, the IRA managed to break Westminster's will. The IRA did not win a military victory, but they did achieve a political one. In 1921, Westminster, exhausted by the prolonged and expensive war in Europe and frustrated after centuries of the so-called Irish Troubles, withdrew most of its troops. (The last of the British troops left in December 1922.) The historian Bowyer Bell has summed up the victory thus: 'the IRA, unable to win, had refused to lose, thus bombing the British to the bargaining table'.[22] This provided the lief motif for the future strategy of the IRA. By this stage, the British pattern of behaviour in Ireland had been set. Westminster had already accepted the Unionist position over the North and were now left to coerce nationalists into some form of constitutional settlement that fell well short of their demands.

Thus, by 1921, the IRA had not achieved the victory they had sought, that of a thirty-two-county republic. The 1920 Government of Ireland Act, which established the new Irish Free State in the south, also set up a separate Northern Irish Government to rule the six counties (Fermanagh, Down, Antrim, Londonderry, Armagh and Tyrone) in the North, in recognition of Unionist

21 Hopkinson, op. cit., p. 10. See also Jeffrey, op. cit., p. 171.
22 J. Bowyer Bell, *A Time of Terror – How Democratic Societies Respond to Revolutionary Violence* (Columbia, NY: Basic Books, 1978), p. 206.

wishes. This was the compromise measure taken by the British Government to satisfy both North and south. This decision was taken after much controversy in London, not so much over the exemption of Ulster from the treaty, but over what geographical space constituted Ulster. The Irish Committee, established in 1919 to consider the future of Ireland, had originally proposed that the nine counties which had historically constituted Ulster be separated off. The Unionists, who dominated the Cabinet of Lloyd George, insisted that only six of these counties should make up Ulster.[23] The Unionists effectively defeated the nationalist claim to incorporate Ulster on the basis of a three-to-one majority in Ireland as a whole, while having their claim to Ulster upheld on the basis of only a 55 per cent majority. This anomaly worried the British Government. The British Cabinet would in fact have preferred an arrangement whereby nine counties, with only a narrow Unionist majority, were exempted from the agreement, but the Northern Irish nationalists were boycotting Westminster and the Unionist wish prevailed. Lloyd George justified the six-county division as a temporary measure. The Cabinet committee dealing with the Irish question claimed that it had done everything that it could to bring about Irish authority, without infringing on the freedom of Ulster.[24] The Cabinet committee went so far as to claim that their proposals encouraged Irish unity. Indeed, the treaty envisaged a reconciliation between North and south. For example, it set up a Council of Ireland, consisting of both Northern and southern representatives to facilitate this process.[25] The two Irish Parliaments were still free to cooperate in transferring to the Council any of the services they wished.[26] This notion of a Council of Ireland would become a familiar theme of English attempts to resolve the Irish question and at least in theory gave southern Ireland some influence in the future of the North. Yet, despite British protestations of the supposed impermanence of the arrangement and their attempts to persuade the Unionists to accept this proposition, in reality they had long accepted that Ulster could not be persuaded. Unionists would have preferred to be governed directly from Westminster as an intregal part of the

23 See John McColgan, *British Policy and the Irish Administration* (London: George, Allen and Unwin, 1983), p. 3.

24 HC, vol. 127, cols 1333–4, 31 March 1920.

25 Government of Ireland Act, section 10.

26 Committee on Ireland, Fourth Report, CP series 247 (2 December 1919). PRO CAB 241/94. Quoted in McColgan, op. cit., p. 38.

United Kingdom. These discussions produced a lingering distrust of the British administration. The Ulster Unionist leader, Sir Edward Carson, actively opposed the Act of 1920 and strongly advised against forcing upon the people of Ulster a parliament 'they had not sought and which they did not want'.[27] Nevertheless, Unionists also saw that acceptance of the 1920 Act gave them certain benefits. Not least, they believed that the establishment of a separate Irish administration in the North foreclosed the possibility of any future incorporation into an All Ireland arrangement.[28] The Act underwrote the British connection to and responsibility for Ireland. The newly created Northern Irish political system was modelled on that of Westminster, with upper and lower chambers, while the British Crown was represented by a governor of the Province. This arrangement strictly limited Northern Irish powers and subordinated them to Westminster where Northern Ireland was assigned twelve members in the House of Commons, plus a university representative.

The 1920 Act effectively set the framework for the future, sanctioning partition and destroying any immediate prospect of a united Ireland. It also meant that any future change in the status of Northern Ireland would have to come about with the consent of the North. The southern Irish Government attempted to hedge on the treaty in an attempt to achieve a more favourable outcome, but after two months of negotiation with Lloyd George's Government and the threat of war against them, Collins and Griffith settled for an agreement, in December 1921, known as the Anglo-Irish treaty. This conferred dominion status on the twenty-six counties of southern Ireland, making it, at least in formal terms, the equivalent of Canada. Article 12 set up a boundary commission which, in theory, had powers to modify the partition line, but the full extent of its powers remained unclear. The nationalists hoped that in time it would oversee the reincorporation of the North into a united Ireland.

The nationalist movement violently divided over both the treaty and its future strategy. In March 1922, the IRA split into pro- and anti-treaty factions. In pursuit of the lost ideal of a thirty-two-county republic, anti-treaty IRA members, or irregulars as they became known, engaged in a brief and bloody civil war with the

---

27 HC, vol. 123, col. 1198, 22 December 1919.
28 Carson, in HC, vol. 123, col. 1202, 22 December 1919. See also Sarah Nelson, *Ulster's Uncertain Defenders: Protestant Political, Paramilitary and Community Groups and the Northern Ireland Conflict* (Belfast: Appletree Press, 1984), p. 28.

new Government of the Republic, but it was defeated and forced underground.[29] The IRA remained a potential threat to the new Irish Free State using tactics of intimidating jurors, bombings and assassination attempts. In response, the Irish state inserted Article 20 (a public safety bill) into the Irish constitution permitting the establishment of military tribunals, the arrest of 'radicals' and proclaiming the illegality of subversive groups.[30]

The North-South divide

Just as some of the Irish nationalists disputed even the legitimacy of the new southern Irish Government, they also opposed the establishment of the six counties in the North as a separate entity. In this they were in some ways supported by Dublin. The actions of the southern Irish Government after the signing of the treaty compounded the division between North and south. The nationalists tried to organize a boycott of Belfast goods and attempted to cut all economic links between North and south. Collins, in his position as head of the Provisional Government, used his power to block the removal of civil servants and documents from the south to the North. These attempts reinforced the fears of the Unionists that they could not expect cooperation from the south. Nineteen-twenty saw the final separation of Ulster from the rest of Ireland. During this year the IRA launched a series of attacks on Government offices, including some in the North. In 1922 the IRA began a major initiative designed to break the North. The Ulster Unionists, fearing that existing forces would prove inadequate for maintaining the law, created a special constabulary – the infamous B-Specials.[31] Also fearing pressure from the south and from its own Catholic communities, the Unionists used its new police forces vigorously to enforce the sectarian divide in the North. During August, violence erupted in Belfast. In the ensuing strife, 8,000 Catholic workers were driven from their jobs.[32]

29 J. Bowyer Bell, *The Secret Army. A History of the IRA* (Dublin: The Academy Press, 1970), pp. 32–7.

30 Ibid., p. 41.

31 Charles Townshend, op. cit., p. 341.

32 For an account of the violence and the response of the Northern Irish Government, see Bryan A. Follis, *A State Under Siege: The Establishment of Northern Ireland 1920–1925* (Oxford: Clarendon Press, 1995), pp. 106–15.

The historian J.C. Beckett has argued that the establishment of Northern Ireland was entered into not 'because anyone wanted it locally, but because the British Government believed that it was the only way of reconciling the various interests'.[33] Indeed, given the centuries of dispute between the Catholics and the Protestants, partition did appear inevitable and at least it was a pragmatic recognition that two variants of Irish nationalism existed and had to be accommodated. Yet, this was not quite the full story. The arrangement whereby the six counties were turned into Northern Ireland had a persuasive logic for upholding the Protestant Unionist position and the British connection in Ireland. Within the nine counties, which were traditionally held to constitute Ulster, there were 900,000 Protestants, most of whom wanted to continue the connection with Westminster, as opposed to 700,000 Catholics who wanted to end it. In the six counties, however, the religious breakdown was 820,000 Protestants and 430,000 Catholics. C.C. Craig, the brother of the first Northern Irish Prime Minister James Craig, put the case for the six counties thus: 'in a nine-county parliament, with sixty-four members, the Unionist majority would be about three or four; but in a six-county Parliament, with fifty-two members, the Unionist majority would be about ten'.[34]

That the division of Ireland was premised upon Unionist demands is undeniable. The institutions in the North were also geared to this principle. It is difficult to dispute the nationalist interpretations of British and Protestant collusion at this point.[35] For example, the actual political constituencies established under the Government of Ireland Act were arranged to maximize the winning of Unionist seats at the general election of 1921. In May, the Unionists did in fact carry forty out of the fifty-two seats.[36] The county councils of Fermanagh and Tyrone were dissolved when they declared allegiance to the southern Irish Parliament in late 1921.[37]

This inbuilt political dominance by the Ulster Protestant majority was further reinforced by the refusal of many of the Catholic community to participate in committees or local structures. Many of the minority refused to recognize the new state in which they were living, so at the very moment when the new

33 J.C. Beckett, *The Ulster Debate* (London: Bodley Head, 1972), p. 11.
34 HC, vol. 127, col. 990, 29 March 1920.
35 For nationalist interpretations, see Whyte, op. cit., pp. 117–46.
36 D.W. Harkness, *Northern Ireland Since 1920* (Dublin: Helican, 1983), p. 9.
37 Ibid., p. 25.

institutions were being established, a number of citizens refused to participate in its structures. Many of the Catholics were, however, excluded because of the Local Government Franchise, which until 1969 was based on property ownership. This meant, in some cases, the exclusion of non-ratepayers, while property owners had extra votes. The vast amount of property was owned by the Protestant population. Indeed, the maintenance of Unionist dominance was ensured through the gerrymandering of constituency borders, most notably in Londonderry.

Law and disorder

The establishment of other institutions in the North also fed the sectarian divide. Mention has already been made of the establishment of the Ulster Volunteer Force (UVF) in 1913. This was soon reorganized into a three-tier outfit that was exclusively Protestant. By August 1922 there were three classes of soldiers: class A on full-time duty; class B who were part-time in their own areas; and a reserve force, class C. The latter class had, by 1922, 17,000 members who had the right to bear arms. The implications were fairly obvious – a large proportion of the male Protestant population had access to firearms.

All of this reflected the siege mentality of the Protestant population. The Catholic population was seen not only as the enemy to the south, but also as the enemy within – as a 'fifth column'. This view was translated into the apparatus of law and order in the North. The Civil Authorities (Special Powers) Act of 1922 was renewed annually until 1928, then extended for a further five years, and by the end of 1933 had become a permanent feature of the regime.[38] The Act provided for the imposition of curfew, the restriction of public meetings, arrest for the possession of unlawful documents and flogging. A constant watch was maintained over the suspect Catholic communities and whenever the Unionists felt threatened, as for example during the periods when the IRA was most active, the Northern Irish authorities used the Act to justify the introduction of measures such as internment.[39] Given these circumstances, the 1920s proved to be the most violent in the history of the Province.

---

38 *Belfast Gazette* (26 May 1922), quoted in Follis, op. cit., p. 99.
39 Ibid., p. 99.

It was not only internal disorder that Craig feared in the decade after the Government of Ireland Act. In March 1922, Craig and Collins had met under the auspices of the British Government in London. They met to discuss the position of the Catholic minority in the North. For Collins, the situation which had developed after the treaty was complicated. Dublin had no desire to see the North succeed in establishing a separate state, but the priority had to be stability in the south. Indeed, Collins struggled to control the anti-treaty forces in the south and he could not have really expected that the Northern parts of the IRA would stand by and allow Catholics in the Province to be discriminated against. Collins therefore met Craig in London to sign a pact which protected minority rights, which in some ways settled the status of Catholics.[40] Despite this meeting, Craig feared that the south might invade. This fear took a concrete form when, in May 1922, the North called more men to arms. The period was characterized by Craig as one in which Ulster had to be mobilized.[41] Specifically, Craig feared that recent events in the south marked a deter-mination on the part of both Collins and De Valera to intervene in the affairs of the North. De Valera and Collins had signed an electoral pact which for many Unionists represented an attempt to provide for southern unity *before* attempting the integration of the North. It was against this backdrop of suspicion that the Belleek and Pettigoe incidents took place. Belleek was and is a predominantly Catholic village located in the Northern county of Fermanagh, and isolated from the rest of the North by lakes and mountains. The road connecting Belleek to the rest of the Province actually ran at some points through the south. Forces loyal to Collins, identified at first as part of the IRA, occupied Pettigoe and an old fort just outside Belleek. These men seized a few Unionists and a crisis ensued over the status of the area. Class A and B specials were alerted and sent in to recover the area but had to retreat under fire. By the end of May there were no Unionist forces left in the area and the IRA appeared to be parading through the streets freely. Part of the debate over this rather curious incident revolves around whether it was actually the IRA involved, or a group of over-enthusiastic and ill-disciplined 'Free State' troops. It now appears to have been the latter. At the time, however, Craig, fearing that this was the thin end of the southern wedge, telephoned the Cabinet in London for support.

40 See *The Times* (31 March 1922).
41 HC, vol. 152, cols 1087–97, 20 March–7 April 1922.

In particular he demanded that Churchill take some form of military action.[42] British troops retook the village on 4 June, while other troops occupied the fort at Belleek and stayed garrisoned there to reassure Unionists until August 1924. A neutral zone was established for a couple of miles either side of the border near the village, and a major crisis between North and south was averted. Some historians claim that Churchill's actions were actually ludicrous and a massive over-reaction to the activities of a few ill-equipped troops.[43] Yet, Churchill claimed that he had to reassure the Unionists that the integrity of the territory of the Province would be enforced.[44] While the British Government had more or less resolved the Irish question with the Act of 1920 and the treaty of 1921, they could not entirely contract out of the running of the Province. From the 1920s, it was the British troops who underwrote the division of Ireland and upheld the position of the Unionists.

Sectarian violence in the Province was exacerbated by the economic depression of the 1930s and continued to threaten the stability of the new Province. Between 1930 and 1939, unemployment did not fall below 25 per cent.[45] The fierce competition for jobs created sectarianism. The Ulster Protestant League, founded in 1931, encouraged the exclusive employment of Protestants. Unionist ideology found its most cogent channel through the Orange Order which had been founded over 200 years earlier. While members of the Orange Order were highly placed in most aspects of Northern Irish life, the most public expression of Protestant ideology was the staging of the annual 'Orange' march on 12 July to commemorate the defeat of the Catholic forces at the Battle of the Diamond in Co. Armagh in 1795. This display of triumphalism did much to ensure that historic hatreds were not forgotten in the 'new arrangement'. By 1935, violence in Northern Ireland reached a peak during an outbreak of severe communal rioting. Twelve people were killed and over 600 injured. A privately sponsored inquiry into the violence by the National Council for Civil

42 Craig to Churchill, 30 May 1922. PRONI CAB 4/46/3, quoted in Follis, op. cit., pp. 102–5.

43 See Michael Farrell, *Arming the Protestants. The Formation of the Ulster Special Constabulary and the Royal Ulster Constabulary 1920–1927* (London: Pluto, 1983) p. 134.

44 W.S. Churchill, *The Aftermath: Being a Sequel to the World Crisis* (London: Macmillan, 1941), p. 336.

45 John Darby, 'The Historical Background' in J. Darby (ed.), *Northern Ireland: The Background to Conflict* (New York: Appletree Press/Syracuse University Press, 1983). See also, 'Cabinet Memorandum by Sir Dawson Bates', 8 July 1932, quoted in Hepburn, *Minorities*, op. cit., p. 163.

Liberties (an organization based on the mainland) in 1936 suggested that a not inconsiderable source of the conflict was the fact that Catholics were discriminated against by the Special Powers Act of 1922.[46] This perspective on the causes of discontent was ignored by the Northern Irish Government, which was itself under intense pressure from the Protestant community to alleviate the economic recession, not to inquire into the grievances of the minority. Indeed, one disquieting trend during this period was the appearance of a new sectarian body among working-class Protestants – the 'Protestant League'. It first appeared during the early 1930s in Scotland and then in Ulster and was dedicated to the 'rights', above all else, of Protestant citizens.[47] This was a timely reminder that the legacy of the Protestant 'plantation' of Ulster remained in force.

States of Ireland

As the 1930s progressed, the triangular relationship between North and south, between Dublin and London and between the two communities in the North appeared to grow ever more strained. Tensions between the North and the south in particular were exacebated by the increasingly nationalistic actions of the southern Irish Government under Eamon De Valera. In particular, the formation of the new Irish constitution in 1937 reaffirmed the distinct territorial and political integrity of Ireland. Article 1 of the document declared that the Irish nation reaffirmed its inalienable, indefeasible and sovereign right to choose its own form of government and to determine its relations with other nations, while Article 2 proclaimed that the national territory consisted of the whole island of Ireland. While a republic was not at this point proclaimed, the nature of the constitution was republican both in nature and content, and from a Unionist point of view immensely provocative.[48]

The constitution upheld the nationalist view, which was frequently reiterated by De Valera, that partition had been a short-term solution and that it had been forced upon a reluctant south. Roy Foster has recently pointed to the sophisticated and

---

46 See Hepburn, *Minorities*, op. cit., p. 166.
47 Ibid., p. 166.
48 Nicholas Mansergh, *The Unresolved Question. The Anglo-Irish Settlement and its Undoing 1912–1972* (New Haven, CT: Yale University Press, 1991), p. 299.

effective actions of De Valera in publicly advocating separatism from Britain but actually adopting gradualist policies *vis-à-vis* the mainland. Not least, Foster points out that it was De Valera who signed an important series of economic agreements with London during the 1930s. However, nationalist orthodoxy, which was publicly upheld by De Valera, holds that if it had not been for the British connection, partition would never have taken place.[49] At one level this is obviously true. The British connection in Ireland, from the 'plantation' period onwards, forms the backdrop to the rest of the story, but by 1920 this interpretation flies in the face of the reality of an entrenched Unionist opposition to the south. As it was, Articles 1 and 2 of the Irish constitution were pretty well calculated to provoke the Unionists, as indeed was Article 44 which enshrined the special position of the Catholic church within the state and did nothing to soften Unionist attitudes towards the south.

De Valera, recognizing British preoccupation with the growing Nazi threat, seized the opportunity to pressurize Westminster over nationalist aims. The IRA too, sensing British vulnerability, entered a new period of militancy. In 1938, on the eve of World War II, the IRA attempted to take the nationalist war to the British mainland. On 12 January 1939, the IRA Council sent the British Government an ultimatum to withdraw its troops from Ireland. Three days later, with no British response, they issued a proclamation of war. The subsequent campaign in Britain consisted of random bombings of cinemas, public houses, shops and post offices. The worst incident was an explosion on 25 August 1939 in Coventry which killed five people.[50] The bombing campaign was politically ineffective. It took place when the British Government was concerned not with sporadic terrorist bombings but with the looming Nazi threat. During World War II, the IRA failed to dent the British position in Ireland.

The events of the late 1940s undercut even further the ambitions of the IRA. The Dublin Government moved further to confirm its status as both a republic and a sovereign whole. The 1948 Republic of Ireland Act confirmed both its status as a republic and its withdrawal from membership of the

---

49 Whyte, op. cit., pp. 117–46. For Foster's account, see 'Anglo-Irish Relations and Northern Ireland. Historical Perspectives' in Dermot Keogh and Michael Haltzel (eds), *Northern Ireland and the Politics of Reconciliation* (Cambridge: Cambridge University Press, 1993).

50 Moss, op. cit., p. 92.

Commonwealth.[51] Despite this declaration of additional independence, however, the Governments in Dublin and Westminster
continued to maintain and even reinforce their close political and
economic links. One contemporary commentator spoke of the
British determination to hold Ireland within the orbit of 'sterling'
and the Commonwealth.[52] The UK Ireland Act, which was
introduced the following year, recognized the new status of the
Republic *vis-à-vis* the Commonwealth, but also had within its terms
a guarantee to the Unionists from the mainland that the partition
of Ireland would not occur without their consent.[53] All of this was,
of course, interesting because it appeared, at least superficially,
that the British Government was still operating in a role of trying
to satisfy both the south and the North. Yet, British motives in the
late 1940s were not that simple. Not least, it has been argued that
this guarantee was in part motivated by the post-war interests of
the British Ministry of Defence.[54] The emerging Cold War had
fuelled British fears that a newly dominant USSR could threaten,
through its vast military power, the stability of the European
continent. In practice, the British Ministry of Defence argued that
this meant the maintenance of strategic bases in Northern Ireland.
In particular, the British Chiefs of Staff argued that they needed to
maintain access to Lough Foyle and the Royal Naval Base at
Lishally. One Chiefs of Staff Report in 1948 noted that 'it was
undesirable that there should be any division of the waters
between Eire and the UK as a result of a decision by an
international court which did not give the UK the navigable
channel'.[55] This type of consideration during the period of the
Cold War provided another dimension for the British rationale for
the military presence on the island which was quite separate from
worries of ethnic conflict in the Province. British strategic
concerns were further fuelled when the southern Irish refused to
join the North Atlantic Treaty Organization (NATO). Potentially,

51 See R.F. Foster, *Modern Ireland 1600–1972* (London: Penguin, 1988), pp.
566–7.
52 Reported in Ian McCabe, *A Diplomatic History of Ireland, 1948–1949* (Dublin:
Irish Academic Press, 1991), p. 154.
53 Foster, op. cit., pp. 566–7. Foster points to the shock on the Irish side when
the British Government issued the guarantee to the Unionists. In fact, the southern
Irish had hoped to use their potential involvement in NATO as a lever against the
British Government to reopen the issue of partition.
54 See McCabe, op. cit., p. 15.
55 PRO DEFE 59. Chiefs of Staff (COS) Committee memorandum, 16
November–31 December (0) series 165–234, quoted in McCabe, op. cit., p. 137.
(Former reference 43/214. Cited as PRO DEFE 5. 9. COS (48) 18 December 1948.)

this meant that a neutral Ireland could, in a future war, be given over to hostile forces.

All of these strategic considerations by-passed the IRA. In 1949, after reflecting on its abortive strategy of the war years, the IRA formulated a new policy, declaring war solely against the administration in the North. This strategy was proclaimed at Borderstown by Christrar O'Neill, the Vice President of Sinn Fein (the political wing of the IRA). He declared that 'the aim of the army is simply to drive the invader from the soil of Ireland and to restore the sovereign independent republic declared in 1916'. To that end, the policy was to prosecute a successful military strategy. Previously, the IRA had waged war against the Government in Dublin, but these military actions were now 'outlawed' in the south and the IRA reverted to war against British rule in the North. The IRA orders issued in October 1954 made this new policy explicit; it stated that the policy was 'to drive the British forces of occupation out of Ireland'.[56] The lines of the conflict were drawn between the Republican aims of a united Ireland and the Unionist/British desire to uphold partition.

At the beginning of the 1950s, members of the IRA crossed the border from the south to perpetrate raids on military barracks in the North. The assaults on British training posts in Armagh in June 1954 produced sizeable arms hauls. The IRA concentration on Northern Ireland was in part a recognition that De Valera's actions had satisfied much, if not all, of nationalist sentiment in the south. The introduction of the 1937 constitution, the Anglo-Irish Agreement of 1938, had provided the Republic with independence and a degree of confidence. The issue of Irish unity, while still an emotional subject, was no longer at the forefront of the agenda. The emphasis on the North reflected the recognition of the IRA that it had to target a different audience to proceed with its agenda of unity by violence. Sinn Fein, for example, ran an enthusiastic campaign in the North and in the Westminster elections of May 1955 received the bulk of the nationalist vote.[57] These activities were the prelude to the guerrilla campaign the IRA initiated with a series of cross-border attacks in 1956. During 'Operation Harvest', as it was known, the IRA attacked barracks and British troops in a style that would be later

56 Tim Pat Coogar, *The IRA* (Glasgow: Fontana, 1980), p. 327.
57 B. Purdie, *Politics in the Streets* (Belfast: Blackstaff Press, 1990), p. 41, quoted in M.L.R. Smith, *Fighting for Ireland: The Military Strategy of the Irish Republican Movement* (London: Routledge, 1995), p. 69.

replicated in the 1970s. The self-proclaimed mission of the IRA was to strengthen resistance in the so-called occupied areas of the Province to British rule. The means by which this would be accomplished was outlined in the IRA training manual, which argued that the IRA had to adopt 'guerilla warfare . . . through a series of little blows'.[58] Despite the emphasis which the IRA claimed to make on the primacy of guerrilla tactics, and specifically the notion of winning hearts and minds, their attacks did not evoke popular support among the Catholics in the North.[59] The notion that the IRA claimed that it was actually a 'people's army' does not really stand up to scrutiny.

The failure of the IRA to gain support for its aims in the North may be explained by certain societal developments in the North. Since the 1950s there had been a significant improvement in economic conditions in the North. The Catholic minority had, on the whole, found its position improved. For example, the 1947 Education Act, which provided for free secondary schooling, meant that a higher proportion of Catholics were able to attend university. This type of change created a trend within the minority community to see its future as part of a Northern Irish state that was offering greater opportunities.[60] Acceptance by the Catholic communities of the Northern Irish state was borne out in the elections of 1959, when Sinn Fein lost both its seats at Westminster.[61] The campaign expired in 1962, with the aims of the IRA apparently redundant and irrelevant to the concerns of the Catholics in the North. In its final campaign message of early 1962, the IRA blamed its recent defeat on the general public and the lack of interest in what it designated as the primary purpose of the Irish people – the unity of Ireland.[62]

The IRA also lost momentum because of the actions of the Irish Government. In July 1957, the Dublin Government introduced internment as an instrument for dealing with the IRA. So successful was this strategy that by the end of 1958, nearly all the IRA executive were in jail and the IRA was unable to function properly without its command. By the end of 1962, the IRA accepted that they had 'lost' the battle and following the failure of the border

58 'Handbook for Volunteers of the Irish Republican Army: Notes on Guerilla Warfare, IRA GHQ, 1956', pp. 5–6, quoted in Smith, op. cit., p. 68.
59 Moss, op. cit., p. 93.
60 Darby, 'The Historical Background' in Darby (ed.), op. cit., pp. 24–5.
61 Ibid., p. 24.
62 See Smith, op. cit., p. 72.

campaign, entered a period of internal dissension and schism. The appointment of a new Chief of Staff, Cathal Goulding, meant a period of reappraisal before engaging the British Army again.

By the late 1960s, the Republican vision of a thirty-two-county state was no closer to realization than in 1923. Events in Northern Ireland would later provide the setting and conditions in which the IRA could once again challenge the British state, but in the interim, Northern Ireland appeared to have entered a period of calm and at least superficially the partition of 1920 appeared to have resolved the Irish question: two Irelands, a nationalist Catholic Republican south and a Unionist Protestant North with a connection to Britain.[64] The linkage with the mainland had, when necessary, been underwritten by British troops, as in 1922. Rather neatly, or so it seemed at the time, the 1920 Act had provided a compromise of self-determination for the south and self-government for the North. As A.J.P. Taylor wrote of Irish partition, 'Lloyd George appeared to have "conjured" the Irish problem out of existence'.[63] It might also be argued that this 'conjuring trick' provided the British Government with an excuse for not having to think too hard about an all-Ireland solution, at least in the short term. Yet, a longer-term problem remained. This was that two nationalisms or identities co-existed on one island. These two groups had different cultures, religions and, most critically of all, different aspirations *vis-à-vis* the mainland. It was especially problematic because the division of the island had not provided homogeneity on both sides of the partition. It had left an enclave of Catholics in the North. This group, potentially, provided the rationale for multi-layered disputes between both North and south, within the Province itself and with the British Government which had sanctioned the division of Ireland and guaranteed its enforcement. In the late 1960s, it was indeed the dissatisfaction of the minority in the North which disrupted the arrangements of 1920–21 and provided the forces of nationalism with an opportunity to challenge once again the British connection in Ireland.

63 A.J.P. Taylor, *English History 1914–1945* (Harmondsworth: Penguin, 1976), p. 213.

64 Whilst taking into account the early distinction between Republicans, who advocated physical force to achieve a united Ireland, and the nationalist Party who advocated constitutional means, this text uses the terms nationalist and Republican interchangeably to describe those opposed to the British presence. See Whyte, op. cit., p. 74.

CHAPTER TWO

The Resurgence of the Two Irish Nationalisms

As far as the British were concerned, by the early 1960s Ireland was not a problem. The Government on the mainland was not really engaged in the affairs of the Province, nor was it involved in the activities of the Northern Irish Government. Despite this sanguine attitude, however, it was in this period that the Province entered its most unsettled period since partition. Indeed, the explosive resurgence of nationalist grievances in 1968–69 threatened to undo the settlement of 1921. This chapter examines how this happened and what, specifically, were the roots of the challenge to the governments in both Northern Ireland and on the mainland.

Reform and resistance

The apparent and immediate catalyst for 'the Troubles', as they became known, was the advent of a Civil Rights movement, which took to the streets in 1968. This symbolized the grievances of the Catholic minority who began to rebel against what it perceived to be the inherent discrimination of the political and economic structures of the Province. Rather ironically, but perhaps not surprisingly for students of history,[1] these protests came about in a period during which Northern Ireland was undergoing a period of economic and political restructuring. The period of reform can be dated from 1963, when the newly elected Prime Minister, Captain Terence O'Neill, attempted to change the basis on which both society and industry operated in the Province. He took office

---

1 On this point in Ireland see Sabine Wichert, *Northern Ireland since 1945* (London: Longman, 1991), p. 113. For a broader perspective on historical reform see Alexis de Toqueville, *L'Ancien Régime et la Revolution*, trans. Henry Reeve (London: John Murray, 1856), p. 333.

determined to modernize and eradicate some, if not all, of the biases upon which government operated.[2]

It is interesting to ask what motivated O'Neill to undertake reform. Some analysts have argued that the character of the man was important to the endeavour and have pointed to the educated and enlightened nature of O'Neill's personality.[3] He was, it has been argued, not like most Northern Irish politicians in that he was not trapped in the parochial nature of Irish politics. He had travelled extensively, been educated abroad and had a vision, which was quite radical for Ireland in the 1960s, that the Province could operate on lines of greater, if not full, equality between its two communitites.[4] Specifically, he advocated toleration towards the Catholic minority. There was, however, another side to this liberal agenda. O'Neill believed quite pragmatically that the implementation of reform could incorporate the Catholics into the life of the Province, and resolve the continuing problem of the nationalist minority. To put it bluntly, this was a more civilized way of dealing with an ethnic minority than had hitherto been adopted by Protestant leaders.[5]

In addition to the pragmatic, but liberal, agenda, a substantial part of O'Neill's reform agenda was inspired by the economic situation in the Province. During the 1950s and early 1960s, dire predications had been made in economic forecasts for the region. In particular, experts argued that much of the industry in Northern Ireland was outdated and that the entire economic infrastructure needed modernizing.[6] It was under O'Neill that economic planning began to be taken seriously, primarily because unemployment in the Province had risen quite dramatically. A number of important sectors, such as agriculture, shipbuilding, textiles and clothing had experienced a continuous decline. Employment in these four sectors, which dominated the Province's industry, declined by half between 1950 and 1979.[7] As a

2 Martin Wallace, *Northern Ireland: 50 Years of Self-Government* (Newton Abbott: David and Charles, 1971), p. 71.

3 Ibid., p. 71.

4 Ibid., p. 71.

5 See David Millar, *Queens's Rebels* (Dublin: Gill and Macmillan, 1978) and A.T.Q. Stewart, *The Narrow Ground: Aspects of Ulster 1609–1969* (London: Faber & Faber, 1977).

6 See Report of the Working Party on the Economy of Northern Ireland, Cmd 446, 1962. See also Wallace, op. cit., pp. 136–7.

7 Leslie McClements, 'Economic Constraints' in David Watt (ed.), 'The Constitution of Northern Ireland: Problems and Prospects', *Studies in Public Policy* 4 (National Institute of Economic and Social Research, Policy Studies Institute, Royal Institute of International Affairs, London: Heinemann, 1981) p. 101.

consequence, social problems related to the high levels of unemployment developed. These were most marked in Catholic areas. Within the overall decline, it was notable that employment rates varied quite radically across the Province. In the south and west and in western Belfast, predominately Catholic areas, unemployment was double the regional average.[8] In 1961, a joint working party of senior officials from the mainland and the Province was established to investigate the factors which were causing the high rate of unemployment. The outcome of these investigations, which became known as the Hall Report, was published in October 1962. It contained a bleak analysis of the prospects for dealing with employment.[9] Worried by this prognosis, O'Neill commissioned Professor Thomas Wilson, of Glasgow University, to prepare a report on economic development. The subsequent Wilson Report, which was published in 1965, pointed to substantial weaknesses in the economy of the Province, but it also made positive recommendations for the improvement of a series of key sectors of the economy: in transport, tourism, agriculture and capital investment.[10] It also recommended a wholesale house-building programme to replace slum dwellings.[11]

In attempting to implement reform, O'Neill's economic programme ran headlong into the problems of trying to modernize a divided society. There were numerous obstacles to change as far as both communities were concerned. Even what might appear as trivial questions to an outside observer had serious political ramifications. Many of these arose because of the peculiar resonance that the past still exerted over the populations in the North. This meant that the naming of a new bridge, town or college, evoked deep passions. One suggestion that a new bridge be named the Carson Bridge, after the key strategist of the Province, caused upset in the Catholic communities.[12] Equally, the siting of a new university at Coleraine caused a stir in the rival site of Londonderry where Catholic leaders led a protest (which included some Protestant councillors) against the decision and alleged that the siting of the new institution reflected a bias

8 Ibid., p. 102.

9 Hall Committee (Report) 8 Nov 1962, House of Commons Debate (hereafter HC), vol. 666, cols 1134–7, 30 October – 9 November 1962, pp. 1134–7.

10 See The Wilson Report, Economic Development in Northern Ireland, Cmnd 479, 1965 (Belfast: HMSO, 1965).

11 Ibid.

12 See Richard Rose, *Governing Without Consensus: An Irish Perspective* (Boston, MA: Beacon Press, 1971), p. 98.

against that part of the region and a desire not to upset the electoral geometry of the city. Some analysts have argued that this was part of a desire to uphold the Protestant east of the Province, which was always strengthened with new initiatives. In Londonderry itself, Catholics outnumbered Protestants by more than two to one, but manipulation of electoral boundaries ensured a Protestant dominance was maintained.[13]

Despite constant sectarian wrangling, O'Neill believed that his economic and modernization programme could eventually reduce inter-communal tensions and reconcile Catholics to the rule of Northern Ireland. Not least, he envisaged that a greater level of general economic prosperity would ameliorate rifts between the communities. In purely economic terms, O'Neill's reforms showed signs, albeit limited ones, of success. In the period 1963–68, numbers in employment rose; the population grew by 3 per cent and there was a substantial programme of new house-building.[14]

O'Neill also persisted in his attempt to normalize the relationship between the Government and the Catholic communities. To this end, the Prime Minster visited a number of Catholic institutions and organizations, something that his predecessors had neglected. Yet such gestures, while important, did not make any significant inroads into the Protestant domination of either employment or government structures.[15] Catholics still remained under-represented on committees and government bodies.[16] Despite the limited nature of the reform process, O'Neill's very attempts aroused deep resentment within his own community and it was from this quarter that he first began to encounter opposition.

In no sphere was this more marked than in O'Neill's plan to recruit Catholics into the heart of Unionism – the Unionist Party itself. It had appeared possible to O'Neill that, as reform began, there could be a significant increase in the number of Catholics who were party members. This soon came to little since the power to accept or reject new applicants rested with local associations, many of which took the view that it was safer to exclude Catholics than to upset the current Protestant membership.[17] The Unionist

13 Ibid. See also Frank Wright, *Northern Ireland: A Comparative Analysis* (Dublin: Gill and Macmillan, 1987), p. 190; and Tim Pat Coogan, *The Troubles: Ireland's Ordeal 1966–1995 and the Search for Peace* (London: Hutchinson, 1995), p. 42.
    14 Rose, op. cit., p. 99.
    15 Rose, op. cit., pp. 442–3.
    16 Ibid., pp. 442–3.
    17 For O'Neill's view of how the Unionist Party should operate, see 'Speech, Queen's University and Conservative and Unionist Association', 26 Jan. 1968, quoted in Terence O'Neill, *Ulster at the Crossroads* (London: Faber & Faber, 1969), p. 59.

Party remained at its core deeply anti-Catholic. Part of the objection to Catholic membership rested not just on a sectarian bias, but also on the belief that it would fundamentally alter the *raison d'être* of the Party – the protection of Unionism and the Province.

Many in the Catholic community also remained wary of O'Neill's intentions. Not least, some believed that reform stemmed less from a desire to improve the lot of the minority, than from a scheme to reduce the rising Catholic birth-rate. It was claimed that the Prime Minister, like many in the Protestant community, feared that at some point in the future, a situation would develop in which Catholics could outnumber the Protestants. In 1969, O'Neill admitted that this concern was part of his agenda, bluntly explaining that 'the basic fear of the Protestants in Northern Ireland is that they will be outbred and outnumbered by the Roman Catholics',[18] but he went on to say that it was only by raising the living standards of the minority group that the Protestants could be assured that they would conform to Protestant norms: 'It is frightfully hard to explain to a Protestant that if you give a Roman Catholic a good job and a good house, they will live like Protestants because they will see neighbours with cars and televisions and want to live like them.'[19]

Yet, even this type of pragmatic argument made little headway with many in the Unionist fold, who regarded it as foolish and dangerous to believe that Catholics could be conciliated to the regime. Some who opposed O'Neill's programme of reform, thought that he was naïve to believe that the Catholics, who had traditionally been hostile towards the Province, could be made loyal. Yet, it was not just old sectarian prejudices, although these were many in number, underwriting Unionist objections to reform. There was also a genuine fear of any political change in the Province. O'Neill's politics challenged traditional assumptions in a way that all the old certainties of life in the Province were turned upside down. Nowhere was this more apparent than in the approach that O'Neill took to the Government in Dublin. The two Irish Governments moved closer than they had been at any time since partition. This new Irish–Irish relationship culminated in 1965, when the southern Taoiseach (Prime Minister), Sean Lemass, visited O'Neill at Stormont Castle, the seat of Northern Irish Government. The two parts of Ireland seemed poised, at this

18 Wallace, op. cit., p. 73.
19 Radio interview with O'Neill quoted in Wallace, op. cit., p. 73.

stage, for unprecedented economic collaboration and both leaders stressed the need for close cross-border cooperation. It should be stressed that O'Neill did not believe that the border could or should be abolished, but rather that the border need not be a political issue. In tune with the spirit of the Stormont meeting, newspapers and articles eagerly recorded the view that 'ancient rifts had been binded'.[20] In all his reforms, O'Neill was actively backed, and in some respects urged on, by the Labour Government on the mainland. In August 1966, Harold Wilson, the Prime Minister, and the British Home Secretary held a meeting with O'Neill. During the course of the meeting they praised the attempts at reform that had already been made, but they also drew attention to the fact that the Province obtained heavy financial assistance from the British Treasury and that this was difficult to justify to some MPs and some members of the Cabinet without a continued liberalization of the regime in Northern Ireland.[21]

Even before civil disorder broke out on the streets of Northern Ireland in 1968, all of this proved too much for some Protestants. Some of the anger at the usurpation of traditional Unionism gathered around the figure of Ian Paisley, the son of a fundamentalist Baptist preacher from Ballymena, in North Antrim. This area was characterized by the term 'bible belt'. Paisley studied theology at the Reformed Presbyterian College in Belfast and was a well-known figure in evangelical circles. He had long aspired to be a spokesman for the more conservative forces at work in the Province and in 1951 formed the Free Presbyterian Church of Ulster, which opposed the growth of ecumenism in the church.[22] He first publicly challenged the Unionist Party during a row with the then Prime Minister, Lord Brookeborough, over the failure of the Party to expel two of its MPs who had advocated the admission of Catholics to the Unionist Party.[23]

It was the advent of O'Neill's reforms and the relative liberalization of the Province that gave Paisley his chance to rail

20 Terence Brown, *Ireland: A Social and Cultural History 1922–1985* (London: Fontana, 1985) p. 280. See Terence O'Neill, *Ulster at the Cross-roads* (London: Faber & Faber, 1969), pp. 157–9.

21 D.G. Boyce, *The Irish Question and British Politics 1868–1986* (London: Macmillan, 1988), p. 104. See Harold Wilson, *The Labour Government 1964–1970: A Personal Record* (London: Weidenfeld and Nicolson, 1971).

22 Sarah Nelson, *Ulster's Uncertain Defenders: Protestant Political, Paramilitary and Community Groups and the Northern Ireland Conflict* (Belfast: Appletree Press, 1984), p. 55. See also Steve Bruce, *God Save Ulster! The Religion and Politics of Paisleyism* (Oxford: Oxford University Press, 1986).

23 Nelson, op. cit., p. 55.

against change in the Province, but also specifically against O'Neill's liberalism *vis-à-vis* the minority community. In 1964, Paisley emerged more fully on to the political scene when he backed four Protestant Unionist candidates in the Belfast corporation elections. In the same year, he heightened his political and public profile by leading thousands of followers in protest at the display of a tricolour by Sinn Fein candidates at their headquarters in west Belfast (the display of nationalist emblems was actually illegal under the Flags and Emblems Act of 1954). The furore over the removal of the flag created a riot. In May 1966, he published the first edition of a virulently anti-Catholic paper, the *Protestant Telegraph*, which ritually condemned O'Neill's appeasement policies.[24] Again in 1966, Paisley came to prominence when he organized demonstrations against a so-called 'Roman way' within the Presbyterian church. He was, however, subsequently convicted of 'unlawful assembly'.[25] Paisley publicly disavowed O'Neill's form of Unionism and of the Prime Minister's stated intention to act as a bridge to the Catholics, stating that: 'A traitor and a bridge are very much alike, for they both go over to the other side.'[26] All of this underlined the hostility and suspicion with which the majority regarded the minority community, but when the Protestant paramilitaries decided to use force against Catholic agitation, Paisley disassociated himself from the more violent acts of those who claimed to follow him. Paisley, although anti-Catholic, drew lines past which, at this stage, he was not prepared to go in defence of the Union. Paisley's reluctance stemmed partly from the composition of his base of support – the bulk of Paisley's adherents were individuals from rural areas who, although committed to the Union, had no desire to actually break the law.[27] What is interesting and worthy of further analysis is why the Protestant community (or at least some parts of it) objected so virulently, and in some cases so violently, to O'Neill's reforms. Certain characteristics of those who supported Paisley have been identified. First, there were those Protestants who were attracted to his platform quite simply because of his anti-Catholic stance. This was premised on a strong, historic hostility towards Catholics that was part of a religious and cultural tradition within Northern Ireland. The Catholic church was regarded as malign and an

24 Ibid., p. 55.
25 Ibid., p. 55.
26 Rose, op. cit., p. 101.
27 Ibid., p. 351.

enemy of the North, a view that was particularly prevalent among the skilled working classes.[28] Secondly, many Protestants were suspicious of the Catholic adherence to the Pope in Rome which, to them, represented allegiance to an 'alien' force which held a manifesto to spread an 'alien' religion. This was, in itself, a challenge to Protestant Ulster. When, after 1962, the IRA began to identify itself as communist, Protestants regarded this as even more suspicious – an enemy which advocated Catholicism was now twinned with communism. When the Catholic communities began to protest against their 'lot' in the Province, many Protestants feared that this was the rising of an enemy within, inspired by malevolent external forces. Thirdly, there were others who were simply opposed to O'Neill's reform programme. Part of O'Neill's plans for economic modernization included a drive for external investment in the Province by powerful multinational corporations. The advent of such investment threatened the traditional dominance of the Unionist industrial classes. It also caused concern among the working classes, who saw that traditional industrial practices, not least that of a preference for Protestant workers, would not be upheld by the new companies that were more interested in pure profit than local prejudices.[29]

On the whole, Protestant objections to the reform process took fairly peaceful forms, such as the blocking of Unionist Party membership, but in the mid-1960s resistance took a more extreme form, orchestrated by the behaviour of the recently reformed Ulster Volunteer Force (UVF). The UVF had rearmed and regrouped in order to oppose nationalist plans to celebrate the anniversary of the 1916 Easter uprising. On 21 May 1966, the UVF declared war against the IRA and engaged in a spate of sectarian killings. As a result of these murders, O'Neill outlawed the organization in June 1966. This merely forced it underground until the spring of 1969.[30]

All of the above factors create the impression of a unified Protestant resistance against reform. This is, in one sense, accurate but in another, misleading. Any such discussion of the Northern Irish Protestant community must have a caveat attached – the difficulty of discussing the Protestant community in Northern Ireland as if it was a monolithic grouping. A key question which

28 Ibid., p. 351.
29 See Coogan, op. cit., p. 41.
30 Steve Bruce, *The Red Hand: Protestant Paramilitaries in Northern Ireland* (Oxford: Oxford University Press, 1992), pp. 14–15.

has been posed by analysts is: did (does) Protestant Ulster have a mind? As A.T.Q. Stewart has pointed out, this is not meant as an offensive question but as a deadly serious one.[31] Can, he asked, one outlook be discussed when Protestant society was class-riven, economically divided and split between its Presbyterian roots and those of the established church? This is an important question and to answer it requires a certain boldness. There is little doubt of the complexity of discussing Protestant mindsets, but what is critical to the discussion of resistance to reform in the 1960s is that Northern Irish Protestants as a group had one defining quality – the entrenched siege mentality which had developed *vis-à-vis* the Catholics since 1921. Protestants agreed, in the 1960s, as they always had, that the minority had to be managed, but they were divided on what mechanisms could be used. For example, O'Neill had an approach that was essentially liberal, which was about managing the Catholics on a more equitable basis. Equally, Paisley had a view of management but it was rather less civilized and premised not on the inclusion of Catholics, but rather on their exclusion from Northern Irish structures. More radically, Protestant paramilitary groups such as the UVF, which represented the extreme edge of resistance to O'Neill, saw the Catholics as the enemy within, to be subdued and coerced.[32] It was this issue of the management of the minority that defines Protestant struggles in the mid-1960s. How should the Catholic minority be treated? How far could or should reform go? Such questions were rendered increasingly critical for Protestants, not only by the reform process but also by the subsequent agitation for Civil Rights. The lack of consensus on the Protestant side meant that any reform was controversial, piecemeal and relatively slow to answer growing Catholic grievances.

Catholic grievances

While some in the Protestant community were quick to demonstrate their disapproval of change, signs of dissatisfaction with O'Neill's reforms were at first slow to come from the Catholic community. Initially, nationalist politicians were in favour of the notion of bridge-building between the two communities. Yet they

31 A.T.Q. Stewart, 'The Mind of Protestant Ulster' in Watt, op. cit., p. 31.
32 See Steve Bruce, *The Red Hand*, op. cit., pp. 14–19.

would go only so far in their support of O'Neill, not least because they did not want to lose votes to the Ulster Unionists. More radical nationalists suspected that successful bridge-building between the communities would only delay the day when the border between the North and the south could be eradicated.[33] It is also accurate to suggest that Catholics, although hopeful of O'Neill's reforms, were less concerned about his economic programme than their rights as citizens, and specifically their rights under local government legislation which oversaw housing and education.[34]

It was precisely this type of local government issue – specifically the allocation of housing – that gave rise to the first stirring of a Civil Rights movement. The first inkling of the storm to come was when the issue of housing Catholic families in Dungannon, in Co. Tyrone, was taken up. A local woman, Patricia McClusky, organized the Homeless Citizen League in the town to protest against the conditions in which Catholics were housed and to agitate for their removal to a group of good quality council houses which were literally standing empty.[35] Despite the reservations of the Protestant-dominated council, she succeeded in rehousing the Catholics and, buoyed by this success, founded, along with her husband, the Campaign for Social Justice.[36] This group was dedicated to publicizing cases of injustice within the Province. Initially it was non-political and non-partisan but was willing to use access to MPs of all persuasions to highlight the social injustices of the minority in the Province.[37] The movement was also dedicated to non-violent methods of agitation. In 1965 the campaign became affiliated to the National Conference of Civil Liberties in London, and two years later the Northern Irish Civil Rights Association was formed (NICRA). This movement presented Stormont and the Unionist Party with a new threat. Previous Catholic challenges to its rule may have been violent but they had, on the whole, been episodic. The Northern Irish Government had been able to subdue such challenges quite easily through its police force. The non-violent methods of the street protesters was rather different. It

33 See Paul Arthur, *The People's Democracy 1968–1973* (Belfast: Blackstaff Press, 1974), pp. 14–15.
34 See Rose, op. cit., p. 101.
35 Ibid., p. 101.
36 See Lord Cameron's Report, *Disturbances in Northern Ireland* (Belfast: HMSO, Cmd 532, 1969).
37 For an analysis of the various groups that made up NICRA, see Rose, op. cit., p. 161.

represented, certainly in Irish terms, a modern form of peaceful protest that could not be easily coerced away.[38]

The Northern Ireland Civil Rights Association was born more out of frustration within the Catholic community than from any other factor. For many Catholics, the years of reform were ironically ones which had fostered, not suppressed, growing frustration. Michael Farrell has described the situation as one in which Catholics were, it is true, enjoying greater levels of good housing and better access to higher education, but they were still suffering from relatively less opportunities than their Protestant counterparts. In the post-war era, he claimed 'Catholics had benefited from a free education system and an increase in university scholarships. This in turn had created a much larger, better-educated, ambitious Catholic middle class, which was anxious to participate in politics and to end their second-class status'.[39] What is interesting though is that the Catholic community did not look to Dublin, which in comparison with the North had a relatively underdeveloped welfare system, for redress of their grievances, but rather sought reform of the Northern Irish structures in a more equitable fashion.[40] This dispute was therefore not about a united Ireland, but initially at least, about the rights of the minority within the Province.

Reform increased expectations but did little to deliver the goods quickly as far as Catholics were concerned. In particular, Catholics began to organize themselves to apply pressure for change in the political system and in areas of social policy. By 1968 much was made on the Catholic side of alleged discrimination in the political system in the Province. Catholics objected to the great dominance of the Unionist vote in Stormont. However, this was a tricky issue because the Unionist Party was the single largest party in the Province and so obviously dominated the Parliament; the other parties were smaller and more disparate in their outlook. Unless partition was to be removed, or unless proportional representation was introduced, there was little that could be done about such a 'first-past-the-post' system.[41] This, therefore, was less of an issue than the abuses at the lower levels of government,

38 Ian McAllister, 'Political Parties: Traditional and Modern' in John Darby (ed.), *Northern Ireland: The Background to Conflict* (New York: Appletree Press, Syracuse University Press, 1983).

39 M. Farrell, *Northern Ireland: The Orange State* (London: Pluto, 1976), p. 238.

40 Ibid., p. 238. See also Rose, op. cit., pp. 298–300.

41 On this issue, see Rose, op. cit., p. 441. As he points out, the Northern Irish system was of a type that was and remains quite customary in the Western world.

specifically in the realm of local government, where most inequalities occurred. These arose primarily from the practice in the Province of allowing laws which restricted voting rights to property owners or tenants with statutory rights. Such restrictions meant that about a quarter of the people who qualified to vote in national elections could not vote in those for local governments. Compounding the problem of exclusion was the retention of laws that allowed multiple property owners multiple votes; company votes were also preserved. In addition to this, there was a denial of rights to some Citizens through a process known as gerry-mandering. In Londonderry, for example, Catholics outnumbered Protestants by two to one, but on the council this situation was inverted, and Protestants outnumbered Catholics.[42] The manipulation of ward boundaries ensured that a greater number of Protestant councillors were elected despite Catholic numerical superiority.

Historians disagree as to the extent of discrimination that existed in the Province before 1968. At one extreme, some depict it as all pervasive. At the other end of the spectrum, some claim that there was nothing wrong in the Province at all.[43] The centre ground has tried to assess the evidence in a more balanced fashion, and in some of the best work on the issue, John Darby argues that although some of the allegations of discrimination against the Protestants cannot be upheld, there was 'a constant and irrefutable pattern of deliberate discrimination against Catholics'.[44] That discrimination existed at some levels and in some regions against Catholics does seem beyond dispute, but it should also be signalled that the electoral laws relating to property franchises in some areas disadvantaged working-class Protestants. By 1968, however, it was Catholic grievances about their status within the Province that sparked street protests.

The IRA

Nationalist protest has a long history in Ireland; nationalists have opposed the British Government, the Protestant landowners, the

---

42 Rose, op. cit., p. 442. See also Wright, op. cit., pp. 190–1.

43 John Whyte, *Interpreting Northern Ireland* (Oxford: Clarendon Press, 1990), pp. 166–7.

44 John Darby, *Conflict in Northern Ireland: The Development of a Polarised Community* (Dublin: Gill and Macmillan, 1976), p. 76, quoted in Whyte, ibid., p. 167.

Irish Government after 1921, and in 1968 the Stormont regime. In nearly all of these battles after 1916, the IRA have been present. One of the key questions is whether the protests of 1968 were the same as those in the past that were orchestrated by the IRA. There has been much debate in the historical literature as to whether the IRA were directly responsible for the setting up of NICRA and the other protest movements of the late 1960s. The question has been posed as to whether NICRA was a guise for the activities of a regrouped IRA. Members of the IRA were indeed around and involved in some of the organizations, but in a quite different mantle from that of their traditional one. After the failure of the border campaigns of the 1950s, the IRA had entered a period of dissension and reflection on the failures of the decade. There was little military dynamism left and on 26 February 1962 the IRA announced that it 'had ordered the termination of the campaign against the British occupation. All full-time service volunteers had been withdrawn.'[45] Militarism ceased, apart from a series of raids on banks. The remainder of the IRA membership, under the leadership of Cathal Goulding, decided to take a more political role in Irish affairs and agitate for change from within bodies such as trade union organizations. Specifically, the organization was now communist and dedicated itself to the ideas of Marx. In the south, the IRA met in various groups, many of which were in Dublin. They were routinely monitored by the Irish Special Branch. In the North, members were involved in Republican clubs. Members of the IRA certainly attended some of the first meetings of the Civil Rights movement, but were not present in any paramilitary sense.[46] Rather, they appeared as ideologues with little grasp of the reality of protest against government. Cathal Goulding admitted in 1970 that three years earlier the movement had become dormant:

> It wasn't active in any political sense or even in any revolutionary sense. Membership was falling off. People had gone away. Units of the IRA and the Cumainn (local branches) of Sinn Fein had become almost non-existent.[47]

When the IRA conference took place in 1967, the leadership realized in a rather embarrassed fashion that they had no

45 Tim Pat Coogan, *The IRA* (Glasgow: Fontana, 1980), p. 418.
46 See Coogan, *The Troubles*, op. cit., p. 63.
47 Interview with Cathal Goulding, *This Week* (31 July 1970), quoted in M.L.R. Smith, *Fighting for Ireland? The Military Strategy of the Irish Republican Movement* (London: Routledge, 1995), p. 80.

movement at all.[48] The nadir of the movement was confirmed when Sinn Fein contested the local elections of 1967 but fared extremely badly. Even formerly loyal voters saw little point in wasting their votes when there was no real campaign to support.[49] The Civil Rights movement consisted of a broad church of aggrieved groups and individuals which set out to reform the Northern Irish system. It was not a paramilitary force, at this stage, and the IRA as an organizational force was dead. This became obvious as the troubles began.

The troubles

Austin Currie, a nationalist MP representing Co. Tyrone, decided to make the issue of housing for Catholic families the central plank of Civil Rights demonstrations. He had been refused by the Unionists in his bid to secure council accommodation for a large Catholic family. After a 'sit in' at the house that the family had been refused, a Civil Rights march was organized for 16 August in Dungannon.[50] The march, inspired by the success of the black Civil Rights movement in the United States, passed off peacefully and another was planned for October. This one was to be in Londonderry.

The site of the march, like much else in Northern Ireland, evoked considerable controversy. Londonderry, or Derry as it was known to Catholics, had traditionally been a bastion of Protestantism. Gerrymandering had ensured, though, that Protestants dominated local structures.[51] The thought of a Civil Rights march through the streets of the town brought strong Protestant opposition. The organizers of the march claimed that it was not sectarian but about the rights of citizenship. William Craig, the Minister of Home Affairs, banned the march.[52] This gave the organizers a choice of whether to cancel or to demonstrate their disapproval of the regime. The march went ahead.

The Royal Ulster Constabulary (RUC) and the Reserve Force (of the B-Special Constabulary or the riot squad) 'policed' the

48 Ibid., p. 80.
49 J. Bowyer Bell, *The Secret Army: A History of the IRA* (Dublin: The Academy Press, 1970), p. 346.
50 Rose, op. cit., p. 102. Terence O'Neill hardly noticed the march; he was in England on holiday. Terence O'Neill *The Autobiography of Terence O'Neill, Prime Minister of Northern Ireland 1963–1969* (London: Rupert Hart-Davis, 1972), p. 99.
51 Rose, op. cit., p. 103.
52 Rose, op. cit., p. 103.

march in a way that brought widespread disapproval from outside the Province. The protesters were treated roughly and among the injured were seventy-seven demonstrators and four constables. The Northern Irish Government, along with the Secretary of State for the Home Department, James Callaghan, later claimed that the police did nothing to provoke the violence.[53] An official commission found otherwise and criticized the police for its indiscriminate use of batons and the use of water canons.[54]

Despite the official line, as espoused by Craig, the Home Office Minister, that the RUC had not behaved badly, in November the Northern Irish Government admitted that the minority group had some grievances and suspended the Londonderry Council. Its powers were placed in the hands of a special commission.[55] Stormont also recommended that new principles for housing allocation be formulated. As far as the Civil Rights people were concerned, this was too little, too late. The reforms did little to resolve the issue of 'one man, one vote' which had now become a central plank of the protesters' manifesto for change.

O'Neill's administration was increasingly under pressure. The concessions that O'Neill had made to the Catholics in November sparked an angry counter-protest led, once again, by Ian Paisley. He and his supporters held a vigil in Armagh cathedral that they used to try to prevent a Civil Rights march. Searches of the Protestant protesters led to a find of two guns and numerous home-made weapons. Paisley himself was later sentenced to a short term of imprisonment for his involvement.[56] Afterwards, on 9 December, the Prime Minister went on television to outline a programme of change for the Province. This did little to prevent a further explosion of violence. In January 1969, the Civil Rights protesters decided to hold another march. On this occasion they were reinforced by a group of Civil Rights activists from Queens University known as 'People's Democracy'.[57] They decided on 1

---

53 Minister of Home Affairs, Craig, vol. 788, col. 50, 13 October 1968. Quoted in Ronald Weitzer, *Policing Under Fire: Ethnic Conflict and Police–Community Relations in Northern Ireland* (New York: State University New York, 1995), p. 60.

54 The Cameron Commission Report: Disturbances in Northern Ireland, Cmnd 532 (Belfast: HMSO, September 1969).

55 Rose, op. cit., p. 103.

56 See M. Farrell, op. cit., p. 62.

57 The relationship between the People's Democracy and the NICRA was problematic and grew increasingly so from 1968–70. Although a ginger group within the NICRA, the declaration of the People's Democracy as a socialist organization caused problems. See Paul Arthur, *The People's Democracy 1968–1973* (Belfast: Blackstaff Press, 1974), p. 75.

January to stage a march from Belfast to Derry. On 4 January, along the route at Burntollet Bridge, the marchers were ambushed by a group of Protestants, including members of the Ulster Special Constabulary (USC). It emerged that RUC officers had chatted casually with the ambushers before the attack.[58] On arrival in Londonderry the marchers were again set upon by indignant Protestants and in the few days that followed, RUC men entered Catholic areas and randomly attacked people.[59] The only IRA activity at this time was stone-throwing and petrol-bombing.[60]

O'Neill decided to resolve the crisis and, in an attempt to regroup both his Party and the Province behind his reforms, called a general election for February. He failed to gain sufficient support. After the election the Unionist Party remained as deeply divided as ever over reform and Catholics had not been persuaded to place their confidence in the Prime Minister. In April, O'Neill announced his resignation. He was replaced by Major James Chichester Clark. Under him, the Government announced that it accepted the principle of 'one man, one vote'.[61] Yet again, this did little to prevent the escalation of violence between the Civil Rights protesters and angry Protestant groups. The climax was reached in August 1969 when a Protestant march, the annual march of the apprentice boys commemorating the relief of the city from the siege of 1689, was stoned by Catholics in Londonderry. August was always a sensitive month in the Province, marked by the tribal and ritualistic marching and counter-marching of the communities. On this occasion, the RUC's reserve force (the B-Specials) retaliated by storming the 'bogside' – the area inhabited by Catholics. They rampaged through the district, causing damage to both people and property. The inhabitants, fearing a Protestant invasion, responded by erecting barricades. The RUC attempted to bulldoze the barricades and a continual siege developed. The so-called 'siege of the Bogside' provoked riots and bloodshed throughout the Province. In Belfast, Catholics began building barricades on street corners and asked the IRA to provide arms. The IRA had little to offer – assessments made of IRA ammunition at the time put their total resources at ten guns! – although individuals, who

58 See *The Sunday Times*, 27 April 1969, and for a full story of the march, Bernadette Devlin, *The Price of My Soul* (London: Pan, 1969).

59 The Cameron Report, op. cit.

60 Coogan, *The IRA*, op. cit., p. 468.

61 Brian Faulkner, *Memoirs of a Statesman*, ed. John Houston (London: Weidenfeld and Nicolson, 1978), p. 54.

later became centrally involved with the IRA, did lead individual defences of parts of Catholic areas.[62] William McKee, who would later lead one of the Belfast brigades, conducted a defence of a church in the face of an attack. Angry Protestant mobs, who gathered at the edge of Catholic areas, burnt empty houses to intimidate the community. They were aided either directly by the RUC or abetted by them when the RUC did nothing to prevent the attacks.[63]

The subsequent investigations into the cause of the troubles, the Cameron Commission and the Scarman Tribunal, pointed to the lack of sufficient manpower available to the RUC to control such wholesale disturbances. Both commissions argued that the lack of people meant that the RUC was forced to depend on methods that inevitably caused casualties and escalated tensions: baton charging, water canon, tear gas and the use of gun fire.[64] The Scarman Tribunal, in an understanding of the Protestant mindset, in particular pointed out that the behaviour of the RUC had not been aided by its belief that it was actually confronting an uprising by the minority community.[65] It also underlined RUC fears that if the Protestant extremists should get out of control, the police were not certain of their ability to control the situation, but on past experience they believed they could deal with the rioting. Both investigations, however, were deeply critical of the behaviour of the RUC, not least its failure to act against crowds hostile to the Civil Rights protestors.[66] The upshot of the rioting was a complete breakdown in the relationship between the communities in the Province and a crisis in the relationship between the Catholics and the police forces.

By this stage the arrangements of 1921 were increasingly under threat and the regime was engaged in a last-ditch enterprise to hold it together. What had brought the Province to the brink? The interpretations, like so much else in Irish history, are hotly contested.[67] One explanation was that of the problem of the minority. Nineteen-sixty-eight was, it could be argued, the endpoint of Irish nationalist rebellion against the Protestant regime in the North. A second and alternative explanation was

62 Coogan, *The IRA*, op. cit., p. 461.
63 Max Hastings, *Ulster 1969* (London: Gollancz, 1970), p. 145.
64 See Weitzer, op. cit., p. 60.
65 Scarman Tribunal: Violence and Civil Disturbances in Northern Ireland in 1969, Cmd 566 (Belfast: HMSO, April 1972), p. 16.
66 The Cameron Report, op. cit.
67 See Whyte, op. cit., pp. 113–94.

that of the problem of the majority. The dogged resistance to change by parts of the Protestant community meant that minority rights were not conceded easily. History is full of ifs, buts and maybes, *but* if O'Neill had succeeded in reforming the Province, at least only partially, perhaps the Catholics might have been reconciled to the rule of Ulster. The indications were in 1967–68 that the protests were about rights *within* the regime, not about the right to dismantle it. But the problem in Northern Ireland was always the problem of how to 'rule' and how to respond to the minority. The Province had been set up to ensure Protestant rights in Ireland. Any political change *vis-à-vis* the minority challenged that fundamental premise. The years 1968–69 saw the knee jerk reaction of a traditional regime confronted with political change. The use of violence in the summer of 1969 saw the regime's authority and legitimacy crumble as far as the minority was concerned and, as in the past, Stormont appealed to the Government on the mainland to uphold the line established in 1921. In August 1969, British troops were deployed into Ireland once again to shore up a contested regime.[68]

68 A small garrison of British troops had been maintained in the Province since the time of partition. British politicians maintained and continued to maintain that the troop deployment in 1969 was merely additional and not extraordinary. See for example H. Atkins in HC, vol. 6, col. 1172, 18 June 1981.

CHAPTER THREE

From Peacekeeping to Containment: The Campaign of the British Army in the Cities, 1969–74

So in August 1969 a Labour Government, at the request of the Northern Irish authorities, committed the British Army on to the streets of Belfast and Londonderry. Civil disorder between the Catholic and Protestant communities had escalated to such a degree that the Northern Irish police forces were no longer capable of subduing the violence or maintaining order.[1] The committal of troops was in some ways a reversion to the position in Ireland before independence – British troops were once more on Irish soil to subdue rebellion against the Government. However, for a short period in the summer of 1969 there was a significant difference in the task of the military; while its role would soon change, the British Army was initially directed to protect the Catholic areas against the onslaught of the Unionists.

There is a debate in the academic literature over the role of the British Army in Northern Ireland in 1969. Analysts have been divided over whether in fact it represented a neutral force placed between warring ethnic factions or whether it was committed to shore up Unionist power. Very simply, the Labour Government of the day expected it to do both. The first task of the British Army was indeed to control the estranged communities – to try to separate the warring Catholics and Protestants. In geographical terms this meant occupying the areas between the two factions. The British soldiers placed themselves between the two and a so-called peace line was established. To mark this boundary, a 'wall' consisting of corrugated iron, barbed wire and look-out posts was

---

1 Desmond Hamill, *Pig in the Middle: The Army in Northern Ireland 1969–1984* (London: Methuen, 1985), p. 6.

constructed. The Irish 'Berlin Wall' as it became known was an attempt to prevent either faction attacking the other.[2]

During this initial period the IRA did not constitute a threat to the Army. Indeed, ironically, at this juncture the British Army was regarded as the 'cavalry' by a besieged Catholic community.[3] It has been observed that there was something unnatural in Catholic approval of the presence of British soldiers[4] but in fact in 1969 relations were so good between the two that this time became known as the 'Honeymoon' period – a reference to the fact that soldiers drank tea provided by grateful Catholic housewives and British officers negotiated with leaders of the Catholic community to dismantle the barricades erected in August 1969 when the fighting was at its most violent.[5]

Some of the British soldiers believed that the Irish 'problem' could be managed without real difficulties; as one officer expressed it, 'I felt that given three weeks I could sort my patch out fairly easily'.[6] This tendency to regard the presence of the troops as short-term was not, however, shared by the British Government. When the soldiers were committed, the British Home Secretary, James Callaghan, stated that 'this is a limited operation',[7] but in private Wilson commented that British troops would have to stay in the Province for at least seven years.[8] The idea was that the Army would keep the peace while necessary reforms and adjustments were made and the Province returned to normality under a reconstructed Unionist rule. As part of the price of a military presence, Wilson demanded a number of concessions from the Unionists. Two reports were commissioned by the Wilson administration – the Cameron and the Hunt Reports – both of which specifically examined the causes of the riots. The Hunt Report recommended that the B-Specials be abolished and replaced by a special reserve force, a new part-time military force under the command of the British Army. Discrimination in housing and gerrymandering of the local politics were outlawed. These were laudable attempts to make the Northern Irish

2 Robert Moss, *Urban Guerillas* (London: Temple Smith, 1972), p. 103.

3 Interview with Major N. Kench, Information Officer, Army Headquarters Lisburn, 30 July 1985.

4 Conor Cruise O'Brien, *States of Ireland* (New York: Pantheon Books, 1972), p. 245.

5 Sunday Times Insight Team, *Ulster* (Harmondsworth: Penguin, 1972), p. 158.

6 Quoted by Christopher Wain, *The Listener*, 23 August 1984.

7 Quoted by Hamill, op. cit., p. 7.

8 Interview with Jo Haines, quoted in Ben Pimlott, *Harold Wilson* (London: HarperCollins, 1992), p. 549.

Government politically and socially more acceptable to the Catholics, but the reforms made were all short-term measures. Long-term constitutional and political changes were shunned. For example, the introduction of proportional representation was considered as a solution to the political mistreatment of the Catholics but it was rejected by the Labour Government because 'it was a long term measure' and 'in 1969 Wilson and his colleagues were interested only in immediate steps in Ulster'.[9] There were several reasons for this hesitancy in confronting the roots of the Irish question. First, the crisis had caught the British Government by surprise and there had long existed a tendency within British politics to avoid confronting the problem of Ireland.[10] Secondly, it was recognized that the Unionists would not accept radical changes easily and any major reforms would have to be introduced into the Province with great caution.[11] The findings of both the Cameron and Hunt Reports, which were deeply critical of the security operations of Northern Ireland, had indeed produced Unionist anger. On 10–11 October, outraged Protestants attacked the British Army and the first RUC officer was killed, somewhat ironically by a Protestant sniper. The British military were literally the target of both communities.

The tinkering of the Wilson Government with the political system in Northern Ireland did little in reality to ameliorate the condition of the Catholic community and antagonized the Unionists. It soon became apparent that the truce between the soldiers and the Catholic communities was not going to last forever. In early 1970 the nature of the conflict in Northern Ireland began to change. In his work *Urban Guerillas*, Moss asserts that the nature of the conflict altered in June 1970. He believes that it was at this juncture that the rioting in the Province assumed a new character; riots were no longer a spontaneous sign of disaffection but consisted of orchestrated attacks on the British Army by a regrouped, reorganized and more professional IRA.

After the failure of its border campaign during the late 1960s, the IRA had rethought its role in Irish politics and actually contemplated participation in legitimate political activities. During the outbreak of the conflict in the North the IRA leadership was incapable of mounting an effective response to the Unionist

---

9 Sunday Times Insight Team, op. cit., p. 145.

10 Padraig O'Malley, *The Uncivil Wars, Ireland Today* (Belfast: Blackstaff Press, 1983), p. 207.

11 Sunday Times Insight Team, op. cit., p. 144.

onslaught on the Catholic communities. In the wake of this failure, the IRA in Belfast rid itself of those members in favour of a non-violent path and reverted to a semi-military strategy. The IRA had split into two in January 1970 and the newly constituted Provisional IRA (PIRA) had taken control of the struggle. This group, driven by taunts of the besieged Catholic areas (according to graffiti in the Bogside, IRA had become synonymous with 'Irish ran away'), had taken it upon themselves to rekindle the battle with the British. Paramilitary snipers began to operate from behind the crowds and systematic bombing and assassinations became common as the PIRA endeavoured to drive the Army out.[12]

The inability of the Labour Government to initiate change immediately in Northern Ireland fed the frustration of the Catholic population and allowed the PIRA room to operate freely within those communities. Nationalist politicians in the North were ill-prepared to take the political initiative. It was not until the summer of 1970 that MPs of Republican inclinations joined together to form the Social Democratic and Labour Party under the leadership of Gerry Fitt. This was fully one year after British troops had arrived and too late to rally Republicans under its political flag; in the intervening period the PIRA had embarked on a campaign against the troops.

The spiral of violence in the Province escalated with the defeat of the Labour Government and the election of a Conservative Government under Edward Heath in June 1970. While the new Prime Minister was primarily interested in the domestic crisis on the mainland, his Party committed itself to defeating the PIRA. Whereas Callaghan and the Labour Party had been cautious in its military actions, the new Home Secretary, Reginald Maudling, was prepared to give the Army its head to crush the rebels.[13] Few analysts have much that is positive to say about Maudling's handling of the Irish situation or indeed his knowledge of the intricacies of the Irish problem,[14] and it was under his Home Secretaryship that the Conservative Party redefined the roots of the problem in Northern Ireland. They perceived the roots of the conflict as lying with the rebellious Catholic communities led by the PIRA. The Army concurred in this view. During the remainder

12 Moss, op. cit., p. 103.
13 Hamill, op. cit., p. 35.
14 See, for example, Foster's view of Maudling in R.F. Foster, *Modern Ireland 1600–1972* (London: Penguin, 1988), p. 591.

of 1970 relations between the Army and the Catholic community steadily deteriorated. Violence mounted: after two nights of rioting in Belfast in June, five people had been killed and 248 injured.[15] It was at this point that the British troops reverted to their historic role of subduing anti-Government forces in Ireland.

The offensive

During July 1970 the British Army imposed a curfew on the Lower Falls area of Belfast, a predominantly Catholic area. During the curfew house-to-house searches were undertaken and a sizable haul of weapons was made, including 100 bombs, 250lbs of explosives and 21,000 rounds of ammunition.[16] While the size of the haul represented a success for the Army, the imposition of such a curfew also suited the strategy of the PIRA, who wanted to provoke a campaign of repression which would turn the people against the government.[17] The searches resulted in five deaths[18] and aided the PIRA in their endeavour. The imposition of the Lower Falls curfew had precisely the effect of allowing the Provisionals to claim that the historic British enemy was once again flexing its muscles on Irish soil. British tactics were presented as a strategy of repression exercised purely against the Catholic communities. Despite the obviously counter-productive nature of the searches in terms of Republican sympathies, the use of house searches continued throughout the next year. In many ways this illustrated the difficult role that the Army was increasingly expected to fulfil. The British Government expected it to both stem the rise of rebellion against the state but also not to fuel support for the paramilitaries. This meant in military terms depriving the paramilitaries of support and materials, which demanded searches of suspects, but the presence, attitudes and actions of the Army during these searches was calculated to drive Catholics if not into support for the PIRA, then at the very least into passive acquiescence of its activities. As one leading authority on Irish politics has commented on the searches of 1970–71: 'The Army may have behaved with relative restraint by comparative

15 Moss, op. cit., p. 104.
16 Hamill, op. cit., p. 37.
17 Moss, op. cit., p. 102.
18 J.J. Lee, *Ireland 1912–1985* (Cambridge: Cambridge University Press, 1989), p. 434.

military standards – but the victims of the 17,262 house searches in 1971 were not in a position to ponder average behaviour.'[19]

British troops were not in an enviable position. The Stormont administration, which at least in theory ran Northern Ireland, looked increasingly fragile, with a leadership trying to introduce limited reform against the wishes of the Unionist Party. The indigenous security forces of the Province were discredited and the British military were left in an alien environment, attempting to subdue rebellion while constitutional solutions were sought. The British military found Ireland a paradoxical and difficult theatre in which to operate. The troops went into Ireland in 1969 against an operational background of colonial counter-insurgency. Many offficers had had experience of rebellions in places such as Borneo, Malaya and Kenya. A strain ran through military thinking that Northern Ireland and its peoples were the equivalent of the restless natives encountered in far-flung places of the British Empire – a view that was reflected in the range of military techniques used by the Army on the streets of Belfast during the period 1970–71: the curfew, searches and the use of special legislation were resonant of previous British campaigns in the colonies. Indeed, the catalyst that finally transformed the nature of the conflict in Northern Ireland was exactly this type of colonial technique – the introduction of internment without trial which began in August 1971.

In the months before August, the activities of the PIRA had escalated. Each month had brought new heights of destruction and viciousness. Between January and August 1971 a total of thirteen soldiers, two policemen and sixteen civilians died.[20] Rioting during this period had grown increasingly organized and violent; in February 1971 the first British soldier was killed in the modern conflict. Internment, it was claimed, was designed to halt the escalation of violence.

Internment without trial had been used by the British Army in many of its colonial campaigns. In Malaya, for example, internment had been regarded as an effective tool for use against insurgents. The Army had used it selectively, arresting twenty-five carefully picked suspects every month.[21] This was not how it

19 Ibid., p. 434.
20 David Barzilay, *The British Army in Ulster,* vol. 1 (Belfast: Century Books, 1973), p. 25.
21 Richard Clutterbuck, *The Long War, The Emergency in Malaya 1948–1960* (London: Cassell, 1967).

happened in Northern Ireland. Internment was introduced with the agreement of the British Government on 9 August. The aim was to remove or suppress Republican political opposition to the Government.[22] The operation was brutal and in many ways random. In one night, 346 men were arrested. Far from being carefully selected, since the intelligence sources used by the Army were so out of date, one of the arrested men was blind and some of the others named had been dead for several years.[23]

The officer in charge of the Army in Northern Ireland, Lieutenant-General Tuzo, claimed he was actually opposed to the use of internment at this juncture on two grounds. First, he believed that the Army was being rushed into the operation without adequate preparation because both Westminster and Stormont believed that internment might provide an instant solution. Secondly, he feared that internment on such a scale would alienate the Catholic community completely. This proved, not unsurprisingly, to be the case, particularly as not one Protestant was arrested during the operation.[24] In retrospect, soldiers like Tuzo, who were involved in the internment operation, claimed that the operation was conducted on too large a scale. Major-General Chiswell, for example, expressed the view that the weapon of internment should have been used as it had been in the colonies, with only a few suspects removed at any one time.[25] Internment, which had been intended to stop the rise of violence, in fact had the opposite effect. As one serving officer wrote of the process: 'It has in fact increased terrorist activity, perhaps boosted PIRA recruitment, polarized further the Catholic and Protestant communities and reduced the ranks of the much needed moderates.'[26]

By the end of 1971, 174 people had been killed and 2,375 people injured, 15,000 troops were stationed in the Province[27] and the Catholic population perceived the conflict once again as a battle between Irish nationalism and the forces of the British Crown. The very presence and actions of the British Army had

22 On this point, see Paddy Hillyard, 'Law and Order' in John Darby (ed.), *Northern Ireland: The Background to Conflict* (New York: Appletree Press/Syracuse University Press, 1983), p. 37.

23 Hamill, op. cit., p. 60.

24 Hamill, op. cit., p. 64.

25 Interview with Major-General Chiswell, Army Headquarters Brecon, 24 July 1985.

26 Quoted by Hamill, op. cit., p. 63.

27 Hamill, op. cit., p. 70.

exacerbated the initial crisis of August 1969 into outright conflict two years later. Why was this? If any force in the world appeared suited to the task of countering and subduing terrorism, it was the British military which had enjoyed extensive experience in dealing with political violence in the post-war period. During the withdrawal from Empire, the British Army had been involved in campaigns in Aden, Borneo, Cyprus, Malaya and Palestine. According to some sources, 'calling out the military to aid the civil power used to be a straightforward matter . . . the rules were simple, the chain of command direct and the objective clear'.[28] However, as Townshend points out, this myth of a golden age in countering political violence was highly misleading; there were no easy answers to the problem of how a state should respond to the threat and use of political violence.[29] This problem was enhanced by the fact that it was not possible in post-industrial Northern Ireland to behave as if it was Aden, Borneo or Cyprus. This point has been missed by many analysts who argue that:

> The major lesson of recent urban guerilla campaigns around the world is that they can and have been defeated by efficient armies provided that the troops are not made to fight with their hands tied behind their backs.[30]

In accordance with this view, it has been suggested that the British Army was held in check too long, allowing the violence in Northern Ireland to escalate. Perhaps, it is suggested, the British military could have defeated the PIRA by reacting more forcibly at the beginning of the conflict. Moss, for example, points out that this had been the method chosen by the Canadian Prime Minister Trudeau to deal with the terrorist group the Front de Libération Québec (FLQ) at the time of the Montreal kidnappings in 1970.[31] Trudeau aroused a storm of criticism over his handling of the terrorists but by that stage they had already been crushed.

Wilkinson points out that the Israeli state (a parliamentary democracy) used violent methods against the Arabs in the Gaza Strip in 1971.[32] But these were not comparable cases. The state of Israel had been under siege from surrounding enemies since its inception, and violence seemed to be the accepted mode of

---

28 Hamill, quoted in *The Times Literary Supplement* (November 1985).
29 Charles Townshend, quoted in ibid.
30 Paul Wilkinson, *Terrorism and the Liberal State* (London: Macmillan, Second Edition 1986), p. 158.
31 Moss, op. cit., p. 113.
32 Wilkinson, op. cit., pp. 158–9.

response. For many reasons these types of response would not have been appropriate for Northern Ireland. First, at the beginning of the crisis it was generally recognized that the Catholic community did have genuine grievances that required and deserved political, not military, solutions. By the early 1970s, given the widespread appeal of the Civil Rights movements in North America and Europe, the British Government had, at least initially, to be seen to be responding to these. A second and more pragmatic reason why the British Government could not act as forcibly as some might have wished was that Britain is not Israel – it would not have been suitable for the British security forces in a region of the United Kingdom to indulge in the Israeli tactics of dynamiting houses in reprisal for harbouring suspects. It must also be added that those analysts who claim that the British Army did not react forcibly enough to subdue the violence ignore much of the evidence that reveals that during the prolonged and bloody conflict in Northern Ireland the British Army has been involved in abuse of the civilian Catholic population. Tough actions against the minority community merely exacerbated existing tensions and did not do anything to bring a political settlement closer to fulfilment. This was increasingly the case during 1970–71 when the military regarded itself as on the offensive against the PIRA.

This 'offensive' was clearly demonstrated during the process of internment in August 1971 when the Army carried out its orders to detain suspects. The conduct of the Army during the process of internment should not be glossed over. In August 1971 in the early hours of the morning people were dragged from their beds in front of their families and summarily taken to jail. As O'Malley has written of internment, 'the brutal knock in the middle of the night . . . the random brutality, the abuse of rights . . . the uncertainty . . . all reeked of totalitarianism'.[33] Small wonder that the Catholic communities were alienated.

The situation was made worse when it became clear just how defective the information on which the Army had operated was. It had mainly been supplied by the RUC, who had kept files on the old IRA command but knew little about the new and more professional Provisionals. In fact, the information was so faulty that the Prime Minister of Northern Ireland, Faulkner, refused to issue the detention orders for ninety-seven of the first 337 suspects.[34]

33 O'Malley, op. cit., p. 208.
34 Brian Faulkner, *Memoirs of a Statesman* (London: Weidenfeld and Nicolson, 1978), pp. 122–3.

The débâcle also had the effect of creating huge sympathy for the PIRA in Eire. More and more aid and arms began to cross the border into the North and the southern Irish Government did little to impede their progress. Taoiseach Lynch himself demanded the abolition of Stormont.

What is interesting in retrospect is the manner in which the decision-makers of the time now claim to have been opposed to the use of internment. Senior Army officials and Faulkner himself assert that they harboured severe reservations about the use of selective detention and yet it was still implemented. It is not unusual for politicians and senior military figures to distance themselves from controversial decisions, but if there was such opposition to internment what motive was there for proceeding with such a process?

One answer is that by the summer of 1971 neither the Unionist Government, Westminster nor the British Army had a strategy for defeating the PIRA or a way of subduing Catholic support for PIRA. Internment was percieved as a risky strategy but one that might work by taking out the communities' 'troublemakers'. It also had the added virtue of allowing both the Unionist Government in Northern Ireland and the Heath Government in Westminster to claim that they were actively engaged in combatting terrorism. Faulkner himself had successfully implemented a policy of internment during the border wars of the 1950s and was hopeful that it would again defeat the paramilitaries. The possibility of introducing internment into the Province had been discussed within the Cabinet committee set up to deal with the Irish question, which was known as GEN42.[35] It was Faulkner who appeared throughout the summer of 1971 to have urged the committee, of which Lieutenant-General Tuzo was a member, to back internment. Initially, however, he encountered opposition. However, by 5 August, when the committee again met, there was increased support for the idea from Tuzo and from Harold Smith, who was a Foreign and Commonwealth Office (FCO) adviser.[36]

There was powerful internal imperative for Faulkner to do something about the PIRA. During the summer months the marching season in Northern Ireland took place. Traditionally, both communities triumphantly marched through the streets provocatively parading the symbols of their ideologies. In 1971

35 Tim Pat Coogan, *The Troubles: Ireland's Ordeal 1966–1995 and the Search for Peace* (London: Hutchinson, 1995), pp. 124–5.
36 Ibid., pp. 124–5. See also Faulkner, op. cit., pp. 118–19.

Faulkner hoped to curtail the marching, in particular he wanted to ban the march of the apprentice boys but he did not dare take on the Unionist community without an inducement. The prize they were offered was the implementation of internment against the Catholic communities. However, the introduction of internment was not just brought about by the skilled advocacy of Faulkner. In this period many in the ruling political-military circles of Northern Ireland were concerned that 'something' had to be done about the PIRA. It is also clear that it had been under consideration in some quarters for some time but that there was political hesitation over its implementation. The practical preparations for it had been in place for a considerable period. For example, lists of those to be interned were prepared well in advance, as were the places where internees would be kept. Once the decision had been taken, troops moved swiftly to implement the process of internment.

Internment marked an irrevocable change in the nature of the conflict. The lifting of 'suspects' from their homes into camps provoked some of the worst violence seen in the Province. In the eight months before internment thirty-four people had been killed; four months after, 140 people died.[37] Rioting once again marred the streets of Northern Ireland and by 31 August levels of public outrage were such that a committee of inquiry under Sir Edward Compton was set up to examine the process of internment. During the following autumn, three more battalions were deployed, bringing the troop level in the Province to nearly 14,000. At this point it became apparent that the British Army would be a fixture in Northern Ireland for the foreseeable future. Callaghan's idea of the Army as a temporary measure lost any of its remaining validity. An indication of how permanent the Army's position had become was that by early 1972 it had implemented a system to deal with greatly increased troop levels on a long-term basis. Three catogories were devised. The first consisted of those battalions which formed part of the permanent garrison, serving in Northern Ireland for two years. The second category was made up of the great majority of battalions removed from the forces of the British Army on the Rhine, serving four-month tours of duty in the Province. And the third consisted of those battalions kept on standby to perform emergency duties in an unexpected crisis, particularly in the border areas.[38] After the débâcle of the

37 Coogan, op. cit., p. 131.
38 Lieutenant-Colonel Michael Dewar, *The British Army in Northern Ireland* (London: Arms and Armour Press, 1985), p. 55.

internment process, Northern Ireland lurched from one bloody crisis to the next. Republican anger seethed in tandem with Unionist fears that the very structures of security and government that had protected them would be pulled down. Out of this fear grew one of the most powerful Unionist paramilitary groups, the Ulster Defence Association (UDA), which gathered men from the various street vigilante groups in Protestant areas into more organized paramilitary activities. This development provided yet another anxiety for the security forces in the sense that they were now potentially under attack from two forces, but there was more to the Army's relationship with the UDA than this. The UDA would provide a willing source of local information for them. A more sinister development was that UDA members were at times able and willing to perform dangerous and illegal tasks for certain factions of the military.[39] The Catholic communities remained suspicious of British involvement with the UDA, so when, in June 1972, William Whitelaw, Secretary of State for Northern Ireland, held a meeting with UDA leaders to try to persuade them not to set up barricades and 'no go areas' in Protestant communities, this was interpreted as an endorsement of Unionist paramilitary behaviour. In fact, Whitelaw was trying to pursue a broader strategy by talking to 'leaders' on both sides of the divide and would later talk to the leadership of the PIRA.

Yet, talking did little to soothe either community after the events of Sunday 30 January 1972. 'Bloody Sunday', as it became known, is surrounded by many myths and became one of the most emotive leif motifs for the modern conflict. It is alleged by Republicans that British soldiers from the Parachute Regiment deliberately opened fire, shooting and killing thirteen men at the end of a Catholic Civil Rights march in Londonderry (a four-teenth man later died). The Army contended that the soldiers acted only in self-defence, fearing for their own lives. Reports differ widely over these events. The coroner at the inquest into the deaths of the thirteen men accused the Army of 'sheer unadult-erated murder'.[40] *The Guardian* newspaper alleged that the soldiers did indeed fire first at the marchers.[41] However, the report by

---

39 See Steve Bruce, *The Red Hand: Protestant Paramilitaries in Northern Ireland* (Oxford: Oxford University Press, 1992), pp. 49–50; and Coogan, op. cit., p. 144.

40 Hamill, op. cit., p. 91.

41 *The Guardian*, 31 January 1972.

Lord Widgery, although it failed to establish that any of the victims was armed, concluded that the Army did not fire first. [42]

However opinions differ over the actual course of events, one thing is certain – 'Bloody Sunday' represented a massive propaganda victory for the PIRA as the television and press publicized the killings of the Catholic men.[43] Southern Premier Lynch recalled the Irish Ambassador from London and emotions reached a peak when the British Embassy in Dublin was burned down by a mob on 2 February. In the wake of internment and what was at best, on Bloody Sunday, the use of ill-disciplined British troops, a whole host of questions were raised over what exactly Westminster was countering through the use of state force and especially what the British Government hoped to achieve politically through such force. In particular, it had become increasingly urgent to reach a political settlement rather than lurching from one crisis to the next, but the military and the political aims did not appear to be syncronized. Hand in hand with military toughness, Westminster continually held out the hope that nationalist aims might some day be met. The Consultative Paper on the Future of Northern Ireland of 1972 stated openly that Westminster did not harbour any wish to impede the realization of Irish unity, if it were to come about by freely given mutual agreement. This meant that the Republican communities were militarily harassed but that politically Westminster was willing to allow them the hope of British withdrawal. This paradox, which legitimized the aim if not the methods of the Republicans, remained at the heart of British policy throughout the 1970s.

The willingness of British politicians to cede, at least in theory, Republican claims is illustrated by the behaviour of Harold Wilson (at this point leader of the opposition) in the aftermath of Bloody Sunday. He was opposed to the use of internment and visited both Northern and southern Ireland during the autumn of 1971 to discuss 'solutions' with politicians. He made a speech in which he described a possible fifteen-year period of transition, in which steps could be taken towards a united Ireland. After the events of Bloody Sunday he stepped up this theme, arguing in public that a cease-fire might be possible if some of the internees, who had not

42 Report of the Tribunal appointed to inquire into the events of Sunday January 30, 1972 which led to the loss of life in connection with the procession in Londonderry on that day. By the Rt Hon Lord Widgery, OBE. TD; HL 101, HC 220.
43 See Liz Curtis, *Ireland the Propaganda War* (London: Pluto Press, 1984), pp. 41–50.

yet been tried, were released.[44] The command of the PIRA was intrigued by this idea and contacted Wilson's office to arrange talks. In March, Wilson and Merlyn Rees, the shadow Home Secretary, held meetings with three leading members of the PIRA – David O'Connell, who was later to become the Provisionals' Chief of Staff, Joe Cahill, the Provisionals' Commander in Belfast and John Kelly.[45] While little came of this meeting, mainly because Wilson as opposition leader had nothing to offer, it indicates an interesting trend in British attitudes towards the 'terrorists'. Despite the claims of successive British Governments that they do not negotiate with terrorists, they have actively carried out a dialogue with leading Provisional spokesmen. Part of the reason for this was the recognition that without the acquiescence of the PIRA, a settlement would not be possible. Negotiating with the enemy was dangerous and in many ways counter-productive because it fed the Provisionals' belief that at some stage the British would have to include them officially in an open dialogue. In the longer term the PIRA was proved right, but in 1971 the British Government under Heath was not prepared for such a step.

At this juncture there was in fact a battle between Heath and Faulkner over the future conduct of security in Northern Ireland. Faulkner wanted to rearm the RUC and sought the re-establishment of the B-Specials. Edward Heath, the British Prime Minister, refused to allow the RUC a more dominant role and argued that the British Army should be in charge of all security arrangements, including the RUC.[46] This proved unacceptable to Faulkner and in March 1972 the British Government announced that in future Northern Ireland would be ruled directly from Westminster through a Secretary of State. The move was regarded as a substantial if indirect victory for the PIRA, for with the abolition of Stormont they had achieved one of their short-term aims: the dissolution of Unionist rule and the recognition that the partition of Ireland was no longer a solution to the Irish troubles.

Direct Rule

The imposition of Direct Rule, under which Westminster assumed complete responsibility for security in Northern Ireland, resulted

44 Pimlott, p. 593.
45 Ibid., op. cit., p. 593.
46 Lee, op. cit., p. 441.

in a substantial improvement in the position of the British Army in Northern Ireland. The Army felt that Direct Rule gave it a long-term and broad-based political direction that had been lacking from the Stormont Government. Previously, the British Army had found itself in a difficult position, the GOC had taken his military orders from London but overall security instructions, many of which the Army had found to be in conflict with the directives from London, had come from the Northern Irish Prime Minister.[47] General Harry Tuzo reported of his tenure as GOC before the abolition of Stormont that he was

> in effect a sort of Minister of Defence and Chief of Staff to two people. I worked for the Prime Minister of Northern Ireland and I also had to report back to Westminster, and of course I gained all my sustenance from Westminster and was entirely dependent on Westminster for the forces I had, so there were no indigenous forces.[48]

In this sense, after the imposition of Direct Rule, the position of the Army was improved because it now had only one master.

Direct Rule, however, also created problems for the Army. It had been hoped by Westminster that the removal of the Stormont Government, which had long been a Catholic aspiration, would open the way for a fresh round of political initiatives with the Republicans. Accordingly, the security forces were required to scale down their activities to the level of so-called 'low profile' operations. This meant the reduction of hot pursuit by Army patrols, the lessening of street patrols and the diminution of overt surveillance. Such measures, it was felt, were necessary to gain the cooperation of Catholic politicians and the southern Irish Government in discussing possible initiatives. While this was the case, such a downgrading of military activity also enabled the PIRA to operate more freely. New recruits who joined the PIRA in this period were unknown to the British Army, intimidation within the Catholic communities became rife and intelligence sources began to dry up. The Army was also instructed to respect some hard-line Republican areas (known as 'no go areas') as beyond their jurisdiction since the presence of the military could be regarded as inflammatory and upset negotiations.[49] The high point of PIRA

47 Hamill, op. cit., p. 103.
48 Institute of Contemporary British History, Seminar on Ireland 1970–74, quoted in Coogan, op. cit., p. 108.
49 British Army, PQS2 1981/82. Tutor Background Paper, Northern Ireland.

influence occurred in July 1972 when, during a cease-fire with the British Army, PIRA leaders held a meeting with representatives of the British Government in London to try to reach some form of compromise concerning the future of the Province.[50] This move starkly demonstrated the ambivalence of the British position towards the Republican paramilitaries. Despite the fact that officially PIRA leaders were designated as terrorists who wished to usurp the state, by negotiating with the leaders of the movement the British Government in many respects upheld the claim of the PIRA that it acted as the voice of the Republican communities. However, these talks failed to reach any successful conclusion since the aims of the two participants were so divergent. Indeed, it is questionable as to whether the leadership of the paramilitaries regarded these discussions in a serious light. After the breakdown of the talks the PIRA resorted to what were by now their familiar tactics of bombing and assassination. The British Government had gambled on the PIRA respecting the cease-fire but this had failed and, indeed, proved to be militarily expensive. The PIRA had in fact used the cease-fire to regroup and reorganize; they returned to the fight after the thirteen-day truce with renewed ferocity.[51] In response, the British Army reverted once more to an offensive policy and tougher tactics against Republican areas.

The most dramatic manifestation of this tougher policy was Operation Motorman in July 1972. Operation Motorman was designed to re-establish a military presence in both the Catholic and Protestant areas of the cities; 'no go areas' would no longer be tolerated. In a massive show of strength 4,000 extra troops were drafted into the Province, bringing the total number to 21,000 and making the operation the largest that Britain had embarked upon since World War II.[52] The operation was a success. British troops established a presence throughout the cities; they dismantled barricades with tanks and established Army units even in those areas regarded as paramilitary strongholds. Following the operation the Army continued to concentrate its energies upon Belfast, maintaining high troop levels by redeploying troops from the border areas to sustain an intensity of concentration.[53] The redeployment was, however, at the expense of operations on the border where activities had to be scaled down. The Republican

50 Tim Pat Coogan, *The IRA* (Glasgow: Fontana, 1980), p. 492.
51 Coogan, *The IRA*, op. cit., p. 496.
52 Dewar, op. cit., p. 66.
53 See Chapter Four.

paramilitaries were forced out of the cities to the border region where they waged a rural guerrilla warfare campaign in areas less familiar to the British Army. As a result of this more rigorous approach, by 1974 the Army claimed to have had practically defeated the PIRA in the cities. The Christmas truce of 1974 and the redeployment of PIRA activities to the border signalled a shift in strategy and its short-term demise as an urban guerrilla movement.[54]

Special legislation and intelligence gathering

The claim of the British Government to have defeated the PIRA at this stage needs to be examined carefully. It raises the question of what 'victory' looked like in 1974. In particular, if this was indeed a victory, it had been achieved at a very high cost to the democratic processes in the United Kingdom and the rights of citizens in Northern Ireland in particular. Leaving aside events such as 'Bloody Sunday', coercive and undemocratic measures such as 'special legislation' and the 'use of intelligence' had become part and parcel of British military strategy in Northern Ireland. In particular, the use of 'special legislation' proved controversial. Special legislation gave troops extraordinary powers to deal with the PIRA. In 1973 the Northern Ireland Emergency Provisions Act was introduced. This Act gave the Army the power to stop and question any person to establish his or her identity, to arrest and detain for four hours any person suspected of criminal activity, and the power to enter and search houses without warrant. It was reinforced by the Prevention of Terrorism Acts of 1974 and 1976. The powers provided by this legislation were used extensively by the Army. In 1973, for example, 75,000 houses were searched.[55]

Throughout the conflict the British Government have decreed that the Army act within the normally accepted rule of law, but Northern Ireland is an exception to the rule of law operating in the rest of the United Kingdom. The legal system operating in the Province is far from normal. Diplock courts, which try certain offences, operate without a jury and the writ of habeas corpus is at odds with democratic principles. Townshend, for example, describes the 1973 Emergency Provisions Act as a 'remarkably

54 Wilkinson, op. cit., p. 160.
55 Kevin Boyle, Tom Haddon, Paddy Hillyard, *Ten Years on in Northern Ireland, The Level and Control of Political Violence* (London: The Cobden Trust, 1980), p. 27.

coercive measure in the nineteenth-century tradition'.[56] Despite this type of criticism, there was general approval in the military of the Emergency Provisions Acts, and some even felt that it did not go far enough. It was argued, for example, that methods such as the compulsory introduction of identity cards in the Province would have made the task of the British Army easier. It was even suggested that recognition of the conflict in Northern Ireland as a war would have benefited the Army by enabling them to implement tougher military measures.[57] Yet these measures were not attempted and the 1973 Act itself remained the subject of much debate and criticism. The Act had actually arisen out of the considerations of the Diplock Commission of 1972. This commission (chaired by Lord Diplock) was criticized specifically for designing legislation which suited those responsible for law and order in Northern Ireland (the military and the police) while ignoring the political, social and economic dimensions of the conflict. In particular, it has been argued that the commission took no account of the legal rights of suspects and that this was a damaging omission as it not only alienated the Catholic communities but more importantly ignored many of the original complaints of the Civil Rights protesters about the nature of the regime in Ireland.[58] In short, the problem was that while emergency legislation was useful for subduing violence, it did little to reconstruct the underlying causes of rebellion in the Province.[59] In fact, even the British military, which regarded the legislation as invaluable in the short term, recognized that it was more problematic in the longer term. The lessons of the use of repression in counter-revolutionary situations is that not only does it encourage support, both active and passive, for terrorist organizations, but it also raises questions about who are the defenders and the attackers.[60] In Ireland it raised the question of whom the Catholics should regard as their defenders – the PIRA or the British military? The Catholic communities on the whole in the early 1970s chose the paramilitaries. It was this civilian support for the paramilitaries among the communities of Northern Ireland that was recognized by the Army as a crucial factor in prolonging

56 Charles Townshend, *Political Violence in Ireland: Government and Resistance since 1848* (Oxford: Oxford University Press, 1983), p. 402.
57 Robin Evelegh, *Peace-Keeping in a Democratic Society* (London: Hurst and Co., 1978), p. 50.
58 Hillyard, op. cit., p. 39.
59 Ibid., p. 39.
60 Ibid., p. 39.

the conflict. Emergency legislation hardened this resistance to the Army, yet the military were not going to ease the pressure on the PIRA and in fact, through the use of 'intelligence', redoubled their efforts to break the support for the paramilitaries.

To accomplish this, however, they needed a great deal of information on local people. Organizations such as the PIRA, which pursue political violence, are, on the whole, characterized by secrecy, mobility and flexibility, with structures and discipline 'fostered to ensure unswerving obedience to the leadership: offenders against the code being punishable by death'.[61] Correspondingly, a crucial requirement in responding to political violence is the development of high-quality intelligence to locate the terrorists. A major development in the Army's campaign in Northern Ireland during the early 1970s was the increasing sophistication of the use of intelligence. In its colonial campaigns the British Army had learnt the value of building up an effective system of gathering information.[62] It is no coincidence that by 1974, the year when the Army began to defeat the PIRA, the intelligence network in Northern Ireland was beginning to run smoothly.

In Northern Ireland the Army had initially encountered several difficulties in its attempt to establish an adequate intelligence network. First, the RUC had been responsible for the routine gathering of intelligence, but by 1969 its files were out of date and its intelligence concerning Catholic areas was non-existent.[63] Secondly, the Army had taken over responsibility for intelligence operations but felt itself a 'foreign force', unfamiliar with the area, the people and the sources available. Despite these initial handicaps, by 1974 the Army had built up an impressive block of detailed information on over 40 per cent of the population of the Province.[64] Much of this information was collected through the means of P-tests; people would be questioned concerning their personal details, families, occupation and religious and political affiliations. Random house searches, head checks and mobile foot patrols were used and all the information was then fed into a central computer. The process has been described as follows:

61 Wilkinson, op. cit., p. 137.
62 David Charters, 'Internal and Psychological Warfare in Northern Ireland', *Royal United Services Institute Journal* (September 1977).
63 Ibid.
64 Wilkinson, op. cit., p. 160.

First they would start with the profiles of would be IRA recruits . . . then requisition the census records of all persons either born in Ireland or with Irish parents . . . This would be cross checked and brought up to date by payments at the DHSS . . . plus records of rent . . . and of car ownership.[65]

These methods were used by the Army to destroy the paramilitaries by increasing the flow of information to the security forces which was then used to deny members refuge, recruits and finance.

The use of intelligence, like the use of special legislation in a democratic society, is a controversial issue and it became even more so when the Army in Northern Ireland used interrogation as a method to produce information from suspects. During the period of internment without trial in 1971 342 men were interned; twelve of these were subjected to interrogation in depth. This process consisted of the prisoners being deprived of sleep, food and clothing, and being systematically questioned.[66] Such methods had been used in the colonies and revealed a great deal of information in situations where intelligence was a major asset,[67] but the military failed to realize that Northern Ireland, with a free press and television, was not a Malaya or a Cyprus. Although soldiers such as Clutterbuck might approve of interrogation to achieve specific ends[68] it could be a very counter-productive process, especially when, as happened in Northern Ireland, allegations of brutality were publicly made against the security forces.[69] A committee headed by Sir Edmund Compton concluded that there had in fact been no brutality committed by the Army, as the interrogators had not intended to inflict pain or suffering.[70] However, the publicity helped the cause of the PIRA, especially as the use of interrogation led to an appeal by the prisoners to the European Court of Human Rights which found that the men had been subjected to 'inhuman and degrading treatment' and awarded them substantial damages.[71] This was reinforced by the

65 'A Computer Programme To Hunt the Bombers', *The Financial Times* 3 December 1974).
66 John McGuffin, *The Guineapigs* (London: Penguin, 1974), pp. 48–9.
67 Charters, op. cit.
68 Richard Clutterbuck, *Protest and the Urban Guerilla* (London: Cassell, 1973), p. 142.
69 McGuffin, op. cit., pp. 48–9.
70 The Compton Report, Cmnd 4823 (London: HMSO, 1971), para. 156–60.
71 O'Malley, op. cit., p. 35.

findings of the Parker Report which found the activities of the Army 'not normally justified'.[72] Subsequently, British Prime Minister Heath decided that the techniques would not be used again, but the damage had been done, not least in some quarters to the reputation of the British Government in Europe. There was some evidence in the British Army campaign in Northern Ireland that some of the military did have a more sophisticated view of the manner in which terrorism could be defeated. Some serving officers, for example, did in fact try to apply lessons gleaned from other conflicts in trying to implement policies aimed at weaning support from the paramilitaries rather than just repressing whole communities. The famous guerrilla fighter, Mao Tse-Tung, likened 'revolutionaries' to fish that require water (the population) in which to swim and survive – without that water the fish quickly expire. Terrorists seek to keep that 'water' by first posing as the legitimate guardians of the people, exploiting genuine political and social grievances, and secondly, through a policy of intimidation. The PIRA succeeded in securing the loyalty of a percentage of the community which, by inclination, abhorred Unionist rule and resented the British presence.[73] A major part of counter-revolutionary strategy rests in the struggle to win over that support. In Malaya, the British Army had managed to deprive the rebels of their supporters by resettling the people in 'strategic hamlets' and providing them with food and shelter. This meant not only that the rebels could not depend upon isolated villages unfamiliar to the soldiers for refuge, but it also meant that the population had an interest in the success of the Army since it had benefited from the system initiated by the British soldiers.[74] This type of strategy for winning the hearts and minds of the Catholic population was advocated by Brigadier Frank Kitson who in the early 1970s was a brigade commander in Belfast. Earlier, Kitson had served in Kenya, Cyprus, Malaysia and Oman, and on the basis of that experience had developed a theory of counter-insurgency tactics which he presented in his book *Low Intensity Operations*.[75]

Kitson recognized that one of the keys to defeating the para-

72 The Parker Report, Cmnd 4901 (London: HMSO, 1972).

73 For an assessment of the complexities of Republican support for the PIRA in this period, see J. Bowyer Bell, *The Irish Troubles: A Generation of Violence 1969–1992* (Dublin: Gill and Macmillan, 1993), pp. 240–1.

74 Evelegh, op. cit., p. 48.

75 General Frank Kitson, *Low-Intensity Operations: Subversion, Insurgency, Peacekeeping* (London: Faber & Faber, 1971).

militaries was to win the trust of local communities. He believed that in the city areas of Northern Ireland the Army should work very closely with the local civil authorities to promote the health and stability of an area, to improve community relations and win the support of the local population. This was not an easy task. Some of the Catholic areas were actually run by the PIRA who organized local matters such as housing lists and operated mafia-style gangs to impose order.[76] Kitson recommended that this could be countered through the appointments of civilian representatives, along the line of colonial district commissioners, who would be responsible for the area, organizing community matters such as street clearance, lighting and welfare work. These 'Mr Fixits', as they became known, would coordinate local government bodies, the population and the Army. This approach was found to be successful in the areas in which it was adopted, for example in Andersontown in 1972.[77] This district was regarded as one of the hardest PIRA areas, but after Operation Motorman a high number of PIRA suspects had been arrested with a consequence that the local network was greatly weakened. The area was in very poor condition because for many months local workmen had not dared to enter it to carry out necessary tasks. The Army therefore undertook the responsibility for civil duties such as refuse collection and repairs. In military terms at least for this area, the strategy was successful. During the period from January to June 1973, after the military had taken over some of the civil administration, the number of shooting incidents in the area fell from forty-one to twelve per month and the number of riot incidents decreased from ten per month to none. Of equal importance, as experience in Malaya, Kenya and Vietnam had shown, was that information from the district began to increase.[78] It is difficult to assess just how widespread these kinds of policy were in Northern Ireland. Much depended on the local commander of an area, but in general Kitson's ideas were not implemented. Many soldiers felt that the first task was to stop the riots and the terrorists rather than to deal with civil administration.[79] Indeed, by the mid-1970s many believed that a hard-line approach backed up by special legislation was working.

76 Sunday Times Insight Team, op. cit., p. 238.
77 Lieutenant-Colonel Graham, Low-level Civil Military Co-ordinator, Belfast, 1970–73, *The Royal United Services Institute Journal* (September 1974), pp. 80–4.
78 Ibid., pp. 80–4.
79 Hamill, op. cit., p. 42.

The beginning of 1974 was a time of relative optimism for the British forces in Northern Ireland. Not only did the Army believe that it was gaining the upper hand in the struggle with the PIRA, but it seemed, at least to those in Westminster, that Northern Ireland was ready for a new political initiative. On 6 December 1973 the Heath Government had arranged for representatives of the British and Irish Governments to discuss possible initiatives with members of the Unionist Party, the SDPL and the Alliance Party at Sunningdale in Berkshire. The result of these deliberations was the Sunningdale Agreement which was aimed at establishing a powersharing executive consisting of six Protestants and five Catholics. A major aim of those who had created the agreement was to provide the Catholics with a greater degree of control over the affairs of the Province. In January 1974, the Northern Ireland Executive was established at Stormont with Brian Faulkner as chief executive and Gerry Fitt from the SDLP as his deputy. Once more, Westminster included a clause in the agreement that admitted the nationalist goal of Irish unification, stating that if the majority of Northern Irish people should indicate a wish to become part of a united Ireland, the British Government would support that wish. It was ironic, but not surprising, that the 'Loyalists' rather than the PIRA destroyed this political initiative.

The Unionists regarded the proposals as a betrayal of their cause and an outright rejection by Westminster of the Unionist *raison d'être*, the right to be British as well as Irish. They treated the new Executive as if it had no mandate and when Edward Heath called a sudden general election in February 1974 the Unionist vote split between Faulkner's pro Executive faction and the anti-Sunningdale Unionist MPs. The latter won. All the Unionist MPs were opposed to the agreement. The Unionist community itself united against the Sunningdale Agreement and on 14 May organized a Province-wide strike in protest against its implementation. They threatened to bring the services of the Province to a standstill. The Unionists had long been preparing for this crisis as bodies such as the Ulster Workers' Council, the Democratic Union Party and the paramilitary groups made that threat a reality. It was estimated that 30,000 people did not attend work; postal services were interrupted; electricity supplies were interfered with; Protestant vigilantes roamed the streets enforcing order in their areas. By this stage, the Heath Government had collapsed and Harold Wilson was once again in charge. Wilson discussed with the Chief of General Staff, Sir Peter Hunt, the possibility of British troops being used to break the strike.[80] The GOC in Northern Ireland, Sir Frank King, however, was not prepared to use troops to bring the strike to an end and in particular he was not prepared to take on the Unionists. According to some accounts, this view was relayed to Downing Street through the Ministry of Defence and directly aided the Unionist defeat of the powersharing initiative.[81] Other interpretations point to the political difficulties that Harold Wilson faced in relation to the crisis. By 24 May the economy in Northern Ireland had been virtually run down. Wilson invited members of the powersharing Executive to London in an attempt to resolve the crisis. What Wilson wanted was a quick result that would not embarrass him politically and allow him to get on with sorting out the mainland economy which itself was convulsed after the wave of worker discontent under the Heath administration.[82] During the meeting between Faulkner, Fitt and Wilson, a major misunderstanding arose. Faulkner apparently believed that it was Wilson's intention to back the Northern Ireland Executive with British troops if necessary, and that it would be possible to retake the control of vital services.[83] He was sadly mistaken. The day after the meeting in London Wilson launched a major tirade against the Unionists (contrary to Faulkner's advice). He accused them, among other things, of sponging off the British taxpayers. While this speech was mainly aimed at reassuring the British on the mainland that he would not give in to the Unionists, it had the effect in the Province of hardening the strike itself. Wilson was not prepared to use force to break the strike and anyway had tended to believe that Heath's powersharing experiment was bound to fail. Given the solidarity of the strike, the Sunningdale Agreement collapsed and Northern Ireland reverted to Direct Rule.[84]

Northern Irish Catholic politicians had, during the crisis, argued that the British Army should be used to break the strike and uphold the new Executive. The decision not to use the Army was a controversial one; the Catholic members of the Executive

80 Martin Dillon, *The Enemy Within: The IRA's War Against the British* (London: Doubleday, 1994), p. 135.

81 Ibid., p. 135. For a general analysis of the crisis, see also Robert Fisk, *The Point of No Return: The Strike Which Broke the British in Ulster* (London: André Deutsch, 1975). Fisk quotes sources that indicate that parts of the British Army Officer Corps in Ireland demonstrated a considerable distrust of Socialist politicians, pp. 240–1.

82 See Pimlott, op. cit., pp. 633–4.

83 Ibid., pp. 633–4.

84 O'Malley, op. cit., p. 317.

believed that through its inactivity the Army was acquiescing in illegal behaviour. The rationale for non-intervention was that the Army should not be used in what was primarily a civil matter best dealt with by the police.[85] This lame distinction barely hid the real reason which was that the British Army was extremely reluctant to become involved in a battle with the Unionists and face a situation in which it was besieged on two fronts, facing not only the PIRA but also the wrath of Protestant paramilitary groups. This apparent sympathy between the military and the Unionists recalled echoes of the past and the traditional support for the Unionist cause which had existed in the British military at the beginning of the century.

Yet the relationship between the British Army and the Unionists in the current conflict has always been complex. Initially, the Protestants welcomed the Army, perceiving it as an additional arm of Unionist power. Lawrence Orr, a prominent Unionist, proclaimed in 1969: 'we're getting the troops and we're getting them without strings'.[86] However, the Unionists were disappointed with the behaviour of the Army, particularly in the phases when the Army adopted a low-profile approach towards the Catholics, as in 1972 and 1975.[87] The relationship between the Army and the Unionists in the 1970s, as now, is best described as one of uneasy alliance; the British Army, despite the threats issued by the Protestants, require them as allies. It certainly cannot cope with a situation of continual siege on two fronts. Equally, while the Protestants regard the Army with suspicion, fearing an eventual British withdrawal, they desire its presence not only to defeat the PIRA, but also as a symbol of Westminster's commitment to their cause.

The inactivity of the Army during the 1974 strike and its tolerance of Unionist paramilitary groups once more underlined the belief in the Catholic communities that the Army was fully aligned with the forces of Unionism. Some analysts have argued that this has been a major failing of the British Army in Northern Ireland – that it has not realized that in order to deprive the PIRA of its support within the Catholic population it has to accommodate Republican ambitions.[88] It is difficult to envisage exactly how this could have been achieved when the Army has as its mandate in the Province the defeat of the PIRA.

85 Hamill, op. cit., p. 144.
86 Quoted in the Sunday Times Insight Team, op. cit., p. 142.
87 O'Malley, op. cit., Chapter 6.
88 Wilkinson, op. cit., p. 166.

By late 1974 the British Army, which had originally been committed as a temporary expedient in 1969, was deeply immersed in counteracting political violence. However, the Army has found it difficult to adjust to its role. Wilkinson writes that: 'Internal security duties under the strict limits imposed in a constitutional liberal democratic system conflict fundamentally in many respects with the professional instincts, traditions and ethos of the military.'[89]

Northern Ireland required a major change in the outlook of soldiers, for it raised the question of whether troops are suited to a strategy requiring the arrest and conviction of terrorists rather than the straightforward elimination of the enemy. Bloody Sunday proved that some soldiers found it difficult to respond with restraint. However, as many commentators have pointed out, taking into consideration the need of the Army to contend with not just the terrorists but also the abuse of both communities, it has behaved better than many other armies would have done. The process of adjustment has not been easy. This, in part, explains why the idea of a hearts-and-minds campaign along the lines envisaged by Kitson was not fully adopted. Some sections of the Army have had difficulty in adjusting to the notion of community service as a weapon in the fight against the enemy. However, the major impediment to the pursuit of a successful strategy in Northern Ireland has been inconsistency in the aims of the Army's political masters. Policy concerning Northern Ireland has fluctuated widely. At one stage Westminster directed the Army to act forcibly against the PIRA, for example during the internment operation of 1971, but when attempts at political conciliation were undertaken, the Army was directed to scale down its operations and the progress made in activities such as intelligence gathering could be lost, as happened after the introduction of Direct Rule in 1972. In such periods, the British Government has even negotiated with PIRA men, the very men who wage war upon the Army. The British Government, unlike the PIRA, has shown no consistency in its strategic aims. Since the beginning of the crisis in Northern Ireland there has been no overriding principle guiding the Army, apart from defeating the PIRA. However, the Army was not even sure that the British Government would not accede to the demands of the PIRA and announce a withdrawal some time in advance, as had happened during the campaign in Aden when the

89 Ibid., p. 157.

Army was left to deal with rebels who knew they had already won.[90]

By 1974, despite the view that the PIRA was steadily being defeated, the position of the Army in Northern Ireland was a matter of profound concern to the British Government. There was little desire to have troops indefinitely entangled in the Province over the longer term. It was embarrassing for the Government to have armed troops parading the streets of the United Kingdom. In particular, there was concern that the Army would be forced to undertake the long-term responsibility for law and order, to such a degree that the police would come to depend on that support and be unable to manage again without it. A case has been made that active service in Northern Ireland was extremely useful in training troops, particularly at officer level,[91] but the skills needed for a tour of duty in the Province were very different from those required for ordinary duties, and by late 1974 the troops seemed weary of a conflict which appeared unending.[92] After the failure of the Sunningdale Agreement a decision was taken by the British Government to attempt to wean British troops out of Ireland.

'Ulsterization' or 'police primacy' as it was known, was a strategy within which the British Army would gradually begin to shed its responsibility for security in the cities and allow the indigenous forces of the Province, namely the RUC, to take over. The idea had first appeared in April 1974 when the British Government started to consider the notion of 'normal policing' for some areas in Northern Ireland. It was strongly backed by the new senior Deputy Chief Constable, Kenneth Newman, who believed that the RUC should be placed in charge of 'policing' the communities, but it ran contrary to the Army's view. The Army had rather expended much thought on the imposition of martial law in the Province to strengthen their hand in the fight against the PIRA.

It was hoped that so-called 'normalization' would enable the British Army to withdraw troops and, it must be added, maintain a greater 'distance' from the conflict with the PIRA and the nationalist communities. Part of the desire to 'normalize' the conflict seems in many respects an attempt to remove the 'British' element from the conflict. Although this has been openly denied by successive British Governments, it was certainly a consideration in 1974, not least because of the success of the PIRA at operating in mainland Britain.

---

90 Robert Paget, *Last Post, Aden* (London: Faber & Faber, 1969), p. 159.
91 Dewar, op. cit., p. 219.
92 Hamill, op. cit., p. 159.

While the PIRA was being squeezed in the cities in 1974, it turned its attention back to a strategy it had practised throughout the conflict with Westminster – to take the battle to the British mainland. In August 1974 the Provisionals moved to a campaign of bombing the mainland. In October they carried out the Guildford bombings and in November an horrific attack was made on a Birmingham nightclub. In many respects the PIRA regarded these attacks as successful and as most likely to bring about a British withdrawal. The 'success' of the Provisionals' mainland campaign did have some of the desired effect on the British Government as it made it ever more imperative to rearrange the security equation in Northern Ireland. This was the British endeavour during the mid-1970s.

CHAPTER FOUR

From Containment to Ulsterization, 1974–80

By the mid-1970s British troops had been involved in the conflict in Northern Ireland for six years. They had, during that period, turned from protectors of the Catholic communities into a force that was, on the whole, geared to the defeat of the PIRA. Part of the task had inevitably involved taking action against the very people they had been initially deployed to defend. Some progress had been made in dealing with the military situation, not least the Army could claim some success against the PIRA in the cities. But the price of that success had been bought by estrangement from the Catholic communities. This in turn meant that there was little hope of a political settlement. Westminster determined to change the equation with a new security policy which had enormous implications for the military and its role in Northern Ireland.

One of the problems that faced the British Government by the mid-1970s was that the use of troops had in many ways exacerbated the spiral of violence in the Province. From 1969 to 1975 the number of fatalities in Northern Ireland relative to the population was twice that of the losses sustained by Britain during the Boer War and twice that of the deaths suffered by the United States in Korea and Vietnam.[1] The British Army had been involved in the conflict for several years and there was no sign of an end to the confrontation. The British Government believed that it was time for a new initiative aimed at counteracting the violence in the Province. A strategy was devised whereby the British Army would no longer be at the forefront of the conflict. The decision was made to scale down military activities and visibly reduce the

1 C.H. Enloe, 'The Police and Military in Ulster: Peace-keeping or Peace Subverting', *Journal of Peace Research* 15.3 (1978).

presence of the Army in an attempt to restore a semblance of normality to the Province and perhaps aid a political settlement.

There were two imperatives for this change in strategy. The first stemmed from the recognition by the British Government that in many respects the political situation had been exacerbated by allowing the military to bear the main responsibility in the conflict with the terrorists. This realization was one common to states in countering political violence. There is always a danger in committing troops for long periods of time; it has been observed that:

> the effect is to elevate into full-scale war, movements that are basically on a much smaller scale . . . the use of the Army imposes a permanent military dimension on the area which raises communal violence to a more permanent and formal level.[2]

The British Government recognized by the mid-1970s that the Army had become immersed in a situation of continuing violence from which it would not be easily extracted and one in which it had become the major protagonist. A second but connected reason for changing strategy was the belief that the PIRA was steadily being defeated in the cities,[3] and that there was now an opportunity to reduce everyday communal violence and civilian dependence upon paramilitary organizations.

The belief that the PIRA was in fact losing popularity appeared to be confirmed by the growth of the Northern Ireland Peace Movement in 1976. Specifically, the organization arose from the violent circumstances of the deaths of three children from the McGuire family in August 1976. The children were killed when a car containing two PIRA men, who had just robbed a bank, mounted the pavement outside their home, running all three down. The driver of the car had been shot by British soldiers pursuing the men. An aunt of the children, Mairread Corrigan, acting upon the revulsion engendered by the incident, founded the peace movement which united moderates from both communities in a campaign for an end of violence in the Province.[4] In 1977 Mairread Corrigan was awarded the Nobel Peace Prize but by then the movement had lost much of its initial emotional impact and died out. In the 1980s a tendency existed to

2 Charles Douglas Home, *The Times* (19 December 1973).
3 Paul Wilkinson, *Terrorism and the Liberal State* (London: Macmillan, Second Edition 1986), p. 160.
4 Lieutenant-Colonel Michael Dewar, *The British Army in Northern Ireland* (London: Arms and Armour Press, 1985), p. 117.

dismiss the peace movement as of little relevance to the Northern Irish conflict,[5] but in 1976 its impact was such that it did actually weaken the appeal of the paramilitaries in the Catholic community,[6] thus aiding Westminster in its bid to consider new initiatives.

The strategy of 'police primacy' was officially announced in a Joint Directive by the Secretary of State for Northern Ireland in 1977. It was stated that the roles of the Army and the police were to be reversed – the military would act in support of the police.[7] In fact this had been gradually occurring since 1975 when the Bourne Committee had recommended that the police should be prepared once more to take responsibility for the security of the Province. The committee chaired by John Bourne, a civil servant in the Northern Ireland Office, produced a document called 'The Way Ahead'.[8] It envisaged the withdrawal of the Army from those Protestant and Catholic areas regarded as 'safe'. This also meant that many of the activities of the Army were curtailed and soldiers had to defer to the RUC. For example, if soldiers wished to perform patrols, carry out searches or arrest suspects they had first to obtain permission from the RUC.[9] In all but the most 'hard-line' of Republican areas, the Army was moved out and the RUC took over and was responsible for countering the PIRA. However, in hard-line Republican areas the Army continued to operate, while the border remained a special case where the military retained its leading role.

The attempt to implement 'police primacy' represented the first really coherent and long-term strategy implemented in Northern Ireland since 1969 and as such represented a positive improvement in the position of the Army. In counteracting political violence, rapid or incoherent shifts in policy can aid the opposition as terrorists feed off uncertainty or ambiguity in state policy.[10] British policy in Northern Ireland during the 1970s had been full of such contradictions. For example, in 1971 the British leader of the opposition, Harold Wilson, announced a plan for the unification of Ireland within fifteen years, yet when Prime Minister

5 Simon Hoggart, *The Sunday Observer* (12 August 1984).
6 Dewar, op. cit., p. 117.
7 British Army, PQS2 1981/82. Tutor Background Paper, Northern Ireland.
8 Desmond Hamill, *Pig in the Middle: The Army in Northern Ireland 1969–1984* (London: Methuen, 1985), p. 184. See also Mark Urban, *Big Boys' Rules: The SAS and the Secret Struggle Against the IRA* (London: Faber & Faber, 1992), pp. 17–18.
9 Ibid., p. 185.
10 Robert Taber, *The War of the Flea* (St Albans: Paladin, 1971), p. 37.

in 1974 did little to prevent the Unionists destroying a power-sharing Executive.[11] This type of inconsistency in the political programme was reflected in the strategies the Army was permitted to adopt at any given time. By 1977 the Army had undergone phases in which it reacted very sharply against the PIRA with the use of internment without trial, as in 1971, and phases when it did little more than watch as the British Government negotiated with PIRA leaders and violence escalated in the Province. Special legislation was introduced into the Province in 1973 to allow the Army to deal more effectively with the PIRA, but yet again the British Government continued to negotiate with the PIRA, albeit in secret, in the pragmatic hope that some form of political accommodation could be found. The major benefit of police primacy was that it was designed to make the Army less significant. The British Government could attempt to underwrite a political settlement while no longer actively engaged against one of the communities that would have to accept it. This clarified the British position but literally threatened to repeat history by pitting the two Irish communities in the North directly against each other once again – the Republicans versus the predominantly Protestant security forces.

This of course did create problems that were not unfamiliar in Ireland. Following the breakdown of law and order in Northern Ireland in 1969, the Hunt Committee had investigated the structure of policing in the Province. The findings of the committee had greatly discredited both the RUC and the Ulster Special Constabulary (USC). Both forces were criticized as too old-fashioned, and the USC was found to be a sectarian force organized on lines which were not dissimilar to a Protestant paramilitary organization. The USC was subsequently disbanded, while the RUC was reorganized into a force that corresponded to the design of the mainland British police forces.[12] To replace the USC the Hunt Report recommended the creation of a part-time military defence. To that end the Ulster Defence Regiment (UDR) was formed on 1 April 1970.[13] Men, some with military experience, were recruited locally, and immediately assumed military duties

---

11 Nicholas Wapshott and George Brock, *Thatcher* (London: Futura, 1983), pp. 227–9.

12 The Sunday Times Insight Team, *Ulster* (Harmondsworth: Penguin, 1972), p. 160.

13 David Barzilay, *The British Army in Ulster*, vol. 1 (Belfast: Century Books, 1973), p. 160. See also House of Commons Debate (hereafter HC), vol. 797, cols 401–2, 4 March 1970.

such as patrolling and the guarding of key installations. When the new strategy of 'police primacy' was introduced, the UDR, as it was known, had grown in size and importance, and began to replace the regular Army units on duties throughout the Province. This enabled the British to reduce force levels. Indeed, this strategy was implemented so successfully that by 1984 the Army had 7,000 troops stationed in the Province while the UDR boasted 7,500 men.[14] One of the major causes of the riots in 1969 had been the fact that the Catholic communities regarded the policing of the Province as a sectarian matter designed to keep them contained and as second-class citizens.[15] In the eyes of some Catholics the British policy of Ulsterization has appeared as little more than a reversion to the pre-1969 position, in which they perceived a Protestant police force as bound to act against their interests.[16] There was some basis to these fears since the RUC was over 90 per cent Protestant, while the UDR was 98 per cent so. In the first few months of its existence, over half the members of the UDR were formed from the Ulster Constabulary,[17] men who had belonged to the force disbanded because of its sectarianism. There was little hope of these forces winning the confidence of the Catholic communities. The issue of who should police the Province raised a stark question: should the Province be primarily policed by the RUC and the UDR, with the obvious problems of religious bias, or the British Army which had also gained the reputation of being anti-Republican?

There was actually no easy answer. Some commentators considered that although the strategy of Ulsterization might enable Westminster to make troop reductions in the short term, from a long-term perspective the policy was dangerous. It was pointed out that if more troops were withdrawn, Northern Ireland would remain policed by a segment of the British Army whose primary loyalty was almost certainly not to Westminster but to Protestant Ulster. The withdrawal of British troops and the implementation of policies vehemently disliked by Protestant Ulster could, it has been observed, pit one segment of the Army against the other.[18] While this was the worst-case political scenario

14 Hamill, op. cit., p. 273.
15 The Sunday Times Insight Team, op. cit., Chapter 2.
16 Tim Pat Coogan, *The IRA* (Glasgow: Fontana, 1980), p. 566.
17 Barzilay, op. cit., vol. 1, p. 154.
18 Padraig O'Malley, *The Uncivil War, Ireland Today* (Belfast: Blackstaff Press, 1983), p. 217.

there were also other concerns about the strategy, not least as to how the RUC and UDR would fare against the paramilitaries without the British Army. This was the predominant military concern.

During the first seven years of the conflict in the Province the RUC had acted as a back-up force for the Army, which had dictated tactics and directed the fight against the PIRA, and it had been the Army which had suffered the heaviest casualties and been the targets of PIRA attacks. A basic change had taken place by 1977 when the RUC was placed at the fore. It was not, however, an easy transition. In the first year in which the policy was implemented the RUC sustained twice its usual losses[19] and suffered its worst attack ever at the hands of the PIRA at the border village of Belcoo in Fermanagh when three policemen were killed.[20]

Many in the Army believed that the strategy had been rushed and that the British Government was too eager to withdraw troops, leaving the RUC and relatively few troops to counter the terrorists. The Army considered that the RUC was simply not sufficiently trained or experienced to operate on its own. Many experts pointed out that while the police force had more than doubled its size over the previous seven years, it was not a mobile force which could easily be deployed to the areas where it was needed. The RUC had grown in numbers from 3,500 in 1970 to 6,500 in the mid-1970s. The force was organized into sixteen divisions and grouped into three regions: Belfast, the south and the north. Each had an assistant Chief Constable who reported daily to the Chief Constable of the RUC. There were problems within the force though: some police stations were actually overmanned whereas some, such as Newry, were desperately short staffed.[21] More importantly, some personnel in the RUC and the UDR were part-time, which meant that they lacked the overall coherence of British Army units which fought the PIRA twenty-four hours a day from established bases. Part-time soldiers and off-duty policemen presented the PIRA with easy targets. Some of these criticisms arose simply from dissatisfaction of many in the Army with the way in which Westminster expected them once again to lower their profile in the conflict against the PIRA and some from professional rivalries between the two security forces. In theory,

19 Statistics supplied by Army Headquarters Lisburn, 30 July 1985.
20 Hamill, op. cit., p. 193.
21 Ibid., p. 226.

the two forces had a measure of integration right from the beginning. The Chief Constable of the RUC and the GOC met at least once a week at the Security Policy Committee and the Deputy Chief Constables held regular daily discussions to coordinate policy. Yet there were still problems of confidence between the two; some RUC officers felt that the military were not sufficiently sensitive to local conditions and had a tendency to rush into areas without consideration for longer-term community relations. In addition, many in the RUC believed that the very presence of British soldiers gave the PIRA its *raison d'être* as the historic enemy. RUC officers also deeply resented the military allegation that they lacked professionalism. Yet some of the criticisms made by the military against the RUC were valid in the mid-1970s – it did lack the experience or training to take over all the anti-terrorist tasks of the Army.

By 1977 the British Army had had nearly ten years of experience in Northern Ireland. Every regiment performed a tour of duty there and the training for units prior to going to serve in Northern Ireland had grown progressively more sophisticated. In the early stages of the conflict soldiers had encountered the violence in Belfast and Londonderry with little training and out-dated equipment from the colonial campaigns.[22] However, by the mid-1970s before troops arrived in Northern Ireland they were retrained in all basic skills such as shooting, field craft and patrolling. They would then undergo a training course at Shorncliffe, a military centre on the English south coast, to deal with PIRA attacks such as hijacks, vehicle ambushes and hostage-taking.[23] It was this experience that had enabled the Army to resist the PIRA. The military felt that without this kind of intense training the RUC would simply let the advantages that had been gained in the battle with the PIRA be dissipated. Such reservations did have some validity but the RUC was not and never had been just an ordinary police force. For example, it already had specially trained units for intelligence work. It was envisaged that the RUC could be strengthened as a quasi-military force. To that end, during 1976 the RUC was equipped with Special Patrol Groups which acted as its anti-terrorist squads. Five regions were given SPGs and police were retained in anti-riot tactics. But this all took time and Army reservations about RUC competence *vis-à-vis* the

22 Hugh Hanning, *Ulster, Brasseys Annual* (June 1971), p. 748.
23 Dewar, op. cit., pp. 177–207.

paramilitaries were borne out by the increased activity and success of the PIRA. In February 1978 it once more embarked upon a bombing campaign to take advantage of the relative inactivity of the Army on the streets of Northern Ireland. It was a campaign of great ruthlessness, resulting in the deaths of twelve civilians at the La Mon House Hotel in February 1978 and £500,000 worth of damage in Londonderry the next day when the PIRA bombed the Ulster bus depot.[24] The Irish National Liberation Army (INLA) and PIRA also perpetrated other high-profile attacks during the late 1970s. In July 1976, they assassinated the British Ambassador to Eire, Christopher Ewart Biggs, in Dublin while in 1979 the INLA succeeded in killing one of their long-term targets – Lord Mountbatten was assassinated at his holiday home in Mullaghmore, Co. Sligo.[25] On the same day the PIRA achieved one of their most notable successes against the British Army itself when eighteen soldiers were killed during an ambush at Warrenpoint. These incidents reflected the actions of a reinvigorated paramilitary organization. Just as the British Army was being withdrawn from an open role *vis-à-vis* the PIRA it was beginning to enter a more militant and violent phase of the campaign.

The reorganization of the PIRA

The success of the British Army in the mid-1970s had been a cause for concern within the PIRA. During the mid to late 1970s the PIRA was forced to make a searching reappraisal of its strategy and tactics. In particular, the organization wanted to regain the initiative after the cease-fire of 1975. The cease-fire had actually caused problems for the paramilitaries because it had meant that they could no longer target the security forces. Instead, they had had to target ordinary Protestants. This was regarded as less satisfactory and less high profile than their usual activities. The PIRA decided to change its system of operating with the leadership opting to implement a smaller, tighter system of organization. At the start of the 1970s the PIRA had as its main tactic the orchestration of mass civil disobedience on the back of Republican disaffectation. This had meant that large numbers of people were involved which in turn meant that the British Army had had considerable success penetrating the organization. The leadership

24 Coogan, op. cit., p. 480.
25 See J. Bowyer Bell, *IRA Tactics and Targets* (Dublin: Poolbeg, 1990), pp. 71–3.

decided that rather than operate in so-called battalions they would work in cells. These cells consisted of four men and each unit would be specialized in different activities. For example, there were sniping cells, execution cells and bombing cells. The aim was to maximize the efficiency of operations and to eliminate the risk of being discovered.[26] By 1979 the PIRA had improved its tactics to such a degree that the level of violence rose dramatically: in that year fatalities incurred by the security forces rose to 113 from eighty-one the previous year.[27] A senior Army intelligence officer, Brigadier James Glover, testified to the efficiency of the PIRA in December 1978. His report stated that:

> The Provisional IRA (PIRA) has the dedication and the sinews of war to raise violence intermittently to at least a level of early 1978, certainly for the foreseeable future. Even if 'peace' is restored, the motivation for politically inspired violence will remain. Arms will be readily available and there will be many who are able and willing to use them. Any peace will be superficial and brittle.[28]

The report showed that the PIRA had progressed a long way since 1969. It assessed the membership of the PIRA and found that the leadership was 'intelligent, astute and experienced with a growing technical expertise'.[29] Unfortunately for the British Army, the PIRA stole this report from the mail and published it, so demonstrating their ability to outwit the Army.[30]

During the mid-1970s there was also a shift of personnel within the leadership of the PIRA organization. New men began to emerge within the Northern communities and challenged what was becoming an aged and southern-led leadership. In particular, in November 1976 the first meeting was held of the new national command under the auspices of Martin McGuinness and Gerry Adams. Also during this period, the PIRA altered its strategy radically to incorporate a new policy. The leadership had accepted that a victory against the British Army would not be accomplished quickly. Rather, a strategy of attrition should be adopted and that alongside the use of violence, legitimate politics should also be adopted. The leadership decided to 'go political' by contesting local government seats and taking them up if elected. It was also decided to contest seats for Parliament but not use them if

26 Coogan, op. cit., p. 581.
27 Statistics supplied by Army Headquarters Lisburn, 30 July 1985.
28 Quoted in Coogan, op. cit., p. 581.
29 Ibid., p. 581.
30 Dewar, op. cit., p. 158.

elected. This decision was made public in the wake of the 1981 hunger strikes and the publicity generated by the election of the PIRA man Bobby Sands as a Member of Parliament and his subsequent death on hunger strike. The PIRA summed up its new policy as 'By Ballot and By Bullet'.[31] This represented a significant alteration in both the philosophy and strategy of the organization. In 1969 the PIRA had deliberately renounced the political option, preferring a violent one. Danny Morrison, the director of Sinn Fein, explained that the change was to 'undermine British propaganda, which states we have no support'.[32] Despite the adoption of a political strategy, the PIRA had not renounced the use of violence as its major weapon, but the military leadership took heed of key figures in the movement such as Gerry Adams who, after three years imprisonment for terrorist offences, had rethought PIRA strategy and had begun to warn publicly against a purely military strategy. This in turn led directly to the development of Sinn Fein as the political wing of the PIRA, which tried to use the political system to advance the cause of Republicanism. The attempt to 'go political' was a direct result of the British changes towards normalization, but it also arose out of the recognition that the conflict had changed into a long-drawn-out one that required some form of political strategy. During the early 1970s, PIRA leaders had hoped that the British Army would withdraw and had been fuelled in this belief by the willingness of both Labour and Conservative Governments to hold cease-fire talks with the paramilitaries. When it became apparent that this was not the case, they adopted a new doctrine – The Long Way. A political strategy became even more urgent when the British Government embarked upon the second part of the normalization of the Province, known as criminalization.

Ever since the advent of Direct Rule, Westminster had been trying to find ways that would defeat the PIRA but not alienate Catholic opinion to such an extent that a peace settlement was impossible. Part of that process culminated in the findings of the Gardiner Committee which reviewed the emergency legislation in Northern Ireland in 1975. It recommended that methods used by the security forces such as internment should be ended. In addition, the British Government announced in March 1976 that all prisoners convicted of crimes would be treated as ordinary criminals. This was part of a desire to portray members of para-

---

31 *An Phoblact* (Republican News), 5 November 1981.
32 Quoted in O'Malley, op. cit., p. 276.

military organizations as wrongdoers rather than heroes. Since 1972 paramilitary prisoners had enjoyed a special status which included a number of privileges such as wearing personal clothing rather than prison uniforms. During 1975 the Gardiner Committee stated that these concessions had been a mistake. The different treatment of 'political prisoners' appeared to perform two undesirable functions: one was to reinforce a commitment to the Republican cause and a second was to concede that these crimes were different because they were perpetrated in a 'political' cause.

However, the ending of the 'special status' for the paramilitaries provoked one of the bitterest campaigns of the modern conflict in Ireland. It became known as the H-Block protest. Once the decision had been taken by Westminster to treat the prisoners in an ordinary fashion, new prison facilities had to be designed to accommodate them. New cells were built at the Maze Prison in Long Kesh. The subsequent protest by the prisoners took its name from the H-shape of the buildings. Initially, the prisoners refused to wear prison uniforms and donned blankets. During 1978 the prisoners escalated the crisis by turning it into a 'dirty' protest, and then during October 1980 into a hunger strike.[33] By December the strike was abandoned with one of the prisoners at the point of death. The British Government seemed ready to make concessions. However, the concessions were considered by the prisoners as too trivial and new strikes began. On 5 May 1981 the first prisoner, Bobby Sands, died, followed by nine others, until in October the British Government made a number of other concessions, enabling the strike to end. Significantly however, the hunger strikes served only to harden Catholic opposition to the Government and mass demonstrations were again staged on the streets of Belfast against the Government. Indeed, the hunger strikes provided a great deal of publicity for the PIRA and the Republican position in general. It was at this point that Sinn Fein engineered a political breakthrough. This occurred when Bobby Sands was elected as the MP for the constituency of Fermanagh and South Tyrone while on hunger strike. With the death of Bobby Sands, Sinn Fein retained the seat and, apparently on the momentum of the hunger strikes, won 10 per cent of the votes in the elections to the Northern Ireland Assembly in 1982.[34] The new

33 O'Malley, op. cit., pp. 264–6.
34 See S. Elliot and Richard A. Wilford, 'The 1982 Northern Ireland Assembly Election', *Studies in Public Policy* 119 (Glasgow: University of Strathclyde, Centre for the Public Policy 1983).

policy of not only continuing the armed struggle against the British Government but also entering the legitimate political arena was distinctly worrying for the British Government who, in the early 1980s, saw the initiative being snatched from it. It should also be added that the policy of criminalization did not appear to result in a lessening of support for the paramilitaries. The ending of internment and the increased use of Diplock courts had consequences which increased Catholic suspicions of the apparatus and operation of law and order. In particular, the difficulties of securing evidence against suspects led to the most brutal methods of interrogation. Indeed, after complaints of brutality, the Government appointed the Bennett Inquiry which led, in turn, to stricter controls being imposed.

The period of the late 1970s and early 1980s saw Westminster attempting to normalize the situation in Ireland. Yet even as Westminster moved in this direction, the alienation of the Catholic communities, and indeed in some cases the Protestant ones, increased. Most paradoxically of all, as the British Government claimed to be moving towards normalization, its military forces were moving into the most intense and controversial role in the Province – fighting a 'secret' war against the PIRA.

Covert operations and black propaganda

In response to the activities of the PIRA in the late 1970s the British Army began to intensify its use of special units and covert operations.[35] Covert or undercover operations had been used from early on in the conflict with the PIRA. As far as the British military were concerned there were several functions of covert operations.

First, covert operations could be used to pick up information concerning the PIRA. One notable example of such work in Northern Ireland by the British Army was the running of the so-called 'Four Square Laundry'. Soldiers posed as laundrymen calling in Republican areas. The soldiers would collect clothing which would then be analysed by forensic experts for traces of gunpowder, blood or explosive material. In 1972 this operation was uncovered by the PIRA when it ambushed the laundry van.[36] It is difficult to know for certain the full extent of Army involvement

35 Hamill, op. cit., p. 271.
36 J. Bloch and P. Fitzgerald, *British Intelligence and Covert Action* (Dingle: Brandon Books, 1983), p. 213.

in covert operations in the Province. Allegations were made in the early stages of the conflict that soldiers were using massage parlours on the Antrim Road to entice PIRA men or their sympathizers to give information. It was similarly alleged that prostitution rings were used by the British Army to gain information. These allegations were strenuously denied by the Home Secretary of the day, Merlyn Rees.[37]

A second function of undercover work was to discredit the enemy and gain support for the actions of the security forces in preference to those of the terrorists. To this end the Army may use undercover operations to cause disgust at what were supposedly the actions of the terrorists. A former soldier, David Seaman, alleged in 1971 that special squads, including men of the Special Air Service, were engaged in this work. Units would explode bombs in Belfast but then blame the PIRA for the ensuing damage. He also alleged that the members of the SAS were trained in the use of the Russian AK47 assault rifle, the Armalite and Thompson submachine guns. These were not normally used by the British Army but were favoured by the PIRA.[38]

A third function of undercover operations, somewhat ironically, was to establish the impartiality of the position of the Army. It has been alleged that the British Army indulged in an assassination campaign in Northern Ireland to project an image of religious conflict and re-establish Britain as the fair party in a dispute between two factions determined upon a course of sectarian murder. It has been written of what appeared to the numerous sectarian killings in the 1970s that 'most of these murders were either directly or indirectly instigated through pseudo groups'.[39] Bloch and Fitzgerald have argued that in their previous campaigns the British Army did not indulge in these activities[40] and that these activities in Northern Ireland marked a significant departure. This is a difficult issue to verify. Numerous allegations have been made that it was British soldiers who perpetrated assassinations of leading figures but this is again almost impossible to verify. There is little doubt that covert operations have been undertaken by some sections of the British Army. Yet the use of covert operations has, however, quite often proved counter-productive, certainly in political terms. If revealed, the state can be discredited because, by

37 *The Scottish Sunday Mail* (8 October 1972).
38 Bloch and Fitzgerald, op. cit., p. 215.
39 Roger Faligot, *The Kitson Experiment* (London: Zed Press, 1983), p. 37.
40 Bloch and Fitzgerald, op. cit., p. 216.

the very use of such operations, the state is conceding that in order to defeat the insurgents it has to resort to their methods; if, in order to defend the state, democratic principles have to be subverted, in many ways the terrorists have won their battle.[41] More critically in Northern Ireland, the use of these operations have not increased the unwillingness of the Republican communities to believe in a British desire for an equitable settlement and have fuelled the conviction in some quarters that nothing has changed in the English–Irish equation.

From 1977 onwards, as the RUC began to take over the major security role in the Province, the Army appeared to turn to more undercover activities. Special operations became an extremely contentious issue. In particular, it was alleged that both the British Army and the RUC were operating a 'shoot to kill' policy. This in effect meant that both forces were accused of acting as death squads, targeting members of the PIRA and the other Republican terrorist organization, the INLA. As evidence, those propounding this theory, including Northern Irish Catholic politician John Hume, point to the deaths in 1980 of at least two INLA suspects shot by police in suspicious circumstances.[42]

The British Army also made great use of what are known as 'black Propaganda' tactics of 'psychological operations' during this campaign in Northern Ireland. The tactics involved spreading stories concerning the PIRA and were meant to discredit the paramilitaries in the eyes of the world and its own supporters. This was not a recent phenomenon in Anglo-Irish relations. During World War I British propaganda alleged the complicity of the German Kaiser in Irish politics. Later, in 1927, it was also alleged that Lenin and Trotsky pulled the strings of the Irish independence movement in 1921.[43] The British Army Land Operation Manual describes the use of psychological operations as follows: 'the planned use of propaganda or other means to influence the opinions, emotions, attitudes and behaviour of the enemy, neutral and friendly groups'.[44] An early example was the leaking to ITN of a story that the PIRA had used three eight-year-olds to plant a bomb in a pram outside Belfast's Victoria

41 Paul Wilkinson, *Political Terrorism* (London: Macmillan, 1973), p. 37.

42 *Shoot to Kill?, International Lawyers Inquiry Into the Use of Lethal Weapons by the Security Forces in Northern Ireland* (Dublin: Mercier Press, 1985).

43 Faligot, op. cit., p. 37.

44 *British Army Land Operations. Vol. 3 Counter Revolutionary Operations* (Ministry of Defence), 29 August 1969, Preface, paras 1–2 and 122, quoted in Liz Curtis, *Ireland the Propaganda War* (London: Pluto Press, 1984), p. 119.

Hospital. The British Press office later admitted this story was a fabrication.[45] These tactics were part of the campaign by the Army to win support for its cause and unite the people against the PIRA. To this end, a stream of propaganda was directed at the Catholic community, including leaflets and booklets depicting atrocities committed by the PIRA.[46] It is difficult to assess how much impact these operations actually had upon the mainland, although in a survey carried out in 1978 it was revealed that 43 per cent of Catholic people in Northern Ireland regarded the PIRA as motivated by patriotism and idealism.[47]

By the late 1970s the British Army decided that it was in fact counter-productive to proceed with the use of black propaganda tactics. It realized that its headquarters at Lisburn was becoming known as the Lisburn Lie Machine and a decision was taken to stop the widespread use of false stories.[48] But, the more contentious elements of the military campaign were not stopped. Indeed, the military campaign on the border began a new phase from 1976 with the deployment of the SAS into the Province to undertake so-called special operations. A handful of SAS men had been operating on the border since the beginning of the conflict but for the first time Westminster acknowledged their presence and dramatically increased their numbers.[49] The SAS operated from a number of bases in South Armagh and along the rest of the border. Officially, their main task is to operate undercover and gather information on the PIRA. SAS men have infiltrated border communities and indeed even the PIRA itself.[50] The most infamous example of covert operation by the British was the work of Captain Nairac who in 1974 worked as an intelligence officer in the border region, mixing with the local population. In 1976 the PIRA claimed responsibility for his murder.[51] By 1977 approximately 160 SAS men were operating in the border districts and a senior SAS officer was attending all army briefings.[52] The major role of the SAS is underlined by the fact that it is one of the few

45 Curtis, op. cit., p. 119.

46 *Time Out*, 14–20 October 1977.

47 E. Moxon-Brown, 'The Water and the Fish: Public Opinion and the Provisional IRA' in Paul Wilkinson (ed.), *British Perspectives on Terrorism* (London: George Allen and Unwin, 1981), pp. 41–73.

48 Major Nick Kench, Publicity Officer, interview at Army Headquarters Lisburn, 30 July 1985.

49 Hamill, op. cit., p. 189.

50 Barzilay, op. cit., vol. 3, p. 197.

51 The *Daily Mail* (7 May 1977).

52 Barzilay. op cit., vol. 3, p. 197.

regiments committed full-time to serving in the Province. The full extent of the role of the SAS in the Province is difficult to gauge and the Army is reluctant to go much beyond acknowledging that SAS men are used to set up ambushes and do intelligence gathering.[53] Their role has been controversial and allegations have been made that they operate as little more than 'death squads', responsible for the deaths of PIRA men on both sides of the border.[54] There is little doubt that they are engaged in a 'secret' battle with the PIRA that radically departs from normal policing functions. In fact, it might be argued that it is on the border that the British military comes closest to mirroring the historic pattern of British military operations against Republicans. Indeed, some parts of the Army see the border as the area of Northern Ireland which most obviously equates to their training for warfare. The paradox remained that the British Army was more closely engaged in open warfare in parts of Northern Ireland while Westminster was declaring that the Province was been returned to normalcy under the rubric of Ulsterization.

The policy of Ulsterization fundamentally altered the relationship between the Army and the RUC in the cities. While the RUC did indeed begin to operate more effectively in the cities, the border areas were a different matter. Areas in Northern Ireland are graded by the military into different colours, ranging from light grey to black according to the strength of the PIRA and the danger posed to security forces. By 1977, much of the Province was considered to be a shade of grey, denoting the degree of control exercised by the security forces. However, the border areas, in particular Armagh, were still considered to be black. It was in these areas during the late 1970s that major disagreements between the British military and the RUC were apparent over how to police the border. The military had developed a strategy suited to a war situation, in which they lived in enclosed bases and were airlifted in and out after a tour of duty. Soldiers operated from their garrisons, patrolling in special units either by foot or by helicopter. Only rarely were vehicles used in the border areas.[55] The RUC, however, still patrolled the border in vehicles, remaining in close contact with the local population and with the Gardai. The RUC felt that it should be immediately available to the Gardai if an emergency arose. This difference in approach

53 Ibid., p. 97.
54 Patsy McArdle, *The Secret War* (Dublin: Mercier Press, 1984), pp. 61–5.
55 Barzilay, op. cit., vol. 1, p. 141.

between the RUC and the Army has meant in effect that two different strategies are in operation.[56] At some points the two forces regarded themselves as in direct competition with each other. For example, in July 1978, a sixteen-year-old boy was killed during an SAS stake out in Co. Antrim. The RUC had failed to provide the military with sufficient information for the stake out in a bid to protect what it saw as its area of operations, while the Army had not informed the police of its intentions as it wanted to protect its specialized tactics.[57] It was in order to overcome this type of difficulty in part that Sir Maurice Oldfield was appointed to play the role of supremo of both forces and in particular to coordinate the intelligence-sharing of both security forces. Oldfield had had considerable experience of intelligence work as formerly he had been the MI5 spymaster who had run the Special Intelligence Service from 1965 until his retirement in 1977. The idea of a supremo was directly derived from the colonial experience in Malaysia where a district officer had coordinated the actions of both the police and the Army.[58]

Oldfield's appointment did not really alter the problems of policing Northern Ireland in a normal way. In particular, there has been a problem with both the RUC and the UDR and the part-time nature of their occupation. UDR men and women are particularly vulnerable off duty. Unlike the British Army, they do not return to a secure military base. They return home. In the border area this can mean a remote farmhouse or a hamlet vulnerable to attack.[59] The PIRA have taken advantage of this weakness and since the late 1970s have begun specifically to target off-duty members of the RUC and the UDR. Between 1981 and 1984 the PIRA killed 130 members of the locally raised security forces, Protestant political figures or local civilians in the border area. It managed to kill less than thirty soldiers in the whole of Northern Ireland during the same period.[60] It again represented a shift in PIRA tactics away from the cities to the far more vulnerable border areas and local forces.

In part this may be accounted for by the fact that the RUC and the UDR are easier targets than the British soldiers. However, Protestants living in the areas adjacent to the border suspected a

56 Hamill, op. cit., p. 237.
57 Curtis, op. cit., p. 76.
58 Hamill, op.cit., pp. 230, 258. See also J. Bowyer Bell, *The Irish Troubles: A Generation of Violence 1969–1992* (Dublin: Gill and Macmillan, 1993), p. 575.
59 Jim Cusack, *The Irish Times* (12 December 1984).
60 Ibid.

different reason for the PIRA strategy. They believe that the PIRA are operating what amounts to a genocidal sectarian campaign against the Protestant community by killing men who are the only sons or sole earners in a family. They allege that the PIRA is trying to invert history and that Protestants will be driven off the land and then eventually replaced by Catholics who will be left alone. In support of this view they point to cases where only sons farming the estate have been killed.[61] The PIRA deny that they operate any such policy but in many cases their assassinations of off-duty policemen or UDR personnel amounts to the same thing. There is little that can be done in such cases as it has been estimated that it would take three soldiers to guard every off-duty policeman, thus proving too expensive both financially and militarily to implement.[62]

By 1975 it was generally recognized that the PIRA was capable of posing a long-term threat to the security of the Province[63] and although the security forces were containing the PIRA in the cities, there were growing problems in rural areas. Indeed, by the mid-1970s it had become apparent that two conflicts were in fact operating in Northern Ireland. Normalization might be possible in the cities but in rural areas there was a very different type of conflict.

The border war

When British troops were first deployed in Northern Ireland in 1969 their primary task was to control the violence in the cities. Belfast and Londonderry provided the stages for confrontation. However, the border area between the North and the south began to assume an increasing importance in British military thinking, not only because it provided a get-away route for the PIRA, but also as an area in which the terrorists chose to engage the Army in another form of engagement – guerrilla warfare.

Experts on terrorism and counter-terrorism argue that the terrain for guerrilla warfare should be carefully selected. According to Taber, 'The ideal country should be rural rather than urban, mountainous rather than flat, thickly forested rather than bare. The terrain should afford natural concealment and obstacles

---

61 Ibid.
62 Ibid.
63 Ed Maloney, *The Irish Times* (21 January 1985).

which hinder military transport.'[64] The border area provides almost a perfect environment for rural guerrilla operations. Geographically, it is both mountainous and rural with numerous tiny hamlets and outlying farms. More importantly, the demarcation of the border is confusing. It divides Northern and southern Ireland but also divides the North. For example, Co. Donegal, which is politically part of the Republic, is further north than any point within the six counties of Northern Ireland itself. The border takes little account of physical or cultural geography; the village of Crossmaglen, four miles from the border within Northern Ireland, was actually earmarked in 1925 as part of the Republic and it remains avidly Republican and anti-British, as the Army has learnt to its cost.[65] The border itself is 420 miles long and runs through whole villages. It actually divides farms and even houses. The village of Pettigoe is divided between Donegal and Fermanagh.[66] The area around the border consists of some of the wildest and most isolated territory in the British Isles and at many points it is not actually clear exactly where the border lies. This uncertain borderline, with its 346 official crossing places, mountains and rivers, has enabled the PIRA to vex the British Army. Despite the type of terrain which favours the terrorist, the IRA had failed to mount a successful border war during the 1950s. It had aroused little support among the inhabitants of the rural areas, and terrorists need the support and refuge provided by locals to mount operations.[67] During the modern conflict, however, the PIRA have achieved an enduring support along the border. The support of Republicanism was indicated by the fact that it was in the border constituency of Fermanagh that Bobby Sands was elected MP in 1981 while in the Maze jail.[68] It has been observed that the motto of the border community is 'tell them [the security forces] nothing'.[69] This has allowed the PIRA to operate with some advantages against the British Army. However, the major explanation for the Army's difficulties in operating on the border has been the existence of a 'sanctuary' for the PIRA across the border in the Republic. The PIRA operate from bases in the Republic of Ireland, making forays across the border to engage

64 Taber, op. cit., p. 110.
65 Barzilay, op. cit., vol. 1, p. 137.
66 Coogan, op. cit., p. 402.
67 Robert Moss, *Urban Guerillas* (London: Temple Smith, 1972), p. 93.
68 *The Times*, 6 May 1981.
69 McArdle, op. cit., p. 6.

the military and then retreat south for refuge. It has been argued that the very existence of such a border with a 'friendly' government can often result in victory for the insurgents.[70]

The strategy of the British Army on the border

The Army has had two main tasks on the border. The first is to catch members of the PIRA to prevent them operating on the border and escaping across it. The second is to prevent the border from being used as a route for ferrying ammunition from the south into the North.[71] The main concern of the Army during the initial period of the conflict (1969–72) was in dealing with the hundreds of unofficial cross-border roads which had no customs points and were illegal crossing points. It was among these roads that the PIRA operated. The Army decided that in order to prevent the PIRA using the roads and bringing munitions into the cities, the roads should be permanently blocked. To this end the Royal Engineers implanted huge wooden spikes in the roads, but such tactics proved futile as no sooner were the spikes in position than they were removed by the local population. The Army then countered by cratering the roads, but again the local population responded by filling in the holes. It proved to be a very difficult issue as troops could not be employed on a permanent basis on every single country road to ensure that the roads remained impassable.[72] As well as proving ineffective in the longer term, these measures served to aggravate the population of the areas north and south of the border who claimed that not only did it hamper their farming activities, but in some cases only served to cut them off from their relatives and friends on the other side.[73] In addition, the military attempts to seal the border created friction with the south as such endeavours were not politically acceptable to Dublin. In November 1971, the Irish Taoiseach Jack Lynch protested to the British Government.[74]

At an early stage of the campaign the Army set up bases along the border in the towns of Crossmaglen, Forkhill and Bessbrook and from these bases soldiers would patrol twenty-four hours a

70 Wilkinson, *Terrorism and the Liberal State,* op. cit., p. 173.
71 Barzilay, op. cit., vol. 1, p. 137.
72 Ibid., p. 138.
73 McArdle, op. cit., pp. 2–9.
74 Ibid., p. 53.

day.[75] In these early days the PIRA operated a double-pronged strategy on the border. It consisted of first trying to provoke the Army into border incidents such as shoot outs. In particular, PIRA members would attack the soldiers engaged in work such as sealing the border roads, firing from positions on the other side of the border. Secondly, the PIRA indulged in the indiscriminate destruction of civilian property, coordinating their attacks with those made in the cities. In particular, the PIRA targeted the border towns of Newtown Butler, Lisnaska and Belleek.[76] The idea was to put as much pressure as possible upon the security forces in the hope that the British Government would tire of the conflict. In these early stages the border seems to have been merely used to divert the attention of the British Army away from the cities, which were the primary focus of PIRA activity. The Army mounted patrols of the border to try to prevent the PIRA men escaping south and also to try to root out the hiding areas of the terrorists. Operation Mulberry was undertaken with this intention. During this operation 2,000 troops searched the border counties of Fermanagh, Tyrone and Armagh.[77]

In 1972 as the British Army undertook its most intense and controversial efforts to defeat the PIRA in the cities, the PIRA began to operate more effectively on the border. It developed a strategy of destroying specific security force targets – in particular the Army vehicles used to patrol the border. The strategy was developed very adeptly. According to some sources:

> Attacks were generally carried out close to the border where there were two parallel roads, one of which gave a view of the other. The mine was generally placed in the culvert or drain running beneath the road. It would be detonated from the road closest to the border and the IRA would get away the few hundred yards to the border.[78]

In Cyprus the British had had experience of dealing with insurgents who had operated in a similar fashion. For example, George Grivas, leader of the EOKA [Ethniki Organosis Kyprion Agonistan] which was dedicated to removing the British presence in Cyprus, had used his troops in two groupings: one operated in the countryside, creating rural incidents to distract the British

75 Hamill, op. cit., pp. 184–5.
76 Ibid., vol. 1, p. 140, vol. 2, p. 244.
77 Barry Smith, 'Bandit Country; Controlling the Borders in Northern Ireland', *War in Peace*, vol. 8, issue 88 (1984), pp. 1754–9.
78 Ibid., vol. 1, p. 143.

Army away from the other group operating in the cities.[79] The PIRA followed the same strategy successfully and in 1973 the decision was made to withdraw British troops from the border. The primary explanation for this change was that the escalation of violence in the cities following internment called for increased troop levels, but the Army also felt vulnerable on the border and the GOC, Lieutenant-General Sir Frank King, felt that the military was dissipating too many of its resources in an area where it would always be labouring under disadvantages.[80] During 1973, the British Army made the cities, in particular Belfast, the centre of its operations.

Yet by 1975, the military importance of the border area had grown significantly. The British Army had to an extent been successful in the cities as a result of the intense concentration on an urban strategy.[81] Given the decision by the British Government to allow the RUC the lead in policing the cities in 1975 – the strategy of 'Ulsterization' – the Army would be freed up to go back to the border. This had become necessary because during the mid-1970s the PIRA appeared to be concentrating on a rural campaign. In particular, British strategists were worried by the activities of the terrorists in the area of the border known as 'murder triangle' or 'bandit country'. Since the cease-fire of Christmas 1974, the PIRA had killed twenty-six people in the area and was able to mount road blocks at will. Of the twelve soldiers killed in Northern Ireland that year, nine had been killed in South Armagh.[82] Sectarian violence had also spiralled quite dramatically; it seemed as if competing groups of Catholic and Protestant paramilitaries were operating in the border areas. Two particularly vicious incidents of sectarian violence made it imperative that the British Army was seen to be acting against the paramilitaries. In July 1975 the Ulster Volunteer Force hijacked the Miami Show Band as they were returning to the Republic after an engagement in the North and all four Catholic members of the band were killed. In retaliation, a group of eleven Protestant workers were hijacked as they returned home from work and murdered by a group claiming to be the South Armagh Republican Action Group.[83] This group had never been heard of before, but was

79 Anthony Burton, *Urban Terrorism: Theory, Practice and Response* (London: Leo Cooper, 1975), pp. 166–7.
80 Hamill, op. cit., p. 132.
81 Ibid., p. 133.
82 Ibid., p. 186.
83 Ibid., p. 189.

generally regarded to be a splinter group of the PIRA.[84] At this stage the British Army simply did not have sufficient numbers of troops to contend with the activities of PIRA, or indeed the other paramilitary groups, along the border. Large rural towns are quite easily garrisoned but the small rural hamlets are impossible to watch all the time. The Army had only four companies to cover 400 square miles with its innumerable villages.[85] It was apparent that the British Army would never be able to cover the entire border area effectively simply by patrolling and the use of road blocks. Some in the military felt that a solution might be the creation of an artificial border 2,000 metres inside northern territory as this would force the opposition to come into an area that could be more easily defended by the military. A minimum number of soldiers would be based forward but there would be a strong reserve force.[86] No matter how satisfactory this solution might have seemed militarily, it was not acceptable politically since it would have meant ceding parts of Northern Ireland to the PIRA. Instead, rather more justifiably, Home Secretary Merlyn Rees sent another battalion to the Province, to reinforce those troops already operating on the border.

The activities of the Army were severely curtailed by their inability to pursue terrorists across the border or retaliate against attacks made from the territory to the south. To counter political violence successfully it might be argued that any state needs the cooperation of its neighbours, but from 1969 to 1973 there was little cooperation, let alone coordination, between the British Army and the southern Irish security forces. The British military was extremely critical of the efforts, or rather what they perceived as the lack of effort, made by the Irish police (the Gardai) or the Irish Army to combat the PIRA.[87] However, given the nature of Anglo-Irish relations since independence, it was not really surprising that the Dublin Government was ambivalent over the activities of the British Army in the area bordering the south.

The problem of the south

The very *raison d'être* of the PIRA, its desire for a thirty-two-county Ireland freed from Westminster, is actually enshrined in the

84 Coogan, op. cit., p. 550.
85 Hamill, op. cit., p. 187.
86 Ibid., p. 100.
87 Ibid., pp. 205–6.

constitution of the Republic of Ireland.[88] It was not surprising therefore that in 1969, at the beginning of the conflict in the North, the Government in Dublin supported the cause of the PIRA. At first the south expressed a concern for the Northern Irish Catholic minority protected by a Protestant police force and a British Army which was not perceived as congenial to Catholic interests or ambitions. The solution put forward by Jack Lynch was the same as that of the PIRA. He stated that 'the reunification of the national territory can provide the only permanent solution for the problem'.[89] For many in the south the PIRA represented new heroes in the age-old Irish struggle against the British forces. This attitude was reinforced throughout the 1970s as the British Army changed its role from one of protecting the Catholic community to one of taking the offensive against the PIRA. However, the attitude of the Dublin Government, despite its rhetoric early in the conflict, was not simply a matter of support for the terrorists but was complicated by conflicting interests and emotions. The crisis in the North beginning in 1969 had produced traumas in the south concerning the very nature of the Irish state. On the one hand, a southern Irish and Catholic government could not be seen to condone the activities of the British security forces in the North; on the other hand, Dublin did not want to open up once again the issue of the border and perhaps spark a civil war along the lines of the 1920s.[90] A victory for the PIRA in the North would have undermined the stability and the political consensus upon which the south has been built.

These concerns have meant that the Dublin Government has not, during this modern conflict, been consistent in its aims towards the PIRA. For example, the Dublin Government objected most strongly to British actions in the North when internment without trial was introduced in 1971, yet internment without trial had been used widely in the south on numerous occasions. The Dublin Government also opposed the use of the Northern Ireland Emergency Provisions Act in 1973, yet had introduced amendments to the southern Irish Offences Act against the state which were equally severe. Again, the southern Irish Government practically begged Prime Minister Margaret Thatcher to make concessions to the hunger strikers in the Maze prison in 1981, but

---

88 J. Bowyer Bell, *A Time of Terror: How Democratic Societies Respond to Revolutionary Violence* (New York: Basic Books, 1981), pp. 230–1.

89 *The Irish Times* (16 June 1977).

90 O'Malley, op. cit., Chapter 2.

they themselves had made no concessions to hunger strikers in the Port Laoise jail in 1977.[91]

The Irish Government has found itself in a difficult and complex position. It does not want to see the PIRA challenging the position of the Irish Government but it also realizes that the cause of the PIRA has an enormous emotional appeal to the people of southern Ireland, particularly when the PIRA succeeds in depicting itself as the defender of Catholic rights in the North. Many members of successive Irish Governments have actively sympathized with the aims, if not the methods, of the PIRA and this too has made it difficult for the British Government to persuade the Dublin administration to be as cooperative as it would like over security on the border.

In 1969, field hospitals were set up on the southern side of the border to cope with the hundreds of people who fled across the border into the Republic to escape the violence in the North.[92] At this stage the Dublin regime was not prepared to act in conjunction with the British Government against the IRA; a reluctance that lasted up until the imposition of Direct Rule in the North in 1972. The British Government was, at this stage, more willing to open up a dialogue in a bid to ensure cooperation over Northern Ireland. The removal of Stormont and the opening of discussions between Dublin and London meant that the Irish Government could justify acting against the PIRA while also claiming to have some influence on the affairs and future of the minority in the North.[93] During 1972 the Irish Government under the Cosgrave-led coalition initiated strong measures against the PIRA in the south. During November 1972, the Irish security forces arrested the PIRA chief of staff, Sean MacStiofain, and the following February Rory O'Bradaigh, the President of Sinn Fein, was captured.[94] A series of repressive actions was also taken in the south. These included greater restraints on state-controlled radio and television which was designed to counter the appeal of the PIRA. This attitude was reflected in the greater cooperation with the British Army over the issue of the border. By the end of 1975 there were two Irish infantry battalions operating south of the border and contact between the security forces had improved considerably.[95] The main area where cross-border security was

91 Ibid., Chapter 2.
92 Dâil Éireann, vol. 241, col. 1402, 22 October 1969.
93 Bowyer Bell, op. cit., p. 219.
94 Ibid., p. 219.
95 Ed Maloney, *The Irish Times* (21 January 1985).

improved was in the communication and exchange of computerized information concerning suspects and the identification by the Gardai of suspects crossing into the North. Both forces operated in close radio contact. Such measures ensured that the border was under constant surveillance. The process was incremental throughout the 1970s but from 1980 Northern Irish police began to travel south to exchange information.[96] The south, however, remained wary about cooperating too openly with the British Army.

The 1970s revealed many of the ambiguities of the southern Irish position. While paying lip service to the notion of unity, the Dublin administration has been all too aware of the problems that such a vision entailed. Indeed, throughout the decade efforts were made in the south to reform popular attitudes towards the PIRA. It sought to choreograph fundamental change by depicting the PIRA as a band of murderers, as criminals who have little in common with the litany of old Irish patriots and martyrs. Successive Irish Governments have also pointed to the reality of a future Catholic Ireland with an entrenched and bitter enclave of one million Protestants. Dublin could, in theory, have found itself playing the role of Westminster but without the economic resources or military strength to sustain the position.[97] While people in the Republic would have liked British troops withdrawn, Dublin knew that it was in no position to assume total responsibility. Despite this recognition of prevailing realities by Dublin, the old allegiances to the cause of an Ireland freed from British connections still lurked and prevented Dublin from following a consistent path *vis-à-vis* British forces in Ireland.

Indeed, throughout the 1970s, the British military remained unhappy with the south despite increased cooperation. In particular, one issue that the British Army wished to see employed was that of so-called hot pursuit. This would have enabled Army patrols chasing suspects to cross the border and apprehend suspects and then return them to the North. The necessity of having to stop at the border was extremely frustrating. However, it was never politically feasible and, despite the calls of the military, was never officially implemented. Military strategy on the border was confined by the limitations of the Anglo-Irish relationship and in particular by the reluctance of the south to be seen to be acting

96 McArdle, op. cit., p. 38.
97 Ulster Survey 1, *The Economist* (2 June 1984), pp. 38–54.

openly against Republican groups which had a measure of support from its own population. Throughout the late 1980s both the British and Irish Governments sought to define and redefine their relationship with each other over Northern Ireland. The complexities of the political relationship appear to have escaped the military, who perceived Dublin's actions quite often as hindering them in their fight against the PIRA. Yet, as the new Thatcher administration soon realized in 1979–80, without the south there could be no political settlement.

An assessment of police primacy

The increased use of the RUC and the UDR resulted from the wish of the British Government to see a return to normality in the Province. The strategy had two strands. First, the Ulsterization of the conflict so that the Province itself assumed the responsibility for security. Secondly, the scaling down of the conflict, that is rather than allowing the PIRA members political prisoner status, they were treated as ordinary criminals who had broken the law.[98] The Republican response of the H-Block protest marked a new shift in PIRA tactics, with the emphasis placed on pressurizing the British Government to make political concessions through fear of international embarrassment.[99]

By the early 1980s the RUC and the UDR appeared to be gaining the upper hand in the struggle with the PIRA. Fatalities inflicted upon the security forces had significantly dropped from ninety-seven in 1982 to only thirty-seven in 1985.[100] Relations had also improved between the RUC and the British Army. In 1975 the Army had doubted the efficiency of the RUC and had felt that much of its hard-won success against the paramilitaries might have been dissipated by a force that was simply not properly trained. However, by the early 1980s the RUC had shown itself to be capable of taking the leading role, although its position had been the subject of much debate. In particular, PIRA successes, such as those at Warrenpoint, had thrown the notion of police primacy into doubt. In August 1979, after the Warrenpoint attack, the new British Prime Minister, Margaret Thatcher, visited the Province to

98 Coogan, op. cit., p. 519.
99 R. Tomlinson, W. Robertson and T. Prentice, 'Orchestra of Death', *The Sunday Standard* (10 May 1981).
100 Statistics supplied by Army Headquarters Lisburn, 30 July 1985.

boost the damaged morale of the security forces and had expressed doubts over the ability of the RUC. She had had to be convinced that police primacy was really the only option if any political progress was to be made in the Province. On 30 August, the new British Government acceded to the wishes of the RUC and increased their numbers by 1,000.[101] The position of the RUC also improved at the end of 1979 when GOC Lieutenant-General Creasey came to the end of his service in Northern Ireland. Creasey had disapproved totally of the policy of 'police primacy' and had been known to state that he was not going to be run by the RUC.[102] He had resented the lowering of the Army's profile and had not willingly implemented the idea of a supporting role for the Army. With his secondment to Oman in 1979 and the appointment of Lieutenant-General Lawson as the GOC, the Army began to play a more supportive, if lesser, role in the urban conflict.[103]

The mid to late 1970s saw the implementation of a different and difficult strategy in Ireland. This was to move the conflict away from the militarized containment by the Army to a more normal mode of policing by the RUC. This did not really happen. What did occur was that the RUC became more militarized and managed to take control of the cities. The Republican paramilitaries moved the main basis of their operations to the border. This in turn sparked a massive effort by British special forces to eradicate the PIRA in the countryside. The normalization of the Province went hand in hand with the deployment of British special forces in greater numbers. The latter development was to prove extremely controversial and during the next decade involved increasing numbers of soldiers in complex and difficult operational circumstances. Indeed, one of the main ramifications of the use of special forces was to increase the Catholic suspicion of the Army and raise allegations during the 1980s of a 'shoot to kill' policy. Such developments did little to provide the context for a settlement that might reconcile the communities in the North, despite the fact that during the next few years the British Government increasingly attempted to find a political solution to the 'troubles' in Northern Ireland that would include the Irish Government in Dublin and allow a reduction in the British military input. This became the task of the Thatcher Government in Ireland.

101 See Bowyer Bell, *The Irish Troubles,* op. cit., p. 575.
102 Quoted in Hamill, op. cit., p. 260.
103 Dewar, op. cit., pp. 147–63.

CHAPTER FIVE

The Search for Political Solutions: The Move to Military Withdrawal? 1980–85

At the beginning of the 1980s, the Thatcher Government was in power and little inclined to look to radical solutions to deal with the problems of Ireland. Indeed, for Mrs Thatcher, Ireland was not a priority, nor an issue that merited particular debate. Her allegiances in the Province were clear: she was committed to the cause of the Unionists[1] and regarded the Republican paramilitaries as an issue that should be dealt with robustly, using the full powers of the security services. Despite these views, it was under the Thatcher administration that the British Government in the early 1980s took the most radical steps towards altering the pattern of politics in the Province with the signing of the Anglo-Irish Agreement of 1985. This brought the south firmly into the politics of Northern Ireland and made it clear to the Unionists that the British Government would not underwrite their cause for ever.[2] This evolution in the political sphere was not mirrored by positive developments in security arrangements. In the same period that the British Government moved towards a settlement, the use of the security forces in Ireland underwent its most controversial phase. Throughout the decade, not only did the PIRA broaden its appeal through entering electoral politics, but both the RUC and the Army were dogged by allegations of 'shoot to kill' policies. The use of supergrasses also helped to undermine the picture of progress in the handling of the Northern Irish question.

---

1 Margaret Thatcher, *The Downing Street Years* (London: HarperCollins, 1993), p. 385.
2 Anthony Kenny, *The Road to Hillsborough: The Shaping of the Anglo-Irish Agreement* (Oxford: Pergamon Press, 1986), pp. 130–2.

New initiatives

At the beginning of the 1980s, as the H-Block protest came to its end, there were indications that the cross-party consensus that existed between the Labour and Conservative parties was, under the strain of the publicity generated by the hunger strikers, breaking down. At its 1981 conference the Labour Party expressed its support for a united Ireland by consent and two years later the Liberal Party, at its annual conference, passed a resolution calling for the withdrawal of British troops. During 1981 the Labour Party questioned whether the Emergency Powers Act should be continued or whether it should at least be debated. The Labour Party supported a motion introduced in the British Parliament that called for a review of the actual operation of the Act. While this motion was defeated by a vote of 279 votes to 213,[3] it demonstrated that some on the mainland wanted to rethink the approach to Ireland. For Mrs Thatcher this was unnecessary. She was determined to utilize the full range use of emergency legislation. She was not, at this point, convinced that there was room for a new political initiative, let alone one that might mean a relaxation of the struggle with the terrorists or political concessions to the Republicans. In particular, she was opposed to any measure that might allow the Dublin Government a decisive voice in the affairs of the Province.[4] This placed her at odds with some within the Conservative Party who believed that the only way forward was to try to work with the southern Government of Dr Garret Fitzgerald. Even as Mrs Thatcher reiterated the hard line, James Prior, the new Secretary of State for Northern Ireland, began to search for a formula that would ease tensions in the Province. Some of his Conservative colleagues pressed him to implement a notion of integration, that is to treat Northern Ireland as if it was no different from any other part of the United Kingdom, but Prior wisely decided that this was not really a viable option and began instead to look at ideas such the devolution of powers as a new long-term solution to the problems of the North.[5] In the short term, Prior believed, as William Whitelaw had, that

---

3 For a discussion of the Labour Party and Northern Ireland, see Paul Dixon, 'British Parties and Ulster Unionists', *Irish Political Studies* 9 (1994), pp. 25–40.

4 Thatcher, op. cit., p. 402.

5 See Sabine Wichart, *Northern Ireland since 1945* (London: Longman, 1991), p. 192.

tensions could be eased through some concessions or gestures of conciliation to the Republican communities. Accordingly, on 6 October 1981, Prior initiated new rules on prison clothes, remission and visits of relatives for those in the H-Block.

Prior's intentions were good but did little to ameliorate tension in the Province. After the death of Bobby Sands in May, there was violent rioting which continued throughout the autumn. During 1981 alone, the RUC fired 29,601 baton rounds of plastic bullets at rioters.[6] By 1982, the RUC had lost 112 officers, the RUC Reserve 58, the British Army 394 and the UDR 127 in the conflict,[7] but behind the usual pattern of violence the Republicans had begun to shift their activities towards a more sophisticated agenda. In the late 1970s the Sinn Fein leadership had decided to broaden its base of operations, but had not really implemented any new policies. The publicity surrounding the hunger strikes and the international attention that had subsequently focused on the Province after the death of Bobby Sands caused the Northern Command of the PIRA to accelerate its shift to a political agenda. In particular, it was Gerry Adams who sought to reverse the policies of the current leadership of Sinn Fein, which was still nominally under the control of the southerners. Adams argued that the party should reverse its traditional policy of abstention and contest elections in both the south and the North.[8] This was a highly sensitive issue; since the partition of Ireland the hard core of Sinn Fein had prided itself on its absolute refusal to recognize the institutions and political system imposed by the British Government and had boycotted the Irish Dail. Adams sought to establish Sinn Fein as not just a party on the margins of Irish politics, but one that could operate throughout Ireland in legitimate politics. Adams wanted Sinn Fein members to contest elections, but the southerners in the Sinn Fein movement, led by O'Bradaigh, opposed this move. After the hunger strike, however, the momentum lay with the Sinn Fein members in the North. Adams and McGuinness capitalized on the emotional wave of support and sympathy for their cause in the North, using the

6 J. Bowyer Bell, *The Irish Troubles: A Generation of Violence, 1967–1992* (Dublin: Gill and Macmillan, 1993), p. 632.

7 See Robert M. Pockgrass, 'Terroristic Murder in Northern Ireland: Who is Killed and Why?', *Terrorism: An International Journal* 9.4 (1987), pp. 341–57.

8 See Mark Ryan, *War and Peace in Ireland: Britain and the IRA in the New World Order* (London: Pluto, 1994), p. 65.

media to broadcast their views on both television and radio.[9] Adams in particular was seen within the movement as a dynamic figure who had been at the cutting edge of the struggle. O'Bradaigh, on the other hand, was regarded as the old face of Republicanism. There was little the southern leadership could do to challenge the northerners. O'Bradaigh was the subject of an exclusion order which prevented him from entering the North and challenging Adams.[10] O'Bradaigh was also handicapped in the south because of the 1973 Irish Broadcasting Act which banned interviews with Sinn Fein, the IRA and other paramilitaries. This left the way open for Adams to assume the leadership and O'Bradaigh duly stepped down in 1982, finally handing over to his rival in November 1983.[11] Adams denies membership of the IRA, but some sources believe that part of the reason why he defeated O'Bradaigh was because of 'his impeccable track record in the war zone'.[12] Whatever his past, Adams in the early 1980s had a clear vision of the manner in which the Republican movement should evolve. He was convinced that Sinn Fein should participate in elections and fought an internal battle within the party to get his views accepted. By 1986, both Sinn Fein and the IRA accepted that the campaign against the British Government should be one of both armed struggle and electoral strength.[13] In 1983, in the election to the newly established Ulster Assembly (through which Jim Prior hoped to establish some form of rolling devolution), Sinn Fein won 10 per cent of the votes and five seats. In the Council elections of Northern Ireland, fifty-eight Sinn Fein councillors took office, and in Omagh and Fermanagh they won the Council Chairs. Subsequent Unionist boycotts of Council meetings reduced local governments to confusion. The growing attraction of the Sinn Fein party was confirmed in the general election of June 1983, when Adams was elected as the member of Parliament for West Belfast. To many observers this seemed an absurd twist of Irish history – that a man widely regarded as a terrorist was now an elected MP. The degree of support for Sinn Fein caused more than a ripple on the mainland. After the Labour Party had displayed interest in debating the Emergency Powers Act

9 Brendan O'Brien, *The Long War: The IRA and Sinn Fein, 1985 to Today* (Dublin: The O'Brien Press, 1993), pp. 112–13.

10 Ibid., pp. 112–13.

11 Ibid., pp. 112–13.

12 IRA source, interview by Brendan O'Brien, quoted in O'Brien, op. cit., p. 113.

13 Ryan, op. cit., p. 65.

during 1981, some on the left of British politics had grown increasingly interested in the message of Sinn Fein. In July 1983, Adams was received in London as a guest of Ken Livingstone, leader of the now defunct Greater London Council (GLC). This suited the Sinn Fein strategy perfectly. It bestowed public recognition and a way of getting the Republican message directly into mainland politics. It also helped to legitimize participation at the ballot box, while the paramilitaries continued to pursue a parallel strategy of physical force.[14]

During the autumn of 1981 it was this Republican strategy of physical force that seemed to dominate activities. The Provisionals increased their killings and maimings with a vengeance and to maximum publicity, especially when the PIRA decided to once again take the battle to the mainland and mounted a series of vicious attacks in England. On 11 October the PIRA carried out a nail-bomb attack on the Chelsea barracks in London; on 17 October they placed a bomb in which Sir Stewart Pringle, the Commandant General of the Royal Marines, lost a leg, and on 26 October an explosive device in Oxford Street killed a bomb disposal expert. Then, on 14 November, back in the Province, the Provisionals murdered Robert Bradford, an Official Unionist MP.[15] This killing sparked fears that a civil war was imminent. When James Prior attended the funeral of the Unionist MP, he was booed and jostled by waiting Unionists who felt that the British Government had once again failed them in their response to the activities of the Republican paramilitaries.[16] Concern was such that the British Army was reinforced by 600 men in order to shore up the front line of beleaguered RUC forces. As 1981 came to a close the overall statistics for deaths in the security forces were worse than the previous year with deaths increased from seventy-six to 101.[17]

It was not just the PIRA who had stepped up the armed struggle with the security forces. The Irish National Liberation Army (INLA), too, seemed determined to put pressure on the British Government. Since 1977 there had been relative peace between Republican factions, although there were still a few housing estates

14 See Gerry Adams in M. Collins (ed.), *Ireland After Britain* (London: Pluto, 1985). Quoted in M.L.R. Smith, *Fighting for Ireland: The Military Strategy of the Irish Republican Movement* (London: Routledge, 1995), p. 162.
15 Bowyer Bell, op. cit., p. 635.
16 James Prior, *A Balance of Power* (London: Hamish Hamilton, 1986) p. 149.
17 Bowyer Bell, op. cit., pp. 641–2.

or sections of cities which were considered Provo or INLA territory and closed to the rival organizations.[18] But in 1981 the INLA, which had achieved infamy with the murder of Lord Mountbatten in 1979, began once again to step up its operations in the Province, on the mainland and in Europe. At the beginning of the decade the two factions appeared to be competing as to which could cause greatest damage to the security forces.[19] During the latter part of 1982, the INLA appeared to be winning. In December it targeted a public house and disco – the Droppin Well at Ballykelly. It was a well-known haunt of off-duty British soldiers. An INLA bomb killed twelve soldiers and sixty-six civilians.[20]

Despite the increased activity of the paramilitaries, the security forces believed that they were coping well with the level of violence in the Province at the beginning of the decade. Two developments, however, seriously dented the images of both the RUC and the British Army. The first was the case of a 'shoot to kill' policy and the second was the trials of the 'supergrasses'.

'Shoot to kill'

The allegations that the security forces in Northern Ireland operated a 'shoot to kill' policy had often been made by Republican spokesmen. From 1980 onwards, however, the controversy assumed a new dimension. Up until that point shootings by both the British Army and the RUC had evoked suspicion in the nationalist communities that they were deliberately targeting IRA men or IRA sympathizers. Abuses by the security forces had been well documented by a group of priests.[21] The killing of John Boyle in July 1978 had once again aroused these fears in a wider public setting and done little to assuage Catholic fears, especially when the soldiers were later acquitted.[22] Stories about a 'secret war' in Ireland had abounded ever since the early 1970s, but 1980 was a turning point because it was in that year that the law was changed so that killings by the RUC and the British Army were no

18 Ibid., pp. 641–2.
19 Interviews with Superintendent Donnelly and others, N. Division, April 1984, quoted in Pockgrass, op. cit., p. 201.
20 Bowyer Bell, op. cit., p. 657.
21 See Gerald McElroy, *The Catholic Church and the Northern Irish Crisis 1968–86* (Dublin: Gill and Macmillan, 1991), pp. 96–7.
22 Mark Urban, *Big Boys' Rules. The SAS and the Secret Struggle Against the IRA* (London: Faber & Faber, 1992), pp. 63–4.

longer subject to the normal proceedings of an inquest. The rules
of a coroner's court were amended so that open verdicts could not
be recorded. Instead, coroners were restricted to findings saying
when, where and how the person had died.[23] Nationalists believed
that this merely covered up the fact that the security forces were
targeting individuals known to them. In particular, the deaths of
two INLA men, Seamus Grew and Roddy Carroll, in 1982 in
suspicious circumstances fuelled the controversy. In December
1982, two RUC cars were sent into Armagh to try and to pick up
Dominic McGlinchey, a hardened operative of the INLA. Grew
and Carroll were supposedly escorting McGlinchey to Grew's home
but before they arrived, McClinchey had been dropped off. When
the two INLA men arrived in Armagh they drove into some
confusion. One RUC officer had crashed into another, but
another RUC officer, Robinson, gave chase, overtaking them,
cutting them off and then shooting. Both were killed. The RUC
subsequently claimed that the two terrorists had tried to run a
roadblock. Robinson was duly charged, tried and acquitted, but
such were the discrepancies in the RUC evidence that concern was
expressed that this was just a blatant example of a 'shoot to kill'
policy. Indeed, allegations were made that this attack was a reprisal
against the INLA for the Droppin Well attack. On 14 December,
James Prior admitted that there were special anti-terrorist squads
operating within the RUC but denied that a 'shoot to kill' policy
was operating.

International attention was aroused by the issue of whether or
not a 'shoot to kill' policy was operating when Amnesty International
began its investigation into killings by members of the British
security forces in Northern Ireland. It was concerned by the spate
of killings in late 1982 when six unarmed people were killed by
members of what appeared to be an anti-terrorist squad within the
RUC.[24] It emerged that senior police officers had made up their
own versions of what had occurred prior to the killings and had
later instructed lower ranks of RUC officers to collude in this
endeavour. Public concern was such that in May 1984 a British
police officer, John Stalker, was appointed to examine whether
there had been a cover-up. Stalker carried out his own
examination of the evidence in all the cases. He subsequently

23 Tim Pat Coogan, *The Troubles; Ireland's Ordeal 1966–1995 and the Search for Peace* (London: Hutchinson, 1995), p. 258.

24 Amnesty International, *Political Killings in Northern Ireland* (London: Amnesty International British Section, 1994), pp. 5–9.

alleged that he was hindered in his investigation by the RUC and, before he could complete his task, he was removed from duty. The inquiry was completed by Colin Sampson, the Chief Constable of West Yorkshire, another British police officer, but the findings were not published, although eighteen officers were disciplined.[25] Much in the security politics of Northern Ireland remained hidden, but some things were revealed by the Stalker/Sampson investigations. It was clear for example that suspected members of Republican paramilitary groups, who were under surveillance, were killed by covert anti-terrorist squads operating within the RUC. It was also apparent that the original police investigations of the killings were at best incompetent and at worst corrupt. It also raised suspicions of many other instances in which the security forces have killed when it would have been possible to arrest. The list of justifications for the killing of suspects began, as the 1980s wore on, to sound predictably familiar: that the suspect had tried to run a roadblock; that the suspect reached for a gun; that the car carrying the suspect was fired at accidentally. All of this sapped at the confidence placed in the RUC and reinforced the idea that, like its predecessors the B-Specials, it was incapable of non-partisan behaviour.

At this point, despite the strategy of police primacy, the main responsibility for covert operations once again returned to the British Army. Since then, in almost all the controversial incidents involving security forces, it has been British soldiers who have been implicated in allegations of 'shoot to kill'. According to one report by Amnesty International, between 1976 and 1992 the SAS killed thirty-seven members of the PIRA.[26] This is not the whole picture, however. The SAS have had long periods in which they have not killed suspects and other periods of intense activity when many paramilitaries have been shot. For example, between December 1983 and February 1985, ten people were shot dead, eight of them members of the IRA, but this was after a period of five years in which the SAS killed no one.[27] What this points to is that the SAS are deployed more aggressively in periods when it is felt that the paramilitaries are most active. The secrecy which surrounds the SAS and its operations makes it difficult to comment with any degree of certainty as to whether the British military was engaged in a 'shoot to kill' policy when it felt that it was losing the initiative

25 See John Stalker, *Stalker* (London: Harrap, 1988).
26 Amnesty International, op. cit., pp. 11–12.
27 Urban, op. cit., p. 165.

to the paramilitaries, but what is not in question is that SAS personnel were indeed used to ambush suspected terrorists and killed people. It has been argued by one authoritative source that in Northern Ireland, 'There is no shoot to kill policy in the sense of a blanket order to shoot terrorists on sight. Rather the knack is to get IRA terrorists, armed and carrying out an operation, to walk into a trap.'[28] This thinking illustrates the grey area that the British military was operating in – no obvious agenda to kill, but a consensus that if the situation arose, such an outcome would be a positive one.

The controversy over a 'shoot to kill' policy raised the perennial questions of the security problem in Ireland: what behaviour is appropriate for security forces countering the paramilitaries? What actions can and should be justified in pursuit of peace? If these questions were becoming familiar by the 1980s, then the ensuing debate was in many ways ritualistic. The military had no doubt that while the rule of law should be obeyed, it should, when necessary, be amended to allow the forces of law and order to defeat terrorism. The views of General Frank Kitson are illustrative of military thinking on this issue. He argued that there were two possible uses for the law: the first and most controversial was that 'the law should be used as just another weapon in the government's arsenal, and in this case it becomes little more than a propaganda cover for the disposal of unwanted members of the public'.[29] The second was that the law should remain impartial. Kitson actually favoured the second route on moral grounds, although he recognized that it might prove militarily difficult.[30] In reality, most of the military believed that the law should be one more weapon in their fight against the terrorists and provide leeway for them in dealing with suspects. Yet this approach remained at odds with the public commitment to normalization and criminalization; increasingly, extraordinary legislation and the use of the SAS appeared out of step with the desire to make political progress. While the Conservative Party had sympathy with the views of the military, the conflict in Ireland, with its repressive legislation, started to appear increasingly at odds with European opinion and began to draw condemnation from a wider audience than had hitherto been the case. After the hunger strikes, there

28 Ibid., p. 164.
29 Frank Kitson, *Low-Intensity Operations: Subversion, Insurgency, Peacekeeping* (London: Faber & Faber, 1971), p. 69.
30 Ibid., p. 69.

was considerable adverse publicity in the continental press and the European Commission of Human Rights condemned the nature of the British response to the H-Block protest. In 1982, partly because of their use in Ireland, the European Community decided to condemn the use of plastic bullets.[31] All of this meant that the British authorities were subjected to a more complex scrutiny of their activities in Ireland at a time when both the PIRA and Sinn Fein were beginning to operate more efficiently.

The supergrasses

Increasingly, it seemed that everything to do with the Irish question was disputed. The effort to impose law and order in Northern Ireland, which was always difficult, seemed even more problematic after the hunger strikes. Internment had not worked; the Diplock courts had proved controversial and the use of interrogation on prisoners had led to hostile publicity. By the early 1980s the British Government was ready to try something new to secure the conviction of paramilitaries – the use of the supergrass or the 'informer witness'. Supergrasses were normally, but not exclusively, men on the margins of the INLA, the PIRA or the UVF who were willing to 'confess' to, and implicate others in, the carrying out of terrorist offences in return for their freedom and a new identity. Their use, it was hoped, might do what covert operations had only partly succeeded in doing – eliminate the main leaders of the terrorist organizations. The use of supergrasses could provide the security forces with insight in and information on both the PIRA and the INLA. The confessions of supergrasses meant that there was less need to intern or interrogate suspects. Christopher Black, the first IRA supergrass, implicated thirty-eight people by his testimony.[32] Henry Kikpatrick was one of several members of the INLA arrested in 1981. He was regarded as a particularly valuable 'catch' as he was a central figure in the Belfast brigade of the INLA. He gave testimony that led to the conviction of twenty-seven INLA men.[33] These convictions were

31 See Brendan O'Leary and John McGarry, *The Politics of Antagonism: Understanding Northern Ireland* (London: Athlone Press, 1993), p. 214.
32 Bowyer Bell, op. cit., p. 661.
33 See T. Gifford, *The Use of Accomplice Evidence in Northern Ireland* (Nottingham: Russell Press, 1984), see also, John E. Finn, 'Public Support for Emergency (Anti-Terrorist) Legislation in Northern Ireland: A Preliminary Analysis', *Terrorism: An International Journal* 10 (1987), pp. 113–24. In February 1987, the Secretary of

later overturned as unsafe and the men were released in 1986. This effectively ended the use of supergrasses, but during the early 1980s the use of informer witnesses was regarded as successful and, in the case of the INLA, as having led directly to its demise. The INLA, which was a relatively small and fractured organization, was badly hurt by the confessions of the supergrasses. By 1986 the INLA was riven with disputes and degenerated into a spate of vicious tit-for-tat murders, primarily because of mutual suspicions raised by the supergrass system. In the period between 1982 and 1984 the returns from the use of informer witnesses seemed positive. Five hundred people were arrested and charged with over 1,500 offences,[34] while the show-trials of those implicated were designed to demonstrate the ability of the security authorities to deal with the paramilitaries. The success was short-lived, however, and as so often in Ireland apparent successes often had unexpected consequences. Many of the supergrasses turned out to be unreliable witnesses. Under cross-examination they tended to break down and, most damaging of all, some reneged on their confessions, denying their testimony. This did considerable damage to the criminal justice system in Northern Ireland and, as the supergrasses were primarily drawn from Republican paramilitary groups, did little to bolster Catholic confidence in the judiciary. A survey carried out in 1984 during the supergrass hearings found that 72 per cent of Catholics questioned disapproved of the supergrass system, on the other hand only 21 per cent of the Protestants asked expressed doubts.[35] By 1987, the release of many of those tried under the system effectively ended the process, but damage had already been done once again to the judicial system in the Province. All in all, with the deaths of the hunger strikers, the 'shoot to kill' and supergrass controversies, the early 1980s did much to strengthen Sinn Fein. It was fear of Sinn Fein's political advance that, more than any thing else, prompted both the Dublin Government and the SDLP in the North to press Westminster for new political initiatives.

State for Northern Ireland, Tom King, admitted that 52 persons convicted on the evidence of an 'accomplice' had had their convictions overturned on appeal. See HC, 6 series, vol. 110, cols 726–7, 18 February 1987.

34 Bowyer Bell, op. cit., p. 661.

35 See *Fortnight: An Independent Review for Northern Ireland* (November 1984).

The inclusion of the south in the politics of Northern Ireland

While the supergrasses and the 'shoot to kill' controversies unfolded, Jim Prior was seeking political solutions. In this, he was not initially encouraged by the British Prime Minister.[36] Mrs Thatcher was suspicious that any move to build closer ties with Dublin would necessarily antagonize the Unionists. She also believed that the southern Irish Taoiseach, Garret Fitzgerald was seeking to play the British card in domestic Irish politics. By this she meant that he was seeking to make political capital out of pushing Westminster into concessions in the North. Despite Prior's best efforts, Thatcher remained sceptical of taking any new path, but by November 1981, pressure was building for the British Government to move towards some form of political initiative. In 1981 the Anglo-Irish Intergovernmental Council was set up. The southern Irish Government was hopeful that it marked a move towards greater Anglo-Irish collaboration whereas Thatcher believed that it was nothing more than a formalization of existing links.[37] These different perceptions of what had been agreed became somewhat irrelevant in the spring of 1982, when Garret Fitzgerald was replaced by Charles Haughey and Anglo-Irish relations were disrupted by the Falklands War. In April 1982 Prior had introduced the White Paper on Northern Ireland which contained the notion of rolling devolution. Haughey denounced the Paper as an 'unworkable mistake' which was faced with inevitable failure.[38] Five days earlier the Argentinians had invaded the Falkland Islands in the South Atlantic. The Irish reaction to the British war effort effectively destroyed any goodwill in Anglo-Irish relations. Not only did the Irish Defence Minister, Paddy Power, describe the British Government as the aggressors, but the Irish Government, after the sinking of the Argentinian battleship, the *Belgrano*, demanded an immediate meeting of the UN Security Council.[39] On 2 May the Irish Government abandoned its agreement with the European Community to employ sanctions against Argentina. Irish behaviour in the foreign policy arena meant that no progress was made on Northern

---

36 Thatcher, op. cit., p. 394.
37 Thatcher, op. cit., p. 393.
38 Garret Fitzgerald, *All in a Life* (London: Macmillan, 1991), pp. 408–9.
39 Ibid., p. 409.

Ireland throughout the rest of the year. It was only the return of Garret Fitzgerald as Taoiseach in December that gave the opportunity for an improvement in relations. Upon his return to office, he described Anglo-Irish relations as being in a disastrous condition.[40]

Part of the British agenda for reopening talks with the southern Irish Government in 1982–83 was to press Dublin over the issue of security cooperation on the border, rather than to discuss new political ventures.[41] Garrett Fitzgerald was willing to offer improved cooperation along the border and also proposed a direct role for the Irish Police, the Gardai, in the Province as well as hinting at the possibility of a role for the Irish Army itself. This was not even a possibility for Thatcher.

The issue of joint cooperation between Westminster and Dublin was raised again with the setting up of the 'New Ireland Forum' in Dublin. This was the brainchild of John Hume MP, the leader of the SDLP. He believed that members of the Catholic and Nationalist parties should try to take the lead in dictating which way Ireland could be unified by consent and in a manner that would include and incorporate Unionist interests.[42] Hume also had another aim which was to ensure that Sinn Fein did not whittle away the electoral appeal of the SDLP by posing as the only party that could offer unification. Discussions of the New Ireland Forum began in May 1983. All the parties in the country, with the exception of the Unionists, who boycotted it, and Sinn Fein, who were not invited, took part in the forum. It also involved prominent academics, politicians and church leaders. The forum deliberated for over a year. When its findings were finally published, they evoked controversy. For the most part, the report was intensely critical of the British handling not only of the current crisis in the North but also of the historic British role in Ireland,[43] perceiving a British presence as one that had contributed to but not eased conflict. This was part and parcel of the nationalist interpretation of Irish history, and not suprisingly failed to recognize the part that British forces had played in separating the warring Catholic and Protestant communities in 1969. The lack of recognition of the sectarian nature of the conflict was reflected in the somewhat utopian manner in which the forum

40 Ibid., p. 462.
41 Thatcher, op.cit., p. 395.
42 See New Ireland Forum Report, Dublin 1984, p. 15.
43 Kenny, op. cit., pp. 41–3.

hoped that the Unionists could be reconciled to the proposal of a unitary state of Ireland, with one Parliament and one government. The forum proposed that the Unionists would be guaranteed a minimum number of seats in the Parliament.[44] It also held out the possibility that the Unionists might be induced to accept unity, without a British presence, through certain benefits which would accrue from the proposed unitary state. Not least, the forum held out the prospect of an 'all Ireland' economic system that could bring about prosperity through greater efficiency. This was all very well, but in the short term most analysts were agreed that a British withdrawal from Northern Ireland would actually have disastrous economic results.[45] The forum did not actively envisage a British withdrawal, but rather the inclusion of the south and a relative weakening of the British position in the North. Hence, it put the case for equal responsibility between Dublin and Westminster for the government of the Province. This meant, it was claimed, not joint sovereignty but joint authority. There were three different models for the way this might work: a confederal Ireland; a unitary state; or joint authority. On security issues, the forum's sub-committee recommended joint responsibility for a criminal justice regime and discussed the establishment of a new police force – seconded from the existing ones in the south of Ireland and the United Kingdom. Eventually, the operation of such a police force would open the way for a British military withdrawal.[46]

For the British Government the most crucial element of the forum was that not only did it raise issues of sovereignty (the British Prime Minister was not convinced by the distinction between 'authority and sovereignty'), but it also ignored the reality of Unionist wishes. In his response to the forum, made in the House of Commons, James Prior pointed out the reality of an entrenched Unionist opposition to such a proposal. While Prior denied that the Unionists could or should operate a veto on future arrangements, he went on to say that the consent of the majority would have to be obtained before any such vision could be entertained. In effect, therefore, the Unionists did have a veto.[47] This meant little progress could be made.

Yet the years 1983–84 provided much food for thought for the British Government. Not least, the successes of Sinn Fein in the

44 Ibid., pp. 46–8.
45 Ibid., p. 48.
46 Ibid., p. 42.
47 Ibid., p. 65. See also House of Commons Debate (hereafter HC), vol. 87, col. 768, 26 November, 1985.

elections of 1983 gave the British administration a greater incentive to do something in the Province, lest the Republicans create a situation where they could gain enough support to veto future developments. The deliberations of the Kilbrandon Committee, commissioned by the British–Irish Association to put together a response to the forum, supported a wider involvement of the south and was critical of British pessimism over the proposals of the forum, but publicly at least the Thatcher administration was not willing to endorse any great new venture. Behind the scenes, however, Dublin and London were negotiating over what types of joint security operation might be implemented for Northern Ireland. As early as March 1984, Sir Robert Armstrong, the Head of the Civil Service and Cabinet Secretary, presented to Dublin the suggestions of the British Cabinet for improving security cooperation. These proposals included the creation of a 'security band' along the border which would be overseen by a Joint Security Commission and policed by joint crime squads, which might then become a common police force. A Law Commission was also proposed to oversee an all-Ireland court. On the British side there was even a willingness to redraw the existing border with the Republic.[48] These provisions, however, were based on the understanding that the south would provide a guarantee of the status of Northern Ireland by renouncing Articles 2 and 3 of the Irish constitution.[49] This was not acceptable to the south. While the British stuck to the notion of having to maintain full sovereignty over Northern Ireland, Dublin was equally wary of holding hostages to the future by renouncing their historic claims to the Province. During the summer the Irish Government did, for the first time, explicitly put forward the idea of amending Articles 2 and 3 of the Irish constitution, but the British Government remained unconvinced that the Irish could deliver.[50]

Against this background of public wrangling over constitutional positions, throughout the summer the Irish and British Governments, using 'back door' channels, continued to debate the future policing of the Province. In response to Sir Robert Armstrong's proposal of a 'security band' along the border, the south put forward its own views, stressing that in any new arrangement the wishes of the Catholic minority in the North should be considered and, where possible, due deference should

48 Thatcher, op. cit., p. 395.
49 Fitzgerald, op. cit., pp. 494–5.
50 Thatcher, op. cit., p. 395.

be shown in new security arrangements. In this vein, spokespersons urged consideration of a new additional nationalist police force in the Province. This force would not be armed and would work with the RUC, backed by a new joint security force.[51] Mainly though, for the south, any progress on security hinged upon the creation of a new joint political framework along the lines of the New Ireland Forum. The British response was cautiously welcoming to the proposals over security, although they remained sceptical of the value of an unarmed police force operating within the Province. Instead, they raised the possibility of a type of force, based on the German frontier police, which would be armed but which could operate with another force that might be unarmed. It would mean three different forces operating in the same relatively small area, the costs of which were certain to be prohibitive.[52] The British Government also mooted once again the notion of an all-Ireland police force. This was rather curious as an all-Ireland police force raised difficult issues, not least for the British Government, the matter of sovereignty in Northern Ireland. Just how seriously Mrs Thatcher took this debate is difficult to know; she maintained publicly throughout 1984 that the British Government could not and would not be pushed into limiting its influence in the Province and there appeared little real hope of political advancement. What is significant is that the British administration was willing to consider new security arrangements which would affect the position of the British Army and in some respects allow for partial withdrawal. The Irish question was literally thrown on to the political agenda on 12 October 1984 when the PIRA staged a savage attack on the life of the British Prime Minister during the Conservative Party conference at Brighton. Five people were killed. Mrs Thatcher said afterwards that the experience at Brighton meant that 'she was not going to be bombed to the negotiating table' and this, in part, accounts for her attitude to Anglo-Irish relations in the aftermath of Brighton.[53] Five weeks later, after an Anglo-Irish summit meeting at Chequers, Mrs Thatcher put paid to any notion that the Irish forum might have a future. She dealt with the Irish issue, announcing that the findings of the forum were not acceptable. She named the three central tenants of the forum and after each one said 'that one is out'. It became known as the 'out, out, out' speech and sparked

51 Fitzgerald, op. cit., p. 504.
52 Ibid., p. 504.
53 Thatcher, op. cit., p. 399.

an immediate crisis in Anglo-Irish relations.[54] Within a year, however, Mrs Thatcher signed the Anglo-Irish Agreement, which was widely regarded as a milestone in Anglo-Irish relations.

The Anglo-Irish Agreement

Despite the rhetoric, the British shift to a more accommodating position *vis-à-vis* the inclusion of the south in the political processes in Northern Ireland had been slowly occurring since 1980–81. In particular, Jim Prior had played a positive role in encouraging the British Cabinet to accept that in order for progress to be made, Dublin would have to be brought on board. Although James Prior resigned as Secretary of State for Northern Ireland in September 1984 and was replaced by Douglas Hurd, the momentum was building for an agreement to be concluded. The British Government was particulary influenced by the arguments of John Hume of the SDLP that Sinn Fein might make substantial inroads into the nationalist vote if concessions were not made. There was also growing international pressure on the Conservative Party to ease the tensions in Northern Ireland, particularly after the death of Bobby Sands. Specifically, Mrs Thatcher appears to have listened to the urgings of the US President, Ronald Reagan, to act positively on the Irish question.

The American interest in Ireland has been well documented,[55] as has the fact that Americans were and are the IRA's main source of funding,[56] but US political influence in Ireland began to grow from the mid-1970s onwards. As early as 1977, President Jimmy Carter had indicated that the politics of Northern Ireland was a direct concern of US foreign policy, while the powerful Irish-American lobby led a campaign to correct the position of the Catholics in Northern Ireland. In November 1984, for example, the so-called MacBride Principles were established. These aimed at persuading American companies involved in Ireland to adopt programmes to employ Catholics. The principle of positive dis-

54 Garret Fitzgerald revealed that just before the speech Mrs Thatcher had, in private, appeared more committed to the process. See Fitzgerald, op. cit., pp. 522–4.

55 See S. Hartley, *The Irish Question as a Problem in British Foreign Policy 1914–1978* (Basingstoke/London: Macmillan in association with King's College, London, 1987). See also S. Cronin, *Washington's Irish Policy 1916–86. Independence: Partition Neutrality* (Dublin: Anvil, 1987).

56 Jack Holland, *The American Connection: US Guns, Money and Influence in Northern Ireland* (New York: Poolbeg, 1987).

crimination in favour of Catholics was endorsed by the American Labor Federation in 1985.[57] Against this backdrop of pressure, President Reagan, with whom Mrs Thatcher had a close working relationship, urged her to make some concessions. In an address to a Joint Session of the US Congress on 20 February 1985, Mrs Thatcher recognized the depth of American interest when she talked of Ireland and assured the Congress of her desire to work with Garret Fitzgerald.[58] While American influence may not have been the decisive factor, by 1985 the British Government, having suffered a series of embarrassments over Northern Ireland, was prepared to do a deal with the south.

The Anglo-Irish Agreement was signed at Hillsborough Castle in Northern Ireland on 15 November 1985. The agreement (also known as the Hillsborough Agreement) contained thirteen articles which laid out the positions of both London and Dublin on Northern Ireland. The first article confirmed that any change in the status of the Province could come about only with the consent of the majority of the people of Northern Ireland.[59] The second article established an intergovernmental conference through which both governments could discuss policy issues and promote a devolved government for Northern Ireland. The latter point recognized the virtue of a wider Irish dimension in the problems of the Province and gave a degree of legitimacy to southern Irish claims of influence over that part of the island. More significantly, the Anglo-Irish Agreement demonstrated, on behalf of Westminster, a commitment to reform in Northern Ireland and an acknowledgement that reform necessitated an input from the south. As William Shannon, a former US Ambassador to Ireland, wrote: 'Never before has Britain formally acknowledged that Ireland has a legal role to play in governing the north.'[60]

Reactions to the Anglo-Irish Agreement varied widely. Generally, the agreement was well received on both the mainland and in the south of Ireland. Some nationalists perceived it as a triumph of Sinn Fein strategy. In particular, Gerry Adams claimed that the agreement demonstrated that Westminster could be

57 O'Leary and McGarry, op. cit., pp. 214–15.
58 Paul Arthur, 'The Anglo-Irish Agreement: A Device for Territorial Management?' in Dermot Keogh and Michael H. Haltzel (eds), *Northern Ireland and the Politics of Reconciliation* (Cambridge: Cambridge University Press, 1993), p. 221.
59 T. Hadden and K. Boyle, 'The Anglo-Irish Agreement: Commentary, Text and Official Review, 1989', p. 58 in Arthur, op. cit., p. 209.
60 W. Shannon, 'The Anglo-Irish Agreement', *Foreign Affairs* 64.4 (Spring 1986).

pressurized into concessions.[61] In a more controversial vein, the Provisionals, while acknowledging the influence of Sinn Fein's electoral successes, argued that the Anglo-Irish Agreement had only come about because of the Brighton bomb.[62] Despite the triumphalism, Sinn Fein also saw that there was another side to the Hillsborough Agreement. In particular, it was recognized that the improvement in Anglo-Irish relations meant a stabilization of the British position in Ireland; Dublin had, rather worryingly for the Provisionals, been brought into the 'containment' of Northern Ireland. Not least from this perspective, Articles 4 and 5 of the accord were important and signified much greater security cooperation along the border, and while not incorporating the radical ideas discussed during the summer of 1984 for new military forces, it represented an improvement in cross-border policing to deal with Republican paramilitaries. Indeed, there were almost immediate tangible benefits in the security field from the signing of the agreement. Ireland ratified the European Convention for the suppression of terrorism – something it had refused to do in 1977 – and this, in turn, directly led to a greater degree of cooperation between Dublin and London over the extradition of prisoners.[63]

While nationalists pondered the mixed results of the Hillsborough Agreement, the Unionists were in little doubt that it represented a British sell-out. Whereas it is true that some in the Unionist community saw the agreement as a pragmatic one that actually brought the southern Irish into underwriting the present status of Northern Ireland, most were convinced that this was the first step towards a British political and military withdrawal. In some respects they were right; most analysts agreed that it marked a significant step towards a downgrading of the British commitment to the Province.

Unionist anger meant that the Hillsborough Agreement marked the beginning of an upsurge in Protestant mobilization and paramilitary violence. Some Protestants, fearing a British betrayal, reached for their guns.[64] Roads all over Northern Ireland were

61 Interview with Gerry Adams, *The Hillsborough Deal: Stepping Stone or Mill Stone?* (Dublin: Political Sinn Fein Pamphlet, December 1985).

62 Irish Republican Information Service (October 1987), quoted in Smith, op. cit., p. 189.

63 Gerard Hogan and Clive Walker, *Political Violence and the Law in Ireland* (Manchester: Manchester University Press, 1989), p. 181.

64 See Steve Bruce, *The Red Hand: Protestant Paramilitaries in Northern Ireland* (Oxford: Oxford University Press, 1992), p. 236.

barricaded and serious rioting took place throughout Protestant areas. The UDA and the UVF threatened to shoot the collaboraters of the new regime.[65] Protestant protest took many forms. In a re-run of the anger after the Sunningdale Agreement of 1974, Unionist politicians withdrew from meetings with British officials, Unionist councils suspended business and Unionist MPs resigned their seats to force a by-election on the Hillsborough Agreement. The Unionists had not been consulted in the run-up to the signing of the Anglo-Irish Agreement and some Unionist leaders, most notably the Reverend Ian Paisley, had warned Mrs Thatcher of the dangers of letting Dublin into the affairs of the North.[66] Anger was such that the RUC was forced to police the Protestant areas and, after the shooting of one Protestant youth by an RUC officer, some Protestants turned against the police force.[67] Yet for all this anger, the Unionists had a problem in what response to adopt with the government on the mainland in the aftermath of the Hillsborough Agreement. The Unionists were rioting to stay *within* the United Kingdom and were attacking *British* security forces to ensure that they remained stationed in the Province, but, and this was, for the Unionists, the unknown factor, if the British were prepared to withdraw, might not such actions hasten their departure? In other words, how far could the Unionists go to pressurize the British Government to keep troops in Northern Ireland? This would remain a key question throughout the late 1980s.[68]

The PIRA, too, after Hillsborough, sensing the strain upon the security forces, began an offensive against police stations in rural areas. The Anglo-Irish Agreement had caused problems for the command of the Provisional paramilitaries. While they were more than willing to take the credit for having bombed the British to the negotiating table, some analysts argue that the PIRA leadership was aware that an increase in paramilitary activity before the Hillsborough meeting might bring about a security clampdown or, indeed, wreck the agreement itself, and risk the ire of moderate nationalist opinion. Instead, in the month before the agreement was signed, the PIRA leadership stated that it would

---

65 Ibid., p. 236.

66 For the Unionist response, see Arthur Aughey, *Under Seige: Ulster Unionism and the Anglo-Irish Agreement* (London: Hurst and Co., 1989), p. 8.

67 Steve Bruce, op. cit., p. 237.

68 On this issue see John Whyte, 'The Dynamics of Social and Political Change in Northern Ireland' in Keogh and Haltzel, op. cit., p. 106.

not carry out actions to disrupt the accord, but rather would expose the weakness of the agreement and make the case that real gains for Republicans could only be achieved through armed struggle.[69] In effect, this meant that the British Government had, in 1985, scored a victory over both Sinn Fein and the Republican paramilitaries. Through their willingness to include the south in Northern affairs, Westminster had taken the wind out of Republican sails. The British had made concessions and in some respects won over moderate nationalist opinion, a fact which was borne out by the election results of 1986. In the January by-elections, the SDLP candidate, Seamus Mallon, took the Newry and Armagh constituency. The Sinn Fein vote there dropped from 21 to 13 per cent, signifying a weakening of support for the movement after Hillsborough.[70] The return of the Provisionals to a rural campaign in late 1985 was the result of frustration at a British success. Even though the Provisionals had claimed that they were not going to disrupt the Anglo-Irish Agreement through violence, in 1985 they had launched a massive bombing campaign both in Ireland and on the mainland. They claimed to have used more explosives in 1985 than in any other year of their campaign. After the signing of the agreement they intensified their activity with bombings and bloodshed.

The combination of paramilitary activity by both the Provisionals and the Unionist groups throughout the autumn led in the following months to a considerable setback in the policy of 'police primacy'. Despite a decade in which the British had been trying to withdraw troops from the Province and return to normal policing, the upsurge in violence meant that two more British Army battalions were sent to Northern Ireland in 1986, with a consequent rise in the numbers of soldiers stationed there from 9,000 to 10,200. This was regarded as a temporary measure but, as the next few years would demonstrate, there was little real hope of substantial troop withdrawals and British ideas of new security arrangements, discussed with the southern Irish in 1982–83, which might have allowed this, never materialized.

Indeed, by late 1985 there was no real consensus, despite both Labour and Liberal Party policy that British troops should be withdrawn. Only two British soldiers were killed in the Province during 1985 and the Army, despite the 'shoot to kill' allegations,

---

69 See E. Maloney, 'Provos Wait for the Anglo-Irish Offensive', *Fortnight* (21 October 1985), quoted in Smith, op. cit., pp. 190–1.

70   O'Brien, op. cit., pp. 133–4.

were regarded as the best instrument not only for countering the PIRA but for once again keeping the peace between the two communities in Northern Ireland. By 1986, British troops were once more deployed in considerable numbers on the streets of Northern Ireland. This time they were underwriting the political initiative of Hillsborough, which had alienated the Unionists.[71] Yet, it was not only the Unionists who would present the British Army with its greatest challenge from 1985 on, but also the regrouping of the PIRA who in 1986 sought once again to drive the British out of Ireland.

---

71 Tom King, speaking in the House of Commons, stated that it was completely false to see the increase in British troop levels as linked to the Anglo-Irish Agreement. Rather, he claimed, additional troops were needed to combat a growth in terrorism. See HC, vol. 92, cols 1050–1, 27 February 1986.

Stalemate in Ireland: Violence
Institutionalized, 1985–90

The period between 1985 and 1990 was one in which Northern Ireland appeared once again to have settled into a period of unremitting violence, a situation characterized by the Enniskillen bombing of 1987 and the deaths of three PIRA activists in Gibraltar in March 1988. Violence was firmly centre stage. Three factors account for the climate of violence that occurred after the signing of the Anglo-Irish Agreement at Hillsborough. The first was that the Republican movement regrouped around an agenda that included the entry of Sinn Fein into southern Irish electoral politics, but which also sanctioned a renewed commitment to battle with the British Government. A second feature of the period was that the British Cabinet, buoyed by the success of Hillsborough, stepped up its attempts to contain the PIRA. Not only did the British Army reinvigorate the military struggle, they also sought to persuade the Dublin Government to greater efforts in containing the paramilitaries, not least through the adoption of tighter extradition procedures in the Republic. A third feature of the period was that the Protestants adopted a belligerent anti-Hillsborough stance that led to an intensification of the activities of the Protestant paramilitaries. All of the above meant that after a period of initial optimism following Hillsborough, the Province lurched back into the familiar pattern of the modern conflict. Yet beneath the violence, very slowly, new trends began to emerge in Ireland. These included a greater degree of cooperation between London and Dublin over the containment of Republican paramilitaries and, towards the end of the decade, a decisive shift in Sinn Fein strategy. The latter emphasized the pursuit of political legitimacy in preference to violent rebellion. This chapter traces the evolution of those trends.

The Republicans regroup

After Hillsborough, the British Government regarded the reinforcement of links with Dublin as imperative. It feared that Sinn Fein might actually make serious inroads into electoral politics in the south that would result in a concomitant decline in Anglo-Irish affairs. In the mid-1980s this seemed a very real possibility. In particular, the emergence after 1983 of a new type of Sinn Fein leadership, typified by Gerry Adams, had been responsible for ensuring that some of the old tenants of Republicanism were relinquished. Traditionally, Sinn Fein leaders had held that the southern Irish Government, created in 1921, was illegitimate. It had, therefore, refused to contest elections in the south under the so-called 'abstentionist' policy. Throughout the early 1980s part of the Sinn Fein leadership had been rethinking its political strategy *vis-à-vis* elections, and had been pondering the chances of electoral success in the south. The decision of the party to reject 'abstentionism' officially was made public in 1986 when the Sinn Fein leadership agreed to field candidates in southern Irish elections. The timing of the announcement was not a coincidence, but was directly linked to the agreement at Hillsborough. The Anglo-Irish Agreement had, for Sinn Fein, made the issue of political representation in the south an urgent one. Most of the southern Irish population had welcomed the Hillsborough accord and demonstrated little inclination to agree with Sinn Fein that the Irish Government was illegitimate. The Sinn Fein leadership feared that if it did not quickly participate in the political life of the south, the Republican movement might grow increasingly isolated and remain confined to the North. Sinn Fein hoped that through contesting elections in the south, Republicanism would become a powerful electoral phenomenon throughout Ireland,[1] halting Anglo-Irish collusion. Despite British fears and Sinn Fein hopes, electoral success eluded the party. It made little impact on voters in the south. In the elections in Eire during 1987, for example, Sinn Fein secured less than 2 per cent of votes cast. More critically for the leadership, the rejection of abstensionism also sparked a fierce internal battle within the nationalist movement. While Adams had managed to persuade a majority of the nationalist movement, including parts of the PIRA, to reject

---

1 See, for example, Gerry Adams, *Falls Memoirs* (Dingle: Brandon Books, 1982), and *Free Ireland: Towards a Lasting Peace* (Dingle: Brandon Books, 1995).

abstensionism, the more traditional parts of the armed wing had opposed participation in southern electoral politics. The dispute over abstensionism threatened to split the movement, much as it had in the past. Previous attempts at abolishing abstensionism in the early 1980s had failed, primarily because the Mid-Ulster and Kerry brigades of the PIRA had vehemently opposed such a move, while other parts of the PIRA, most notably the South Armagh and Dundalk brigades, had divided over the issue.[2] In 1986, Adams wished to avoid a repetition of such fragmentation. In order to reassure the paramilitaries that acceptance of an electoral strategy did not and would not mean an abdication of the armed struggle,[3] or lead to a constitutional sell-out, certain key terms were negotiated between Sinn Fein and the armed wing.[4] These were that central positions on the army council were to be filled by hard-liners committed to the military struggle; that local units were to be given greater freedom to mount attacks and that Martin McGuinness was to hold a central role on the Northern Command of the PIRA. In addition, two hard-line paramilitaries, who had been previously expelled from the movement for opposing the leadership, were allowed to return as paramilitaries in the Belfast area.[5] The immediate effect of this deal was that the PIRA became less tightly controlled, with a membership more inclined to mount individual attacks on the security forces. This posed problems for the Sinn Fein leadership as it strove to gain legitimacy through the ballot box.

The Sinn Fein strategy of electoral participation combined with violent struggle was fraught with ambiguities. Participation within the electoral framework sat uneasily with an armed struggle that was designed to usurp the very institutions in which the Republicans sought representation. Sinn Fein, for example, believed that the Hillsborough Agreement (although a fruitless endeavour in the longer term) had been forced on the British Government solely through Republican pressure. Adams claimed that it was the result of 'the electoral advances of Sinn Fein and the successes of the Republican movement which had forced the British to

---

2 Brendan O'Brien, *The Long War: The IRA and Sinn Fein 1985 to Today* (Dublin: The O'Brien Press, 1993), p. 130.

3 *The Times* (26 September 1986).

4 Joe Austin, quoted in *Workers Press* (13 September 1986), cited in Mark Ryan, *War and Peace in Ireland: Britain and the IRA in the New World Order* (London: Pluto, 1994), p. 68.

5 O'Brien, op. cit., p. 131.

negotiate with the south'.[6] Sinn Fein was therefore in a strange twist of logic, claiming responsibility for reshaping the very system that the Republican paramilitaries wanted to destroy.

The strategy of violent action and electoral politics had at its heart a deeper and more practical problem than that of mere ambiguity. In a nutshell, this was that the violent actions of PIRA often alienated voters. Sinn Fein attempted to reconcile the two aspects of policy with a succession of claims that the PIRA only targeted 'legitimate' security forces, not civilians. It was hoped that this would soothe electoral fears and allow even those who disapproved of violence to vote for Sinn Fein. Such claims, however, made little impact on voters, and after 1987 Sinn Fein continued to lose electoral ground, even in the North. In the general election of that year, it lost sixteen of its council seats. While leaders such as Gerry Adams did not openly condemn paramilitary attacks, he was publicly critical of PIRA 'mistakes' which cost Sinn Fein votes. At the 1989 Ard Fheis, he directly addressed some of his remarks to the military wing of the party: 'At times the fate of the struggle is in your hands. You have to be careful and careful again.'[7] Yet there appeared to be little that Adams or other leaders could do in the late 1980s, or indeed at any other time, to ensure that the more hard-line members of the Provisionals did not commit 'mistakes'. Sinn Fein leaders expressed exasperation at the timings of some of the Provisionals activities but appeared unwilling or, more critically, unable to stop them.

There was, at this point in the 1980s, a great deal of confidence within the Provisionals that they would be able to escalate the military campaign against the British Government. In particular, they hoped that the connection with Libya would be useful. Contacts between the PIRA and the Libyans dated back to 1981. Since 1985 enormous shipments of arms supplied by the Ghadaffi regime had entered Ireland.[8] The sheer quantity and quality of the arms supplied by the Middle Eastern leader provided the para-militaries with an unprecedented arsenal. The shipments included surface-to-air missiles, rocket-propelled grenades and over 2,000,000 rounds of ammunition.[9]

6 Sinn Fein Document, Dublin Provisional Sinn Fein (PSF), 1987, p. 14, in M.L.R. Smith, *Fighting for Ireland: The Military Strategy of the Irish Republican Movement* (London: Routledge, 1995).

7 Gerry Adams, Presidential Address, 84 Ard Fheis, Dublin PSF, 1989, p. 4, quoted in Smith, op. cit., p. 176.

8 O'Brien, op. cit., p. 129.

9 Ibid., p. 129.

In addition to fostering links with sympathetic foreign regimes and building its military arsenal, the PIRA intensified its campaign against the security forces in rural areas. In particular, it targeted off-duty members of the security forces who lived in isolated areas and rural police stations in remote locations. These were both vulnerable targets. Many rural police stations were still only manned during the day, and off-duty police officers had little or no pro- tection from attacks. The PIRA also sought to make it impossible for the RUC to operate in these areas[10] by targeting anybody who was involved in any way with the police. For example, even the builders who were contracted to work on bombed police stations were designated as security-related targets. In effect, the rural infrastructure of policing was under threat.

In response, both the RUC and the British Army undertook considerable efforts to counter this strategy. In May 1987 the SAS destroyed one of the PIRA's most feared units, the East Tyrone brigade, as it attacked an RUC station at Loughall in Co. Armagh.[11] Eight PIRA men were killed. It was a notable victory for the security forces as it was the single biggest loss suffered by the IRA since the 1920s. Not unsurprisingly, the nature and 'efficiency' of the SAS operation again opened up the debate not only over whether a 'shoot to kill' policy operated in the Province, but also over the nature of covert operations in Northern Ireland generally. In this respect the Loughall attack was particularly interesting because the Army had, at practically every stage of the operation, excellent intelligence on the PIRA's plans. Critics of SAS behaviour during the Loughall operation asked whether or not it might have been possible to end the attack in a manner short of eight fatalities. Could another way not have been found of preventing the attack? Might it have been possible at Loughall to arrest or detain the paramilitaries?[12] Loughall once more starkly raised the question of the nature of the struggle in Northern Ireland. It was claimed by the Army that the soldiers involved in the ambush had followed the 'rules of engagement' operated by the British Army in the Province. These were the rules of the so-called yellow card, under which soldiers had to shout specific warnings before shooting. The Army asserted that these rules had been followed at Loughall and that the ensuing deaths were

10 *The Irish Times* (11 May 1987).
11 Smith, op. cit., p. 188.
12 Mark Urban, *Big Boys' Rules: The SAS and the Secret Struggle Against the IRA* . (London: Faber & Faber, 1992), p. 234.

therefore 'legitimate'. Indeed, when commenting on the deaths, Gerry Adams conceded that Loughall had been a 'fair' engagement between PIRA combatants and the security forces. Yet, even if both sides had developed an 'understanding' of the risks involved in 'military' operations, incidents such as Loughall did little to bring a resolution of the conflict closer. Indeed, it is questionable whether it even dented the ability of the para-militaries to operate. After the losses at Loughall, the PIRA was determined to show that it could still operate both efficiently at home and abroad. In 1987, the PIRA launched an attack on the Rheindalen base in West Germany, and on 8 November it detonated a bomb during the Remembrance Day service at Enniskillen in Co. Fermanagh. The latter detonation killed eleven people and injured over sixty others. The PIRA later expressed regret for the deaths, but argued in a rather spurious fashion that the bomb had actually been triggered by the British Army.[13]

The deaths at Enniskillen and the subsequent public revulsion triggered a massive security alert in both the North and the south. It is, of course, always difficult to quantify public outrage or its impact on public policy but after the bombing, security forces north and south of the border engaged in intense activities to contain further PIRA actions. This period was characterized by a marked improvement in Anglo-Irish collaboration against the paramilitaries.[14] The adoption in the south of a new Extradition Act on 14 December 1987, in particular, marked a turning point. The Act made it more difficult for those members of the PIRA found guilty of terrorist offences to escape extradition to either the North or the mainland. The passing of the bill was, for Mrs Thatcher, one of the successes to come from the Hillsborough accord.[15] The British Government had long sought tougher measures to prevent the south acting as a safe haven for the PIRA and had put pressure on the southern Government to harden its stance on the extradition of paramilitaries. It was a thorny issue. Extradition was a politically sensitive matter for any southern Irish leader. In recognition of this, in 1986–87 the British Government sought to soften Irish sensibilities to the process by reopening the

13 IRA statement, 9 November 1987, quoted in O'Brien, op. cit., p. 142. O'Brien points out that the PIRA claimed in its statement that in the past some landmines had been triggered by British Army high scanning equipment.

14 On the British response to Irish extradition proceedings, see Margaret
• Thatcher, *The Downing Street Years* (London: HarperCollins, 1993), pp. 406–7.

15 Ibid., pp. 406–7. See also, *The Irish Times* (15 August 1987).

cases of some Irish people held in British prisons on terrorist convictions. Accordingly, the British Government ordered a new police investigation into the convictions of the so-called 'Guildford Four' who had already served twelve years for allegedly bombing a pub in 1974, while another group, the 'Birmingham Six', were also given leave to appeal against their convictions for terrorist offences. However, these appeals of Irish people who had been tried in Great Britain only heightened tension in the Republic. The debate over extradition caused a political storm.

The relationship between the United Kingdom and Eire over extradition had always been one of unease and controversy. The return of fugitives between the two had, before Irish independence, occurred under a system of reciprocal warrants. This was a legacy of the colonial relationship under which warrants for extradition in one country had been endorsed in the other. The practice was actively maintained after the Anglo-Irish treaty in 1921 and persisted until 1964,[16] although the system had partly broken down in 1929. The breakdown of relations was a reflection of tensions between the new Republic and its neighbour in the North. Both North and south subsequently refused to endorse warrants originating in the other part of Ireland. More seriously, the practice ceased altogether when, in 1964, the House of Lords refused to endorse Irish warrants and the Irish Supreme Court ruled that the process of backing external warrants was not in tune with the spirit of the constitution. In effect, this meant that after 1964 all three areas – the south, the North and the United Kingdom itself – could act as 'safe havens' for paramilitaries.

As the modern conflict in the North unfolded, it became urgent for all three sides to develop a clear position on extradition processes. The first British military fatality in 1971 was quickly followed by a demand from the North for the return from the south of those suspected of committing offences in the Province. The demand opened a Pandora's box of legal and political issues which starkly exposed the differences between Dublin and Westminster over the Northern conflict. Primarily, differences centred on what constituted a 'political offence'. The southern Irish position, in accordance with its constitution, was that a person accused of a 'political offence' could not be extradited.

16 Paul O'Higgins, 'The Irish Extradition Act, 1965', *International and Comparative Law Quarterly* 15. 2 (9 April 1966), p. 30, quoted in Bruce Warner, 'Extradition Law and Practice in the Crucible of Ulster, Ireland and Great Britain: A Metamorphosis?', *Conflict Quarterly* 7 (1987), pp. 57–92.

The southern Irish judiciary held in a number of cases that suspects could not be extradited to another country if they had committed what the court deemed to be a political offence. It followed therefore that a crime committed in connection with the PIRA could be designated a political offence.[17] The case of a Catholic priest, Bartholomew Burns, who was accused of handling explosives for the PIRA in Scotland, led to a direct statement of this position. The judge involved in the case expressed it thus: 'it seems again impossible to categorise the existing situation in Northern Ireland and Britain as being otherwise than a political disturbance, part of and incidental to which is the keeping of explosives . . . for the IRA'.[18] This did not condone the crime committed, but followed a strictly constitutional interpretation of cases. Yet, as the 1970s wore on Irish judges increasingly found themselves in difficult, not to say untenable, positions. In 1975, the Irish Minister of Justice argued that judges were in an embarrassing predicament because they were constrained by the interpretation of the 'political offence' to release prisoners accused of serious crimes.[19] By the mid-1980s, the strain on the system began to show and Irish politicians were placed under growing pressure to initiate change in the interpretation of a political offence. Some of the momentum for reform came from a recognition that Irish law on this issue was increasingly at odds, not only with the British judiciary but also with the growing body of European law. In February 1987, after a decade of hesitation, Dublin signed the European Convention on the Suppression of Terrorism (ECST), removing the 'political offence' from the list of crimes that could not be extradited.[20]

As part of the price for movement on the issue of extradition, Dublin expected British movement on key Northern Irish issues. Specifically, the Irish Government maintained that Anglo-Irish relations should not be seen as a one-way street under which Ireland merely acquiesced in British wishes for the conduct of policy associated with the North. Dublin pointed out that in spite of the Hillsborough Agreement the British and Irish administrations had not agreed on key aspects of government in the Province. In particular, the Irish sought reform to the criminal

17 Ibid., pp. 57–92.
18 Ibid., pp. 57–92.
19 Ibid., pp. 57–92.
20 See Arwel Ellis Owen, *The Anglo-Irish Agreement: The First Three Years* (Cardiff: University of Wales Press, 1994), pp. 166–7.

justice system in the North. Garret Fitzgerald argued that a new code of conduct for the RUC and reform of the courts had been central to his agreement to the Hillsborough accord.[21] Throughout 1986–87 the Irish Government pressed hard for reform in the North as the price for improved extradition proceedings in the south. These demands met with little sympathy on the British side.[22] The British Government remained vexed by what it perceived as Irish vacillation over extradition and the political capital it believed that Irish politicians gained through appearing tough on British requests for cooperation over the affairs of Northern Ireland.[23]

Some of the British attitude ignored the realities of Irish party politics and the sensitivity of southern Irish voters to events in the North. One of the ambiguities of southern political life was that the Dublin Government itself pursued a hard line against the PIRA and Sinn Fein but was also intensely critical of British actions in the North which more or less replicated Irish restrictions operating the Republic. For example, Dublin had a long history of using 'internment' against paramilitaries but strongly objected to any British implementation of such a policy. Even so, no Irish politician could appear disinterested or objective on Northern Ireland. This meant that as a matter of expedience, British policy had to be vigorously scrutinized. Never mind that Sinn Fein failed at the ballot box in the south, many voters still objected to the British presence and Irish politicians had to respect this allegiance.

British politicians also, at times, appeared ignorant of the battle being fought in the Republic over the 'modernization' of Irish society. This battle had important ramifications for the relationship with the North. Some Irish leaders, against powerful opposition, sought to make the Republic a more modern and secular state. The drive for social transition was led, in many respects, by Garret Fitzgerald.[24] But reforming a predominantly Catholic and agrarian state was not an easy matter and in June 1986 reformers suffered a major blow when the Irish electorate voted against permitting civil divorce. It was a significant defeat for social transformation in the south, and the poll on divorce provided Unionists with evidence that influence from Dublin

21 Garret Fitzgerald, *All in a Life* (Dublin: Gill and Macmillan, 1989), pp. 542–3. See also, *The Economist* (3 October 1987).

22 See Tom King's comments on this issue in the *Irish Times* (22 October 1987).

23 See, for example, *The Independent* (22 March 1988).

24 Fitzgerald, op. cit., pp. 542–55.

equated to Rome Rule, making them even more determined to avoid southern Irish influence through the Hillsborough process. The cumulative effect of the bid to restructure the Republic was that Garret Fitzgerald occupied an increasingly fragile political position that was easily challenged by rivals. In the June elections of 1987 Garret Fitzgerald was replaced by Charles Haughey who not only had publicly stated his opposition to British demands for changes in Irish extradition procedures, but had also been implicated in gun-running schemes to the North. It appeared, after this turn of events, that there was little real hope of Anglo-Irish agreement over the Province, but after pressure sustained from Washington, Haughey agreed to support change and the southern Irish passed the new Extradition Act on 14 December 1987.[25]

The Anglo-Irish Agreement thus survived its first major challenge, and despite public wrangling over extradition, the security forces of both North and south, in the same period, initiated unprecedented coordination against the paramilitaries. On 23 November 1987, both Northern and southern security forces mounted a huge search for Libyan arms. The first big discovery of foreign arms was made in late January 1988 in North Donegal, and in the following month another haul was discovered in Dublin.[26]

Gibraltar

Despite increased collaboration, the issue of security and legal procedures in Northern Ireland continued to provoke unease in the conduct of Anglo-Irish relations. It seems almost unnecessary to note, after a history of the modern period, that the Irish Government continued to lack confidence in the British justice system. But events in early 1988 conspired to promote a near crisis in the relationship between London and Dublin. In January 1988, the Court of Appeal rejected the appeal of the 'Birmingham Six'. In the very same week it was announced by the British Attorney General, Sir Patrick Mayhew, that it would not be in the national interest to prosecute those RUC officers found guilty of perverting the course of justice as a result of the Stalker/Samson inquiry.[27] In

25 *News Letter* (7 December 1987). See also *The Irish Times* (7 December 1987).
26 O'Brien, op. cit., pp. 143–4.
27 House of Commons Debate (hereafter HC), vol. 126, col. 465, 28 January 1988.

February, the only British soldier to have been sentenced so far in the conflict on a manslaughter charge, one Private Thain, was released after three years. In March, one of the most sensational actions of the British security forces took place in Gibraltar in the 'death on the rock incident', which once more highlighted the British military role in Ireland.

Throughout the latter part of 1987, the PIRA had been planning a revenge attack for the eight deaths at Loughall and was also planning to escalate the campaign against the British forces, emboldened by the Libyan supplies. The overall campaign aimed to 'sicken' the British Government into a retreat from Ireland. In this particular instance, the PIRA wanted to stage a spectacular 'hit' against the British security forces. It chose the Royal Anglian Regiment at Ince's Hall, based in the main street of Gibraltar. O'Brien has alleged that part of the motivation for choosing this particular site was as a thank-you to Ghadaffi for supplying arms, indicating that they were to be used for good anti-British purposes.[28] In preparation for the attack, the PIRA placed a 'team' of three active members in Gibraltar. Both the RUC and the British intelligence forces were aware of PIRA plans and on 2 March had flown a team of SAS soldiers to the rock.[29] On 6 March, three Irish people were shot dead by the SAS; all were unarmed, but were well-known members of the PIRA. The subsequent controversy over the killings was intense, not least because of the confusion over whether the suspects were in fact in possession of a bomb.[30] As it turned out, there was a bomb, but it was not, as some newspapers alleged, in the car of the victims – it was later discovered over the border in Marbella.

The involvement of the SAS in this operation, as well as its behaviour at Loughall, underlined the emphasis that continued to be placed on special forces. While the SAS had for over a decade been increasingly important in British Army strategy, by 1988 this trend reached full implementation. Although British soldiers continued to reinforce the notion of police primacy on the streets

28 O'Brien, op. cit., p. 151.

29 See Tim Pat Coogan, *The Troubles: Ireland's Ordeal 1966–1995 and the Search for Peace* (London: Hutchinson, 1995), p. 290.

30 There was also an intense debate after the shootings as to whether the SAS had fired without warning. See Windlesham on the Thames Television investigation entitled 'Death on the Rock' in which Thames alleged several inaccuracies in the official version of the Gibraltar killings. Quoted in W. Harvey Cox, 'From Hillsborough to Downing Street – and After' in Peter Catterall and Sean MacDougall, *The Northern Ireland Question in British Politics* (London: Macmillan, 1996), p. 193.

of the Province, an elite group of soldiers was undertaking specialist operations designed to destroy the heart of the PIRA. This development indicated that rather than trying to defeat the PIRA through broad sweeping operations such as internment, the British military was now using specialist troops to fight single operations. Reinforcing the 30,000 armed forces on the ground, which allowed the British Government to control the Province, small elite military units were used in a bid to eliminate key paramilitaries.[31]

The reverberations from the attack in Gibraltar were felt almost immediately in the Province when the three PIRA members were buried in Northern Ireland. At one of the funerals, which took place on 16 March in Milltown, a Loyalist gunman attacked mourners, killing three of them. Subsequently, as one of the mourners was buried, another tragedy occurred, when Robert Howes and Derek Wood, two British corporals in plain clothes, drove into the funeral crowds. Rather inexplicably they appeared unaware of what was going on. They were savagely dragged from their car, beaten and then shot.[32]

From these bloody events, the Governments in London and Dublin took very different lessons. To the southern Irish, the British administration still seemed more preoccupied with counter-insurgency and the defeat of the PIRA than with a programme of thorough-going reform. Indeed, from an Irish perspective the British Government did not seem to perceive the 'negative' effects that the deaths at Loughall and Gibraltar created. This view was compounded for the Irish during the early months of 1988 when not only was the appeal of the Birmingham Six rejected but it was followed by a similar rejection of the appeals of the Guildford Four, the MacGuires and the Winchester Three. The British perspective of the events of early 1988 was not unexpectedly different from that of the Irish. Not least, officials continued to deplore what they perceived as the unnecessary vacillation over extradition procedures in the southern Irish courts, and in 1988 Westminster embarked on a tightening of procedures in the Northern Irish courts, as well as a review of British security policy in the Province. In her memoirs, Mrs Thatcher lists a number of options she wanted to be considered for use in the Province after the violent events of late 1987 and early 1988. She relates that she

31 Urban, op. cit., p. 247.
32 For an assessment of the killings, see HC, vol. 130, cols 194, 496, 502, 21–31 March 1987–88.

not only considered banning Sinn Fein, introducing identity cards and reintroducing selective internment, but also considered reversing the policy of police primacy.[33] Some of these proposals were indeed quickly taken up in a bid to contain the paramilitaries once more.

The justice system and media bans

One initiative from Mrs Thatcher's list which was activated in the Province was the withdrawal of what was termed 'the right of silence' for those under arrest. This issue had been debated at length since the beginning of the Northern Irish conflict, but its implementation had been rejected in both 1972 and 1984. The idea behind its introduction was that a court would be able to draw inferences from the fact that a person had remained silent when questioned by the RUC. In particular, this innovation was provoked not only by the upswing in paramilitary activity but more directly from the cases of three Irish people convicted of plotting to kill Tom King.[34] They had, under questioning, elected to remain silent. From 1988, although suspects could still remain silent, the failure to cooperate could later be used as evidence against them in court.[35]

Other measures taken to make the activities of the PIRA more difficult included the imposition of a series of bans in the media on Sinn Fein activity. The British Home Secretary, Douglas Hurd, implemented a broadcasting ban on 19 October 1988. It required broadcasters to 'refrain from broadcasting direct statements' by representatives of Sinn Fein, Republican Sinn Fein and the Ulster Defence Association.[36] It was claimed that the ban was in response to the upsurge in paramilitary activity during the earlier part of the year, in particular the PIRA bombing of a coach at Ballygawley in Co. Tyrone in which eight British soldiers died as they arrived back in the Province after leave.[37] With this attack, the PIRA had actually killed more British soldiers in the first eight months of 1988 than in any comparable period during the decade. The *News*

---

33 Thatcher, op. cit., p. 408.
34 See Ellis Owen, op. cit., p. 249.
35 *The Irish Times* (28 October 1988).
36 Douglas Hurd, HC, vol. 138, col. 893, 19 October 1988.
37 Thatcher, op. cit., p. 411. *The Guardian* (22 August 1988). See also Douglas Hurd's view that the Enniskillen bombing had contributed to the necessity for a broadcasting ban. Douglas Hurd, HC, vol. 138, col. 896, 19 October 1988.

Letter stated that the PIRA had, through its actions, challenged Mrs Thatcher to respond and if she did not many more would die.[38]

In addition to media bans, a requirement was placed in the Elected Authorities Act of 1989 that all councillors in Northern Ireland take an oath repudiating the use of violence. The British Government also introduced measures to prevent funds reaching the PIRA.[39] The broadcasting ban in particular was intended to 'silence' Sinn Fein and prevent it from entering the mainstream of Irish politics. It was invoked despite the fact that Sinn Fein had actually been losing popularity since the early 1980s. It might be argued that there was little need to protect the public from Sinn Fein as the electorate had shown little inclination to place the party at the centre of political life in the Province. Yet, for many, if not for the British Government, Sinn Fein held the key to the activities of the PIRA. Any prospect of peace necessarily had to include the armed wing of the Republican struggle. It was the recognition that any real political progress had to include Sinn Fein that encouraged the SDLP to hold out the prospects of talks with its leadership in 1988.

Sinn Fein responded positively to this development. This was partly because of its drive towards electoral legitimacy but also because of the new media restrictions. The increased collaboration between London and Dublin, the renewed vigour of the British approach towards the Province and its failure at the ballot box caused anxiety in the Sinn Fein leadership. The notion that in the years immediately after Hillsborough the Anglo-Irish alliance was lining up against them pushed Sinn Fein into a reconsideration of how it could break out of growing political isolation. Sinn Fein had already established a common framework with two of the smallest parties in the Province, the Irish Independent Party and the People's Democracy, but these could not provide the real political clout that Gerry Adams sought. Sinn Fein therefore sought a formal dialogue with the SDLP. On 11 January 1988 John Hume, the leader of the SDLP, met with Gerry Adams and afterwards set up a series of talks between the parties to try to establish a dialogue with the political wing of the PIRA.[40] Hume had as his prime motivation the desire to end PIRA activities. In particular, Hume argued that paramilitary activity only hardened the resolve of the British Government to remain in Ireland,

38 *News Letter* (22 August 1988).
39 *The Guardian* (27 August 1988).
40 See Coogan, op. cit., pp. 334–5.

whereas the Anglo-Irish Agreement had, the SDLP argued, showed a British willingness to withdraw.[41]

Out of these talks there emerged a better understanding between the two groups but also clear differences, not only on how to put forward the nationalist position, but what in fact the nationalist position was. In particular, the SDLP deplored the use of paramilitary violence to achieve nationalist ends. For example, on 17 March Hume argued that the IRA campaign was actually doing damage to the people whom it claimed to be protecting, and that it was too simplistic to claim that the cause of all violence was the British presence in Ireland. Rather, Hume stressed that the British position was not the source of all trouble in Northern Ireland, but pointed instead to the intra-ethnic nature of the struggle in Ireland. The SDLP leader also argued that it was impossible to think that the British Army could withdraw either immediately or easily. Not least, he pointed out that such a withdrawal would leave 20,000 armed members of the RUC and the UDR in the Province, without the 'neutral' presence of British troops.[42] Not surprisingly, Adams did not agree with this view of a neutral British presence, nor indeed with Hume's interpretation of an island divided between Irish peoples. Nevertheless, Adams sought a common front with the SDLP which would bring the Sinn Fein party into the mainstream of political activity both in the North and the south. He calculated that Dublin would find it difficult to avoid reinforcing a united nationalist position.[43] The SDLP/Sinn Fein talks ended on 5 September 1988. Each group restated its position. Both agreed that self-determination was the key to the future and that the 'Irish people' should be defined as all the people living on the island of Ireland. However, both sides continued to disagree as to how Unionist disagreement could be countered.

While little came immediately from the talks (certainly there was no evidence that a framework had been agreed), the basis for future peace talks had been laid in that Sinn Fein was now openly debating the nationalist position in Ireland. Significantly, however, Sinn Fein did not concede that the use of violence was illegitimate or counter-productive in the struggle to achieve Irish unity.[44] There was no indication that Sinn Fein could be persuaded to harness, if possible, the activities of the PIRA, thus frustrating one

41 *News Letter* (15 June 1988).
42 Ibid.
43 Sinn Fein–SDLP, January–September 1989, quoted in Coogan, op. cit., p. 335.
44 *The Times* (6 September 1988).

of John Hume's primary objectives in talking to Sinn Fein. The talks between Sinn Fein and the SDLP provoked immense controversy among politicians in the Province. The Unionists declared that they would refuse to talk to Sinn Fein while Hume continued his dialogue with Adams.[45] For many Unionists, the period after Hillsborough, culminating in these talks, represented a severe weakening of their position *vis-à-vis* the Government on the mainland.

Protestant grievances

For Protestants, the Hillsborough Agreement contained unambiguous signs that Westminster was finally and publicly ceding control of the Province to the south. In particular, the establishment of a joint ministerial conference of British and Irish ministers, which would be set up at Maryfield in Northern Ireland and would monitor the political, security and legal issues of concern to the minority population, sounded warning bells for the Protestant community. Despite the fact that the mainland Government reserved the right to the final say on all issues, the Protestants believed that this represented a seachange in British attitudes towards the Province.[46]

Protestant responses took various forms. There was, as has been noted in Chapter Five, a violent reflex reaction from the paramilitaries and a more considered political response in the boycotting of various political institutions by representatives of the Protestant community. It is the actions of the various Unionists paramilitary organizations that have excited most comment from those interested in Ulster Unionism.[47] Indeed, Unionist paramilitary violence first came publicly to the attention of the British population in general when the first Unionist paramilitary killing was shown on television. This was the incident at Milltown cemetery when a UDA man, Michael Stone, was responsible for killing some of the mourners at the funeral of a PIRA member.[48]

45 According to Coogan, op. cit., p. 335, the Unionists did in fact meet with SDLP representatives at secret talks held in Germany on 14–15 October 1988.

46 W.D. Flackes and S. Elliott, *Northern Ireland: A Political Directory, 1968–88* (Belfast: Blackstaff Press, 1989), pp. 67–8.

47 See Colin Coulter, 'The Character of Unionism' in *Irish Political Studies* 9 (1994), pp. 1–24.

48 Stone actually appears to have been a maverick member of the UDA, involved with a small group within the Mid-Ulster UDA who used him as a 'freelance' gunman. On this issue see Steve Bruce, *The Red Hand: Protestant Paramilitaries in Northern Ireland* (Oxford: Oxford University Press, 1992), pp. 258–9.

In the investigation into the case of Stone, a rather curious picture emerged of the manner in which the Protestant paramilitaries operated. The picture was one of disorganization and random attacks, many of which were orchestrated by a few die-hards without an overall strategy. In many ways this was hardly surprising. While the PIRA had a coherent target, to destroy British rule in Ireland and unite the Irish peoples, the Unionists had only a negative ambition, that was to hold the Union together. It was widely recognized that paramilitary activity could jeopardize, not strengthen the link with the mainland. Those loyal to the Union could fulfil their ambition of securing the Union through a number of avenues. It was possible, in support of the Union, to become a member of the RUC or the UDR, thus 'legally' reinforcing the state and countering the ambitions of the PIRA and the INLA. A word of warning is necessary, however: it is accurate to suggest that Unionists have and do support the RUC, yet throughout the conflict there have been periods of intense dissatisfaction with the force and the way in which the Province has been policed. Chapter Five noted the violence that characterized Protestant neighbourhoods after the signing of the Anglo-Irish Agreement, and there continued to be a level of protest against the RUC both for 'enforcing' the accord and for a perceived collusion in selling out the Protestant community.[49] Despite this dissatisfaction, the possibilty of joining the RUC and the UDR have necessarily meant that the base from which Unionist paramilitary organizations draw their support is circumscribed and relatively small. In particular, analysts have noted that the middle classes are almost entirely absent from Unionist paramilitary groups, but are well represented in the RUC.[50] It has even been argued that it is the least 'competent' members of society who opt to join Unionist paramilitary organizations, for example those who have been rejected by the RUC, the UDR and other parts of the British Army. All of this means that Protestant paramilitaries have a smaller military base than that of the PIRA from which to recruit. In addition, there are other structural problems that Protestant paramilitaries have to contend with, not least that as they come from the same community as the majority of the UDR and the RUC, they are far more liable to be arrested

49 *The Times* (19 September 1988). On this issue, see Ronald Weitzer, *Policing Under Fire: Ethnic Conflict and Police-Community Relations in Northern Ireland* (New York: State University of New York, 1995), pp. 114–15.
50 See Bruce, op. cit., pp. 270–1.

or 'caught' for terrorist offences. In 1982, for example, when conviction rates for members of nationalist and Unionist paramilitary organizations charged with murder were compared, the conviction rate for Republicans was between 50 and 60 per cent, but that for Loyalist murders was between 90 and 100 per cent.[51]

Despite these disadvantages, the Protestant paramilitaries also operated with certain advantages, not least because of the relationship with the security forces. In many regimes, relations between state forces and pro-state paramilitary groups can be close. Indeed, in some cases, the state may actually accept, either tacitly or not, the claims of unofficial groups to act on its behalf and even fund or sanction extra-legal behaviour. It is difficult to comment on how far this has actually been the case in Northern Ireland. By its very nature, this question is sensitive. Republican sources claim that direct links exist between certain sections of the British military, the RUC and Protestant paramilitaries. This is a claim vehemently denied by military sources. During the mid-1980s, however, serious allegations were made by Fred Holroyd, a former intelligence liaison member, who had seen duty in border areas of the Province in the previous decade. He alleged that certain members of the intelligence services, most notably one Robert Nairac, had been involved in collusion with Protestant paramilitaries to assassinate leading Republicans.[52] These claims have provoked a vigorous debate among journalists and academics who are divided over the 'truth' of these types of allegation.[53] It is difficult to draw any concrete conclusions over whether there was in fact an ongoing conspiracy between the British military and Protestant paramilitaries, although towards the end of the 1980s, some evidence emerged of collusion between the UDR and the UDA/UFF (Ulster Freedom Fighters).

In August 1989, a Catholic man, Loughlin Maginn, was killed by UDA/UFF gunmen. In an attempt to justify their actions, Protestant paramilitaries claimed that they knew from looking at police files that Maginn was an IRA man. Within a month of the Maginn murder, posters appeared on walls all over Belfast, containing the names of paramilitary 'suspects' taken from confidential police files. The Chief Constable of the RUC appointed a British police officer, John Stevens, to look into the issue of how

---

51 Ed Maloney, *The Irish Times* (20 November 1982).
52 See Urban, op. cit., p. 53.
53 See, for example, Martin Dillon, *The Dirty War* (London: Arrow, 1995).

classified documents had gone 'missing'.[54] Two soldiers from the UDR were later charged with the murder of Maginn and were given life sentences for passing on information that led to his death.[55] The Stevens Report, which set out eighty-three recommendations, was published in May 1990. Fifty-nine people were afterwards charged or reported to the Director of Public Prosecutions (DPP). Thiry-two of those arrested were members of Loyalist organizations. Almost entirely, the defendants were charged with the 'mishandling' of intelligence documents or for unlawfully possessing documents. Not one was charged with murder, except for Brian Nelson, whose case later became a major embarrassment because of his links with security forces.[56] The Stevens Report was criticized by those who believed that its remit had not been broad enough to allow a thorough investigation of the issue of collusion between security forces and members of paramilitary organizations. In particular, critics argued that it did not name those members of the security forces who had been responsible for passing confidential information on to the UDA/UFF. A report commissioned by Amnesty International, to look into the behaviour of security forces in the Province, suggested that the Stevens Report, in order to be really effective, should have examined the wider dimensions of the role of British security forces and illegal Protestant organizations. In particular, it argued that the Report should have focused on the possibility that 'a community of interest' existed between the security forces and Protestant paramilitaries, which in turn might lead to 'joint' operations against Republican paramilitaries.[57]

In many ways, however, this suggestion missed the point. There was, and had been from the beginning of the century, an obvious 'community of interest' between the British security services and the Unionist paramilitaries. In short, it was to defeat the PIRA and other Republican paramilitary groups, while maintaining the connection with the mainland. What was important was whether the British Army behaved illegally in either encouraging or tolerating Protestant paramilitary attacks on Republicans. This is an almost impossible question to answer while the Irish conflict continues. The British Army has been and remains reluctant to participate in

---

54 See Amnesty International, *Political Killings in Northern Ireland* (London: Amnesty International British Section, 1994).
55 Ibid.
56 Ibid.
57 Ibid.

any such inquiry, claiming that such an investigation could damage their operations in the Province. Indeed, while the British Army continued to rely on the SAS to implement its policies against the PIRA, whether it be at Loughall or in Gibraltar, there was little hope that the British Government would allow its serving forces to be investigated. Mark Urban, in his work on the SAS in Ireland, argues that the Army's clandestine activities could always be justified in 'military' terms. Urban points out that British Government ministers did admit that misinformation had been used over Irish affairs but, in the words of Tom King, only for 'absolutely honourable reasons'.[58] This type of justification did little to reassure the minority in the Province that they could have confidence either in the British Government or its security forces. Yet, such were the complex twists of the Northern Irish story that nationalist suspicions of the security services could operate in many, sometimes contradictory, ways. Although almost universally opposed to the use of the SAS, some nationalists at times expressed a preference for British troops patrolling the Province, rather than the indigenous forces of the UDR and the RUC. As John Hume pointed out in 1988, how many nationalists would relish the prospect of a complete and rapid withdrawal of British forces, leaving the heavily armed UDR and RUC in place as the only arbiters of law and order? Policing a divided Province had no simple answers.

By 1990, Protestant fears of a British sell-out had not materialized. The Hillsborough Agreement, although now part of the Anglo-Irish dialogue, had not amounted to anything approaching an abdication of political responsibility by Westminster. The combination of intense paramilitary activity and a hard-line British military response meant that although in 1985 Dublin and Westminster had tried to implement limited 'reform', they had failed to alter the pattern of military confrontation in the Province. Indeed, both Governments had, after the Anglo-Irish Agreement, invoked cumulatively repressive measures that effectively ended any real hope for sustained change short of the military defeat of the PIRA. Yet, in this very same period the British Government accepted that complete defeat was not likely.[59] Violence and the instruments of violence had therefore become thoroughly institutionalized. Underneath this grim ending to the

58 See Urban, op. cit., p. 78.
59 See Peter Brooke's comment that the PIRA could be contained but not defeated. Quoted in Coogan, op. cit., p. 337.

decade, however, there were shifts in the pattern of local politics in Northern Ireland. Most notably Sinn Fein had shifted its ground to one of political dialogue, and promised to deliver at some point in the future a profound change in the attitude of the nationalist movement. It was through this change that, twenty years after the beginning of the violence, the peace process of the 1990s began to take shape.

CHAPTER SEVEN

Redefining the Role of the British Military in Ireland: Debates Over Peace, 1990–95

The 1990s were dominated in Northern Ireland by the 'peace process'. This was an attempt by both the British and Irish Governments to find some form of compromise solution to the Troubles. The first half of the decade was marked by attempts to persuade the PIRA to lay down its arms, to debate the decommissioning of weapons and to attempt to impose a durable cease-fire on Ireland. The British Army were, during this period, in the position of having to underwrite these ambitions.

British and Irish attempts to initiate progress in the Province were facilitated by movement on the nationalist side. By 1990 there was a shift towards a different pattern of politics in the Province and hopeful signs that the violent stalemate would be undone. Yet, progress on one side was not in itself enough to end the conflict. The British Government had to be prepared to take the nationalist gambits seriously and, in particular, needed to be convinced that the armed wing of the nationalist movement would renounce violence. Any lasting political settlement therefore hinged both on the ability of the moderates to persuade the PIRA to lay down its arms and a British willingness to underwrite new political structures, perhaps even against the will of the Unionists. No one part of this complex package was easy, not least the question of whether the British could persuade the PIRA to give up its paramilitary campaign.

'Talks about talks'

In 1990, under the influence of Peter Brooke, the Secretary of State for Northern Ireland, the British Government began to take seriously the new correlation of forces on the nationalist side and signalled that it was willing to discuss future options. Brooke sought, in his period as minister, to build upon the Anglo-Irish Agreement to achieve greater devolution in its affairs from the mainland.[1] From late 1989 Brooke tried to find some form of consensus that might allow for a greater devolution of power and permit most of the major players involved in the Province to form a dialogue that would eventually bring about new political structures. This endeavour became known as 'talks about talks'.[2] Out of it came the notion of a three-stranded discussion along the lines which had been consistently advocated by Hume in the 1980s – that talks should take place between the Northern political parties (the internal dimension), between Dublin and Belfast, and between Dublin and London. The Unionists were not keen about any aspect of these talks, fearing that they might lead to a greater devolution of power from Westminster, and resented greatly the inclusion of the Dublin Government. Sinn Fein was excluded altogether.

Over the course of the next year, the Northern Ireland Office tried to start negotiations between all the parties. Even starting the talks was the subject of much contention. The Dublin Government was unhappy because it believed that the three strands should begin in unison and that its input should not be contingent, as the Unionists insisted, on progress in strand one.[3] Progress towards the talks was therefore complicated as Brooke strove to balance the competing views and concerns of all those involved. Argument raged around issues such as where the talks should be held and even who should chair the sessions. The British Government proposed that Lord Carrington should act as chair, but this was blocked by the Unionists because of their belief that Carrington was closely associated with the Foreign Office, a body which they alleged had been instrumental in the signing of the Anglo-Irish Agreement.[4] This particular issue was eventually resolved with the appointment of an Australian, Sir Ninian Stephens, to chair the discussions. Talks did eventually get under way and continued with breaks until the spring of 1992, but the basic problem was that

1 Paul Arthur, 'The Brooke Initiative', *Irish Political Studies* 7 (1992), pp. 111–15.

2 See Tim Pat Coogan, *The Troubles: Ireland's Ordeal 1966–1995 and the Search For Peace* (London: Hutchinson, 1995), pp. 337–40.

3 See Arthur, op. cit., pp. 111–15.

4 W. Harvey Cox, 'From Hillsborough to Downing Street – and After' in Peter Catterall and Sean McDougall, *The Northern Irish Question in British Politics* (London: Macmillan, 1996), p. 189.

there was no agreement as to what the talks should aim for. Analysts are divided in their assessments of these talks: some point to the futility of the discussions whereas others believed that they were the necessary prerequisite for future dialogue.[5] Yet the continuing violence perpetrated by the PIRA pointed to the problems of leaving one of the key players out of any negotiation over the future.

By 1990 the British Government had more or less conceded, in private, the centrality of Sinn Fein to any dialogue about the future. Despite the fact that Sinn Fein was publicly excluded from the talks, throughout the first two years of the decade, a secret channel of communication between the British Government and Sinn Fein was established.[6] This did not mark a new departure in British behaviour. There was by this stage a long track record of secret meetings between Government officials and Irish para-militaries. But these meetings were rather different. The contacts came about in a period not only when Sinn Fein was noticeably altering its political strategy, but when the British Government believed that it might be possible to coerce or lure Sinn Fein through political concessions into exerting pressure upon the PIRA to give up the armed struggle.[7] These contacts began in October 1990, when a top British civil servant held a meeting with Martin McGuinness.[8] In addition to the secret talks, the British Government also authorized the release to Sinn Fein of an advance copy of a speech which Brooke was going to make in London on 9 November.[9] The speech, which was entitled 'the British presence', was a major statement of intent towards the Province. Throughout the speech, Brooke portrayed the British attitude in Ireland as one of neutrality. In line with this theme, he acknowledged the legitimacy of the views of both the Unionists and nationalists. Of the former, Brooke said it was accepted that the Province could not and would not be ceded from the United Kingdom without the consent of the majority, but he also said that it was understood that the nationalist minority had concerns and aims which, if pursued through democratic non-violent means, were equally legitimate. This statement of British neutrality was

5 See Coogan, op. cit., p. 204.

6 See Paul Arthur, 'Dialogue Between Sinn Fein and the British Government', *Irish Political Studies* 10 (1995), pp. 185–91.

7 See Martin Dillon, *The Enemy Within: The IRA's War Against the British* (London: Doubleday, 1994), p. 229.

8 Ibid., p. 230.

9 Ibid., p. 230.

encapsulated in the idea that the British had no 'selfish strategic or economic interest in the Province'.[10] Brooke acknowledged that the British presence had different components – the Army, the Northern Ireland Office, the financing of the Province by the British Exchequer, and not least the Unionist population which regarded itself as British. On the military presence, the Secretary of State argued that the United Kingdom did not want to sustain high troop levels in the Province but that soldiers were there as long as they were needed to protect the police from paramilitary attacks.[11] However, once the threat to the police had been removed, the British Army could be, and would be, withdrawn.

In March 1991, one type of watershed was reached in the politics of Anglo-Irish relations when the Birmingham Six were finally released from prison. The Court of Appeal held that their convictions sixteen years before were actually unsafe. Compensation was promised and it was hoped that this might ameliorate the talks over the future of the Province.[12]

In April 1991, in another attempt to reinforce contacts with Sinn Fein, the British Government informed the paramilitaries that the Loyalists, in preparation for the talks, were going to declare a moratorium on the shooting of Catholics.[13] The cease-fire was duly announced. It lasted almost without exception until July.[14] Throughout this period, Sinn Fein were kept fully informed of the progress of the talks. The British Government continued to forward copies of major speeches to Sinn Fein, including one by Sir Patrick Mayhew, Brooke's successor, made in Coleraine in December 1992. This speech, which echoed the themes of Brooke's initiatives, held out the prospect of holding talks with Sinn Fein within the three-tiered strategy if, but again only if, violence ceased.[15] Mayhew argued that the role of the British Government was to facilitate a real resolution of the division of society.[16] Other initiatives designed to appease the nationalists

10 Peter Brooke, Secretary of State for Northern Ireland (Speech), 9 November 1990.

11 Ibid.

12 J. Bowyer Bell, *The Irish Troubles: A Generation of Violence* (Dublin: Gill and Macmillan, 1993), p. 771.

13 Coogan, op. cit., p. 338.

14 For the exception, on 25 May a Sinn Fein councillor was shot dead, see Coogan, op. cit., p. 338.

15 Culture and Identity; text of a speech by Sir Patrick Mayhew at the University of Ulster, Coleraine, 16 December 1992, provided by the Northern Irish Information Service.

16 Harvey Cox, op. cit., p. 199.

were subsequently announced, including one rescinding the ban on having street names in Irish.[17]

These tactics were designed to tempt Sinn Fein with the chance of inclusion at any future talks and to show British neutrality on the issue of Ireland. But the price was the renunciation of political violence. This took account of changes which had recently occurred in the philosophy of Sinn Fein. It had for the latter part of the 1980s dedicated itself to become a legitimate political force in Irish politics. It had made repeated attempts to contest elections and had become, through its association with John Hume and the SDLP, more of a political force in the Province. Part of the Sinn Fein agenda had also involved establishing links with members of the Catholic church.[18] All of this formed part of the endeavour to establish a broadly based nationalist movement which would gain support from Dublin and create an irresistible pressure upon the British Government for political-military change in the Province. Gerry Adams had long accepted that Sinn Fein individually could not make either substantial inroads in electoral politics or greatly influence either the political process in the south or on the British mainland.[19] He therefore sought to cultivate a movement of nationalist interests. The stumbling block to this ambition, however, was that many nationalists remained loathe to work with Sinn Fein until it had renounced violence. This also formed the main part of the British objection to opening up any public dialogue with Sinn Fein.

At this stage there were few visible signs that the PIRA would renounce violence. Indeed, throughout this period the paramilitaries once again targeted the establishment on the British mainland. In 1990, the Conservative MP, Ian Gow, a vociferous supporter of the Unionists and close friend of Mrs Thatcher, was blown up by a car bomb in front of his house.[20] Attempts to kill notable British figures continued when on 18 September, the former Governor of Gibraltar, Sir Peter Terry, was shot.[21] At this time police raids on PIRA 'safe houses' in both London and

17 Harvey Cox, op. cit., p. 200.

18 Not least, it should be noted that the work of Father Reid is generally regarded as the key to providing the seeds for dialogue between Sinn Fein, the other Northern parties and the Government in the south. On this issue see Coogan, op. cit., p. 372.

19 See Gerry Adams, *The Politics of Irish Freedom* (Dingle: Brandon Books, 1986) and *Towards a Lasting Peace in Ireland* (Dingle: Brandon Books, 1992).

20 Dillon, op. cit., p. 228.

21 Bowyer Bell, op. cit., p. 781.

Belfast revealed a list of names of 235 prominent public figures whom the paramilitaries intended to kill.[22] To many in the nationalist movement, the use of violence was an essential means of achieving a British declaration of intent to withdraw. Indeed, the armed wing was determined to keep the pressure up. In the autumn the PIRA resorted to the use of so-called hostage drivers to deliver bombs. This involved tying alleged informers into lorries loaded with bombs and forcing them to drive straight into British Army posts.[23] Despite the violence, the security forces in the Province believed that their losses were at least acceptable. In 1990, the British Army lost seven soldiers, while the UDR lost eight. The inability of the PIRA to dent the security services in the Province meant that the paramilitaries increasingly turned attention to the mainland bombing campaign. One of its most spectacular hits was in 1991, when the PIRA launched a mortar attack on Downing Street itself. It came close to killing the British Gulf War Cabinet.[24] The Provisionals continued their mainland campaign, detonating a huge bomb in the middle of the city of London in April 1992. As one author has argued, this violence was 'an essential means of achieving a British declaration of intent to withdraw which had formed the central spine of Republican discourse since the formation of the Provisionals'.[25]

The violence continued into the following year with numerous atrocities, one of the worst being the Teeban bomb which in January 1992 killed eight Protestant workmen. On 29 August 1991 the 3,000th person to die violently since the beginning of the troubles in 1969 was killed.[26] The violence overshadowed the debate which had been going on during the preceding year, within both Sinn Fein and the PIRA, over the future use of violence to further aims.

Throughout 1991 the paramilitaries maintained publicly that there could not be renunciation of violence without a British military withdrawal. Yet, this position was increasingly untenable as the movement was put under pressure to relinquish violence. In 1992, for example, Gerry Adams claimed that the IRA could not

---

22 Dillon, op. cit., p. 230.
23 Bowyer Bell, op. cit., p. 781.
24 See *The Economist*, 9–15 February 1991, p. 38.
25 Anthony McIntyre, 'Modern Irish Republicanism: The Product of British State Strategies', *Irish Political Studies* 10 (1995), pp. 97–121.
26 Harvey Cox, op. cit., p. 189.

continue with its 'ballot box and armalite' strategy.[27] In February 1992, as a result of internal debate over future strategies, Sinn Fein published a peace initiative, entitled 'Towards a lasting peace in Ireland', a document which had, according to some sources, the tacit approval of the PIRA.[28] The sentiments behind it represented a clear revision on the part of the movement away from some of the 'historic' truths which had sustained the organization. For example, the document placed an emphasis on the southern Irish Government as an agent for change in the North. No longer was the Dail the illegal representative of the British Government in the south. Even more strikingly, the document indicated a willingness on the part of the PIRA to consider non-violent options, if this would remove the British presence. Sinn Fein also proclaimed a revision of its long-held views of the British troop presence. Rather than demand an immediate withdrawal, it was accepted that Westminster might join the ranks of the 'persuaders' in seeking to obtain Unionist consent to a united Ireland. All this rather left aside the question of the armed struggle, but critics of violence from within Sinn Fein were vocal in pointing to the 'isolating' effect that violent actions had had on the movement and the counter-productive effects of actions such as the Enniskillen bombing.[29]

As the debate continued, Adams seized the political initiative through a dialogue with the SDLP. His bid to engage in constitutional nationalism took the form once again of talks with John Hume. These confidential discussions began in April 1993. In October, the discussions were made public when the Hume/Adams document was delivered to the Irish Government.[30] It held out the hope that the Provisionals might end their campaign of violence in return for some form of British declaration of support for unification. It is now clear that the southern Irish Government, through its special adviser on the Province, Martin Mansergh, had been directly involved in the preparation of the Hume/Adams principles.[31]

The contacts between Hume and Adams gained much

27 Ed Moloney, 'Peace Chronology', unpublished, 1994, p. 15. Quoted in Anthony McIntyre, 'Modern Irish Republicanism: The Product of British State Strategies', *Irish Political Studies* 10 (1995), pp. 97–121.

28 Brendan O'Brien, *The Long War: The IRA and Sinn Fein from Armed Struggle to Peace Talks* (Dublin: O'Brien, 1993), p. 228.

29 Ibid., p. 226.

30 *The Economist* (30 October–5 November 1993).

31 For Mansergh's role in the peace process, see Coogan, op. cit., p. 367.

attention. Specifically, it gave Gerry Adams a high profile as the man who could perhaps 'deliver' a peace with the Provisionals. Nevertheless, doubts were cast over his role less than two weeks after the delivery of the Hume/Adams talks. A bomb planted by the PIRA in a fish shop on the Shankill Road in the heart of a Protestant community exploded, killing ten people including one of the bombers. In retaliation, Loyalist gunmen launched a campaign of random assassinations on Catholics. Adams expressed regret for the Shankill bombing, but just a few days later took his place at the funeral of the bomber, even acting as a pall bearer.[32] This made his regrets over the killings appear, at best, insincere. However, those more attuned to the workings of Sinn Fein and its relationship with the PIRA argued that Adams had little choice but to appear at the funeral to keep faith with the PIRA men he was trying to persuade into peace.

Some analysts have claimed throughout that the British Government was operating a clear and consistent strategy of using political overtures to Sinn Fein to isolate the PIRA.[33] While the British obviously had a sustained interest in restraining the para-militaries, it was not obvious at this stage that there was a coherent plan or even an endpoint in mind for the process of 'splitting the Nationalists'. Not least, the Government of John Major was at certain points circumscribed in its Irish policy because of its weak domestic position, which necessitated a cultivation of the Unionist vote in the House of Commons.

The Conservative Party had long been dependent in periods of political emergency on the 'good will' of its Unionist colleagues within the House of Commons. In 1992–93 this was a critical factor in British politics. The April 1992 general election did not produce the Labour Government that had been widely predicted. John Major was returned but with a majority of only twenty-one. The narrow majority was crucial to the Government as Major struggled to push forward a controversial strategy over Europe. In 1993, John Major faced a severe test to his leadership over his European policies in the vote on the Maastricht Treaty. Both the Unionists and sympathetic colleagues on the backbenches threatened to undo Major's European strategy if he pushed too hard on the issue of contacts with Sinn Fein. As it was, on 22 July 1993 it was the Unionist vote that saved both John Major and the Maastricht Treaty. For those watching, it raised the question of what

---

32 *The Economist* (30 October–5 November 1993).
33 McIntyre, op. cit., pp. 97–121.

concessions the Unionists had managed to exact from the Prime Minister.

The British position *vis-à-vis* the Province was further complicated when it became public that despite its repeated protestations to the contrary, the British Government had been conducting a covert dialogue with Sinn Fein.[34] The Government was not helped in this instance in that the British version of events, which maintained that it had been asked by the PIRA in early 1993 for assistance in ending the conflict, was challenged by Sinn Fein.[35] The latter's version was that it had responded to British suggestions that an eventual withdrawal might be negotiated.[36] The matter proved just how problematic the issue of negotiating with paramilitaries is for democratic regimes.

Generally, when those in power find they cannot destroy their opponents militarily, alternate schemes have to be devised. In many cases this can require dialogue with the enemy. In liberal societies the electorate then has to be persuaded that the Government is right to pursue such a dialogue. As Dillon argues of secret negotiations with paramilitaries: 'the critical dilemma facing governments is whether to begin the process in secret before making a public admission that terrorists are about to be accorded public recognition'.[37] This was the dilemma of the British Government – if and when to announce the contacts with Sinn Fein and the PIRA as preparation for peace. John Major survived the revelations with some boldness. Nevertheless, the British Government came under pressure from a variety of sources to recover the initiative. In particular, Dublin pressurized Prime Minister Major to keep the momentum going in the quest for peace. According to Martin Dillon, by mid-May 1993, John Major had already decided that he would talk to the spokesmen of Sinn Fein. By this stage anyway, the British Government and Sinn Fein had exchanged sixteen letters and four oral messages.[38] But after the atrocities committed by the PIRA on the British mainland, most notably the bombing in Warrington in the spring of 1993 which killed two young children, Major was persuaded by his political colleagues that the risks were, at that moment, too high. Indeed, Major himself said that talking to Gerry Adams would turn

34 *The Economist* (4 December 1993).
35 Kevin Boyle and Tom Haddon, 'Framing Northern Ireland's Future', *International Affairs* 71.2 (April 1995), p. 273.
36 Ibid., p. 273. See also *The Weekly Telegraph* (8–14 December 1993).
37 Dillon, op. cit., p. 225.
38 Harvey Cox, op. cit., p. 201.

his stomach.[39] In October, Albert Reynolds and John Major rejected the Hume/Adams proposals.[40] Yet, this was followed by a burst of Anglo-Irish activity between Dick Spring, the Irish Foreign Minister, and Patrick Mayhew in a bid to put together a joint initiative. In November, the British response to the Hume/Adams proposals came in the form of an Anglo-Irish announcement known as the Downing Street Declaration.

The peace process

Despite the Anglo-Irish rejection of the Hume/Adams suggestions, many of the terms of the Downing Street Declaration had actually been foreshadowed in those talks. Not least of these was the notion that a united Ireland could be achieved through negotiation and constitutional methods. It also held out the promise once again to Sinn Fein of the possibility of inclusion in the peace process on the basis of a permanent end to the use of violence. The British Government undertook to engage in direct talks with Sinn Fein as to how practically the violence could end.[41]

Assessments of the actual meanings of the Downing Street Declaration varied quite dramatically. Some analysts claim that it was an attempt by the British Government to claw back influence after the Anglo-Irish accord of 1985.[42] Conversely, others claimed it was tilted towards one aim and one aim only – a united Ireland. One commentator noted, for example, that there were twenty-seven references to Irish unity in the document but only two to the Northern Ireland within the United Kingdom.[43] Another author argued that British policy was moving inexorably towards disengagement, driven by PIRA violence.[44] One British official, Sir David Goodall, stated 'that the tone of the declaration moves the British Government a shade further towards accepting a united Ireland as an attainable rather than simply a conceivable goal'.[45]

The Declaration was indeed a step towards redefining the British role in Ireland as the arbiter of Irish problems, not least the statement by which Great Britain agreed

39 Ibid., p. 201.
40 *The Economist* (6 November 1993).
41 *The Weekly Telegraph* (22–8 December 1993).
42 McIntyre, op. cit., pp. 97–121.
43 John Wilson Foster, 'Processed Peace' *Fortnight* (March 1994), pp. 35–6. Quoted in Harvey Cox, op. cit., p. 202.
44 Dillon, op. cit., pp. 259–63.
45 *The Tablet* (25 December 1993).

that it is for the people of the island of Ireland alone, by agreement between the two parts respectively, to exercise their right of self-determination on the basis of consent . . . to bring about a united Ireland . . . if that is their wish.[46]

Alongside this concession, came the desire for greater devolution in the Province – but the Unionists were not discarded by John Major. Shortly after the announcement of the Downing Street Declaration, which conceded the possibility of a united Ireland at some point, the British Government also took a step explicitly designed to conciliate the Unionists. This was the setting up of a Northern Ireland Affairs Select Committee (NIASC),[47] long-demanded by Unionists and seen as an integrationist device. Like other select committees it was designed to oversee the operation of government departments, in this case the Northern Irish Office.[48] When the House of Commons debated the creation of the committee, the Labour Party opposed it on the grounds that it was merely a 'payback' to the Unionists for their support over European issues, not least their support for John Major over the Maastricht Treaty. In particular, Labour politicians questioned the British Government's neutrality over the Province when it had conceded to the Unionists what was, in effect, another move towards the integration of the Province into the life and politics of the mainland.[49] Yet again, this was an instance of a British Prime Minister attempting a balancing act in order to keep the Unionists on side in the House of Commons. The British Government was moving slowly, in a piecemeal fashion, towards an Irish solution to 'the troubles', yet there was a long way to go, as the Sinn Fein response to the Downing Street Declaration proved.

The Downing Street Declaration itself appeared to cause some confusion and hesitancy on the part of Sinn Fein. It has been alleged that the Declaration split the PIRA. This was not true.[50] Behind the scenes the paramilitaries had voted not to reject it.[51] Sinn Fein did not want to reject it in an outright fashion. At first, it hedged on its response and called for clarification of the terms of the Declaration. This was an attempt to buy time rather than

46 *Weekly Telegraph* (22–8 December 1993).
47 On this issue, see Rick Wilford and Sydney Elliott, 'The Northern Ireland Affairs Select Committee', *Irish Political Studies* 10 (1995), pp. 216–25.
48 Ibid., pp. 216–25.
49 Ibid., pp. 216–25.
50 Dillon, op. cit., p. 254.
51 Coogan, op. cit., p. 376.

reject the agreement outright. The PIRA, however, sent the British Government a series of contradictory signals. It continued attacks on the mainland to maintain the pressure. Most noticeably it mounted a number of assaults on Heathrow airport in March 1994.[52] At the same time the Provisionals also operated a series of voluntary three-day cease-fires. On 13 May 1994, Sinn Fein sought clarification on some of the issues at stake in the Declaration. All of these moves were designed to wrong-foot Government officials and ensure that any initiative lay with the nationalists. The British Government responded to these activities through a reiteration of the terms offered in the Declaration.

Sinn Fein finally rejected the Declaration after a full-scale party conference at Letterkenny in July 1994.[53] Yet all was not lost. Momentum had been building for the Sinn Fein leadership to underwrite a cease-fire. Throughout the process the Party had maintained a dialogue with Dublin and the Irish Taoiseach, Albert Reynolds, while another line of pressure came from the American White House. Gerry Adams had, after years of being refused entry, finally succeeded in gaining a visa to the United States of America.[54] Despite British opposition, Adams visited the United States three times. After March 1995, Adam used his visits to activate American fund-raising activities. Some sections of American society, most notably the Irish diaspora, had long supported the financing of Sinn Fein and throughout his later trips, most notably in the autumn of 1995, Adams raised enormous amounts of money.[55] A year earlier, Adams had a more political agenda, which was to convince the White House of his sincerity as a peace-maker. In return, he was pressurized to accede to the cease-fire. US influence had an affect. On 31 August 1994 the PIRA did indeed announce a cease-fire.[56] It did not promise that this was a permanent cease-fire but rather stated that this was a 'complete cessation of violence', and according to the PIRA announcement, 'All of our units have been instructed accordingly.'[57] Gerry Adams saluted the bravery of the volunteers. In October, Loyalist paramilitaries also declared a cease-fire. This was a momentous

52 M.L.R. Smith, *Fighting for Ireland: The Military Strategy of the Irish Republican Movement* (London: Routledge, 1995), pp. 207–8.

53 R. Savill and R. Shrimsley, 'Ulster Peace Deal Rejected by Sinn Fein', *The Weekly Telegraph* (27 July–2 August 1994).

54 Coogan, op. cit., pp. 382–4.

55 *The Sunday Times* (19 November 1995).

56 *The Economist* (5–11 February 1994).

57 Ibid.

occasion – at least for a time, there was peace in Ireland after twenty-five years of violence.

The cease-fire was the result of a number of profound changes within the Province. One was, of course, the substantial revision in the attitude of Sinn Fein. It no longer argued in the rather simplistic fashion that had characterized much of its former rhetoric that Britain could simply 'leave' or be pushed out of Ireland. The dialogue with Hume had brought home that Unionist objectives to a united Ireland were not just sustained by a British presence, but rooted in deep cultural and historical beliefs that could not be wished away, even if the British Army left. Much of the evolution of nationalist thinking demonstrated that it was understood that there was little chance of ever achieving a united Ireland without a broad political consensus in the North and a sustained input from the south. In other words, Sinn Fein accepted that it would have to work within a nationalist coalition formed from both parts of Ireland to achieve its ultimate aim.

No less importantly, the British position too had shifted, although not as far as its paramilitary opponents. Since the mid-1970s, the British Government had been trying to create the conditions in which 'the troubles' could be both contained and resolved within a predominantly Irish context. What the peace process of the 1990s demonstrated was that the British Government had come to recognize the centrality of the Dublin Government to this aim, and the fact that no initiative could successfully go ahead without a southern dimension. Indeed, it might be argued that it was this southern dimension that had pushed Britain as far as it had with respect to the Downing Street Declaration.[58] In particular Dublin's willingness to accept the 'consent' principle which effectively negated Articles 2 and 3 of the Irish constitution which asserted jurisdiction over the whole island of Ireland opened up the possibility of real Anglo-Irish cooperation. John Major's Irish policy was not without opponents within his own Cabinet. It has now become apparent that there was deep unhappiness at the inclusion of Sinn Fein in any peace process and continued unease at developments in the Province.[59] The Unionists were also opposed to Major's initiatives and some of the more hard-liners alleged that John Major had done a secret deal with the PIRA. On 6 September 1994, Ian Paisley was thrown out of 10 Downing

58 Coogan, op. cit., p. 379.
59 Ibid., p. 369.

Street for refusing to take Major's word that this was not the case.[60] This signalled that despite Conservative dependence on Unionist votes, there were limits to British patience with Unionist intransigence towards the Peace Process.

Yet perhaps the most important shift was that the British Government had finally recognized that in military terms the PIRA could not be completely defeated and that any Northern Irish settlement was in fact dependent on Sinn Fein. In this context, it is worth noting that the very use of the term cease-fire in the Province conferred some form of military legitimacy on the PIRA. Cease-fires normally end 'proper wars' not conflicts with terrorists. A cease-fire was not really in keeping with British policy since 1975, when PIRA had been depicted in a welter of legislation as common criminals. The term 'cease-fire', used throughout 1994–95, conferred some dignity on the paramilitary opponents of the state.

The cease-fire was not permanent and the PIRA had not gone away, but was rather waiting and still armed for the moment, if it so chose to renew the conflict. After the PIRA cease-fire, this knowledge brought the British administration to a new phase of the military-political battle in the Province. This was an attempt, quite literally, to disarm the enemy through a process of decommissioning.

Normalization to decommissioning

After the cease-fires of August and October 1994 there was a gradual scaling down of activities by the British security forces. Most noticeably, British Army patrols were withdrawn from the streets of Belfast and Londonderry. This was in many ways an extension of the normalization process for the Province which Westminster had long sought. Yet in part, some of these changes in the military were necessitated by the end of the Cold War. It is often tempting to think of the Army in Northern Ireland as separate from the mainstream of the British forces, but the Province did not escape the cuts made in the wake of the so-called

---

60 For a report on the incidents, see *The Economist* (10 September 1994). For an exposition of the distrust which had come to characterize Unionist views of successive British Cabinets, see W. Harvey Cox, 'Managing Northern Ireland Intergovernmentally: An Appraisal of the Anglo-Irish Agreement', *Parliamentary Affairs* 40, no. 1, January 1987, quoted in Arthur Aughey, *Under Siege: Ulster Unionism and the Anglo-Irish Agreement* (London: Hurst and Co., 1989), p. 37.

'peace dividend' after the collapse of the Warsaw Treaty Organization. In July 1991, for example, it was announced by Tom King, who was at this point Minister of Defence, that the British Armed Forces would be cut by 40,000 soldiers within four years. In relation to Ireland, he announced that the UDR would merge with the Irish Rangers to form the Royal Irish Regiment.[61] The newly formed regiment would, he envisaged, be made up of eight battalions – one which would be used globally and seven for use in the Province.[62] There was a pragmatic cost-cutting rationale at work here, but these changes in Ireland were also made in response to the complaints of both Dublin and the SDLP that the UDR remained inherently biased and sectarian in outlook and composition. One hundred members of the UDR had been charged with a series of serious offences and seventeen members were serving sentences for murder.[63] The Royal Irish Rangers was approximately 30 per cent Catholic in terms of its composition. The Regiment had a long tradition of recruiting from the south and it was hoped, after the amalgamation, that more Catholics would be encouraged to join.[64] Unionists, however, alleged that the regiment was being used by London to ameliorate nationalist fears of the security forces as the British Government prepared for a peace process. Yet nationalist suspicions of the security forces remained strong and their actions remained controversial.

The success of the British Army in countering or at least containing terrorism in the Province was apparent by the early 1990s. One semi-official source phrased it in the following way:

> The security forces have been able to cut the number of deaths in Northern Ireland from over 500 in 1972, to 94 in 1991 and 84 in 1992. The number of deaths due to terrorism in Northern Ireland every year since 1977 has on average been less than the toll of an average week on the United Kingdoms roads.[65]

It has been argued that these types of statistic made it obvious to the PIRA that, at the very least, a military stalemate existed in the Province and that the British presence would endure in the island.

---

61 See Tom King, House of Commons Debate (hereafter HC), vol. 195, col. 1043, 23 July 1991. I am grateful to Sharda Tarachandra for this reference. It is taken from her MA dissertation, Leeds 1992.

62 Ibid.

63 Bowyer Bell, op. cit., p. 793.

64 Thomas Bartlett and Keith Jeffrey (eds), *A Military History of Ireland* (Cambridge: Cambridge University Press, 1996), p. 456.

65 Royal United Services Institute, *Newsbrief* 13.2 (December 1993).

British military success therefore had, for more than two decades, helped to pressurize the PIRA to the negotiating table in 1994. It should be stressed however that this was not what the British military itself desired. Some officers would rather not have seen the Government negotiating with terrorists the terms of a cease-fire. In itself, they argued, this represented a failure for military policy in the Province.[66]

Here there is the problem of what constituted success for a military force operating in the Province. To be withdrawn from the streets to soothe nationalist fears was galling when it was obvious that the PIRA had not disarmed. Yet the very presence of a British military force, withdrawn from the streets or not, inspired continued allegations that a 'shoot to kill' policy operated. In this respect the actions of the Army sometimes jeopardize the quest for peace. Critics of the Army argued that in the 1990s the role of the British military was not peacekeeping but was in essence to pinpoint and eradicate the PIRA. It was not, critics argued, about policing nor about prevention, but just about raising the costs of operations for the Provisionals. For example, in February 1992, four PIRA men were shot dead by the SAS in Coalisland during an attack on a police station. This raised questions over the behaviour of the SAS once again.[67] This unit was again under intense scrutiny especially with the publication of a new book in 1993. Mark Urban, himself a former soldier turned journalist wrote a book, *Big Boy's Rules: The Secret War Against the IRA*.[68] In this work he alleged that the British Army had been authorized at times to 'trap' and 'kill' PIRA men, albeit within certain guidelines. He claimed that the SAS had killed thirty-seven PIRA gunmen since 1976. Similar allegations were also made by Martin Dillon in his works on the PIRA.[69] While none of these accusations were completely new, alongside the complex negotiations going on in the Province for peace, it raised questions once again about the British role in Ireland in 1994 and whether a British military force could ever really be neutral in 'the troubles'.

Moreover, nationalists remained unhappy not only with SAS activities but also with the presence of the British Parachute Regiment in the Province. Since Bloody Sunday, this regiment had

---

66 Ibid.

67 Bowyer Bell, op. cit., p. 805.

68 Urban, *Big Boy's Rules: The SAS and the Secret Struggle Against the IRA* (London: Faber & Faber, 1992).

69 See, for example, Dillon, op. cit. and Dillon and D. Lehane, *Political Murder in Northern Ireland* (London: Penguin, 1973).

not been popular with the nationalist community, but after one particular incident when the Paras were accused of 'harassing' locals in Coalisland, there were calls for their withdrawal which reached across party lines. The Unionist MP, Ken Maginnis, the Party's security spokesman, expressed his doubts about the behaviour of the regiment and fuelled calls for its withdrawal. The controversy over this particular regiment gained increased resonance in the case of Private Lee Clegg. In 1993 he was sentenced to life imprisonment for the alleged murder of Karen Reilly. Clegg had allegedly shot her dead when she was a passenger in a car which had driven through an Army checkpoint in 1990. The case aroused enormous controversy both on the mainland and in the Province, as supporters campaigned for his early release arguing that he had acted within the rules of engagement allowed to soldiers in Northern Ireland. The incident provoked calls for different laws to deal with such situations. In July 1995 Clegg was released on licence at a sensitive time both in the Province (because of the marching season) and in the peace process. The release led to rioting in Belfast. It underlined the sensitivity of the nationalists in the Province to the behaviour of the British Army. This type of issue – how soldiers behave – mattered a great deal in the society and culture of Northern Ireland, not least because after a quarter of a century of violence it was one of the most policed societies in the Western world and the actions of all the security forces affected daily conduct and therefore came under intense local scrutiny.

In 1994, after the cease-fire, the British Government turned its attention to the idea of a permanent decommissioning of arms as a way of disarming the paramilitaries. In October, the British Government set out the conditions that would entitle paramilitary-backed parties to enter into political negotiations over the future of the Province. These conditions were that the PIRA would give clear evidence that it was willing to disarm according to so-called agreed modalities and that to prove good faith it would decommission some of its arsenal. Until it did so, it was still barred from joining in the three-stranded talks. These demands by the British Government resulted in an impasse, not least because Sinn Fein argued that decommissioning represented a betrayal of Article 10 of the Downing Street Declaration which had not set it as a prerequisite to talks. The British administration continued to insist on decommissioning and, to break the deadlock, an international committee was set up to talk to all the potential parties involved to try to identify a way in which verifiable decommissioning could take place. This was the first track of the so-called twin-track path to peace; the second part was the opening of preliminary talks with the parties in Northern Ireland. In January 1996, the first joint meeting with Sinn Fein was held. Shortly after that, the decommissioning committee led by US Senator George Mitchell, reported his findings. The appointment of Mitchell was in itself an indication of how far the British Government had moved towards a partial acceptance that Westminster alone could not solve the problems of the Province. The Mitchell Commission recommended that the British Government should abandon its demand that paramilitaries in Northern Ireland give up their weapons before all-party talks. Rather, Mitchell and his team suggested that the party talks should take place along any process of decommissioning. This was a compromise proposal. Mitchell also suggested that six principles be put in place before all-party talks could begin. These were that the parties agree to (1) acceptance of the democratic and exclusively peaceful means of resolving political issues, (2) the total disarmament of paramilitary organizations, (3) independent verification of disarmament, (4) the renunciation of violence and opposition to any other group using force, (5) agreement to abide by the terms of any agreement, and (6) an end to punishment beatings and killings.[70]

The recommendations of the Mitchell Report placed Sinn Fein in a difficult position. Expectations were high after the initial period of the cease-fire that some form of accommodation could be found, but decommissioning was not popular with the PIRA, nor were the terms of the Mitchell Report. Martin McGuinness had argued that if 'weapons' were going to be scrutinized, then the military arsenal of the security forces, including the British Army in the Province, should form part of that process.[71] Indeed, Sinn Fein argued that the logical conclusion for a peace settlement was the demilitarization of the entire Province. The British Government obviously did not accept this. John Major had given the Mitchell Commission the go ahead strictly on the conditions that the weaponry of the security forces was not included and that the commission focused on 'illegal' or

---

70 Report of the International Body on Arms Decommissioning, 24 January 1996. Mitchell Commission Report, p. 3. http://www.unite.customers/alliance/Mitchellrep.html.

71 Royal United Services Institute, *Newsbrief* 16.2 (February 1996).

paramilitary weapons alone.[72] Sinn Fein also demanded that illegal weapons held by Protestants should be included in the decommissioning process in the Province. Again this did not happen, leading some nationalists to the conclusion that decommissioning was a one-way street. If Sinn Fein had agreed to British demands, the PIRA would no longer be a military force and, indeed, would potentially be at the mercy of the private arms in the hands of the Protestant community and of the security forces. Dublin, aware of the concerns of the nationalist community in the North, argued that if decommissioning went ahead there was a need for a newly constituted police force which was drawn from both communities. Deommissioning was dismissed by some nationalists as merely a delaying tactic by the British Government in an attempt to prolong the cease-fire and pressurize Sinn Fein and the PIRA into giving up the military campaign altogether. The logic of this argument was that the longer the people of the Province got used to peace, the more difficult it would be for the PIRA to re-ignite the campaign.

In addition to nationalist objections, there were numerous practical difficulties about the decommissioning process. Many of those involved in decommissioning believed that the process was bound to falter, simply because of the problems of verification. Questions such as how would the inspectors know that the PIRA had indeed handed in all its weapons were, in the prevailing climate of mistrust, simply unanswerable.

The whole idea of decommissioning appeared to die a death after the Mitchell Committee had actually reported to the Government. The debates on the peace process changed in emphasis towards Unionist demands for the creation of an elected assembly for the Province as the way forward. This proposal was outlined in the Irish Framework Document of February 1995. Nationalists were initially opposed to the idea, seeing any new political structures as inherently biased to the Unionists.[73] Such was PIRA frustration at the inability of Sinn Fein radically to influence the peace process that by early 1996 the cease-fire in Ireland was over and the PIRA resumed its military campaign against the British Government. Once again, the British mainland was the subject of a number of ferocious and bloody attacks.

72 Ibid.
73 *The Guardian* (25 January 1996).

New ideas – old problems

The British Government had, during the first part of the 1990s, tried to reinvent its role in the Province. From the time of the appointment of Peter Brooke, it had sought to become 'neutral' participants in an Irish drama. The involvement of Dublin in the talks about peace had made this seem possible, at least for a period. The shift of Sinn Fein into legitimate electoral politics also gave Westminster the chance to see if Adams could persuade the PIRA to lay down its arms. The British Government hoped to use the 'peace process' to further the aim of retreating from Ireland. At this stage, though, it was not envisaged that this would be, or could be, a complete retreat, not least because there was the problem of the Unionists. The Conservative Party needed their support to stay in power and could not use their full power to persuade them to accept radically different political institutions for the Province. However, British policies worked, in some respects, at least in the short term. There was a double cease-fire for a time and debate centred more upon Irish–Irish political issues than the British presence.

Yet, nothing had really changed in the essentials of the Province. The problems of two nationalisms – one wishing to be aligned with Britain – still remained as clearly entrenched as ever. Political progress remained slow and controversial. When in 1994–95 political progress proved illusive, the British Government sought to extend the cease-fire through a process of decommissioning. If this had worked it would have resolved the question of the PIRA and its continued ability to perpetrate violence. But it failed. While Sinn Fein changed its colours, the PIRA did not. Yet the achievement of cease-fire should not be underestimated. At least there were no killings, beatings or other atrocities for the first time in twenty-five years. The paramilitary cease-fire gave the Province a breathing space and some peace. The resumption of the PIRA campaign in early 1996 signalled the end of this particular endeavour.

Throughout the British attempts of the 1990s to reinvent their role in Ireland, the role of the Army has been both controversial and symbolic. Actual numbers of soldiers in the Province were once again being reduced and during the cease-fires themselves the British Army actually left the streets. This was in tune with recent British themes of a willingness to withdraw and attain neutrality in the Province. Indeed, after the Downing Street Declaration Britain did seem closer to disengagement from the affairs of Ireland. Yet, the very presence of the SAS and the Parachute Regiment in the Province gave pause for thought. The use of these troops did not point to a 'neutral' British view, but rather to the old endeavour of rooting out and destroying the rebellious opposition. This was one of the inherent paradoxes of the British attitude towards the Province in the 1990s. Neutrality or the expressed ambition for neutrality did not sit comfortably with the operation of special forces. Even as Government representatives negotiated with Sinn Fein for the terms of a peace process, British soldiers sought to destroy the organization. This approach did little to reassure the nationalists that the British Government was sincere in its desire for peace. On the other hand, how could the British Government not continue the war against an opponent which took every opportunity to take the battle to the British mainland, in incidents from the attack on Downing Street to the bomb attack on civilians in Warrington? Yet increasingly the British military response came under scrutiny. In September 1995, the European Court of Human Rights ruled that the killing of three PIRA members by the SAS in Gibraltar in 1988 was unlawful.[74] This external scrutiny of British behaviour will continue. Until the PIRA are defeated (which seems unlikely) or voluntarily give up the struggle (which is again unlikely), or until the British finally decide to leave (which is not possible while the Unionists operate a veto), the British Army will continue to remain in the Province.

74 *The Economist* (30 September–6 October 1995), p. 29.

CHAPTER EIGHT

Conclusions: The Long Retreat?

Any assessment of the role of the British Army in Northern Ireland is bound to provoke controversy. It has been and remains a highly emotional issue, not least because many have lost their lives, their families or their friends in the violence and, unlike other conflicts, it is not yet over. This work has examined the broad role of the British Army in Northern Ireland. In particular it puts forward the view that the Army has been internal to both the origins and the evolution of the modern conflict. Specifically, it tells a story of how troops have been used in a complicated and volatile conflict during a period in which British policy has not always been clear. It points to the military-political difficulties of policing a 'local' conflict with soldiers. More importantly, it argues that the British Army has had to operate in difficult circumstances, particularly since the mid-1970s when a political determination developed in Westminster to downgrade the British involvement in Ireland. The British Army was then caught between a public commitment by the British Government to the Protestant aim of remaining in the United Kingdom and the reality of a virulent Republican form of nationalism which had inexorably worn Westminster down. The role of the Army in the conflict in Ireland therefore can only be understood in the context of what has been essentially a question of managing a partial retreat from Ireland.

The campaign of the British Army in Northern Ireland in the contemporary period has gone through several different phases. This work identifies the first phase, during the period 1969–70, when the primary task of the military was to separate the warring Catholic and Protestant communities. This aspect of the modern conflict is often dismissed, with many commentators downplaying the sectarian nature of the troubles. This book argues that the

169

ethnic nature of the conflict in Northern Ireland is critical and was most obviously displayed in the initial phase.[1] The book explains that, in this first phase, British troops acted as a quasi police force, engaged in the prevention and control of riots and the policing of 'peace lines' between the Protestant and Catholic communities.[2] British troops were actively involved in the protection of the minority Catholic community. However, the conflict changed quite dramatically with the emergence of a splinter group of the IRA under the new fashioning of the Provisionals in 1970. Their subsequent attacks upon the security forces transformed the function of the British Army; it was recast into a role as the opponent of the type of nationalism associated with Catholic Ireland. The conflict then assumed new dimensions – British military-political might against rebellious Catholic Irish insurrection. This, it might be argued, was a clear reversion to pre-partition politics. But there was a significant and new dimension to the conflict in 1969–70. This was that the British Government, after fifty years of indifference to the views of the minority in the Province, was prepared to reform the institutions and policing structures of the Province. This, the book argues, created a uniquely awkward situation for the British Government. Even as troops moved to subdue the Provisionals, alienating the Catholics, the British Government was actively engaged in trying to improve the position of the minority community, not least through its inclusion in government.[3] However, as Chapter Two argues, the former task prevented the successful completion of the latter. The dual nature of the British agenda in Ireland after 1970, to subdue the Provisionals but also to reform government to include the Catholics, added to the original ethnic tension in the Province.

In the early 1970s, it was the activity of the British military which attracted most attention and controversy. As Chapter Three explains, the British Army responded to the challenge of the PIRA by abandoning its neutral role and engaging in a formidable counter-insurgency campaign against an urban paramilitary opponent. Yet

1 On this issue of ethnic conflict in Ireland, see Arthur Aughey, *Under Siege: Ulster Unionism and the Anglo-Irish Agreement* (London: Hurst and Co., 1989), pp. 1–12. See also D. George Boyce, *Nationalism in Ireland* 3rd Edition (London: Routledge, 1995), and Steve Bruce, *The Edge of the Union* (Oxford: Oxford University Press, 1994).

2 See, for example, Tactics for Street Riots/Battles, 'Report on the Study Period by the GOC Northern Ireland HQNI, 22 January 1970, p. 23, held by the tactical Doctrine Retrieval Cell, HQT Avon.

3 Brigid Hadfield, *The Constitution of Northern Ireland* (Belfast: SLS, 1989).

another layer was thus added to the nature of the conflict – not only was it about managing ethnic conflict, it was also about how best to deal with the armed insurgents who denied the very legitimacy of the state. The British Government chose to respond through military toughness, basing its philosophy on the military experiences in the colonies. Many tactics originally devised for the far-flung reaches of the British Empire, such as Malaysia and Aden, were taken and used in Ireland. Not surprisingly, this turned the Catholic community against the British Army. The introduction of internment without trial in August 1971, for example, saw the complete estrangement of the Catholic community from the security forces.[4] Alongside the military toughness, a full range of 'emergency legislation' was enacted within the Province to make the task of the Army easier. By the mid-1970s, all of this culminated in some British military success. The Army managed to drive the provisional IRA from the cities of Northern Ireland. Yet, the military did not succeed in fully eradicating the threat from the paramilitaries. More seriously, as Chapter Three demonstrates, the actions of the military made the prospect of any peaceful accept-ance of change to the political system in the Province doubtful. Nevertheless, the British Government did try to promote reform in Northern Ireland, not least through the abolition of the Northern Irish Government and the imposition of Direct Rule in 1972. This was an attempt to govern the Province in a more equitable fashion; but Catholic acceptance of such reforms remained tempered by the actions and methods of the security forces.

There is little doubt that the British military made mistakes in this early period. Internment, for example, has been widely commented upon as a disaster, while the behaviour of troops during the internment operation of 1971 was regarded even by military sources as insensitive.[5] Yet, while accepting criticism of the military, this work points out that the Army in the early years was in an unenviable position. In the space of a few short years at the beginning of the decade, there were three changes of government in Westminster and Irish policy was riven at this stage with confusing and contradictory direction. This meant that British troops, committed as a temporary expedient in 1969, became immersed in a long-term campaign, but with no apparent political aim apart from the defeat of the PIRA.

4 See R.F. Foster, *Modern Ireland 1600–1972* (London: Penguin, 1988), pp. 590–1.
5 See Desmond Hamill, *Pig in the Middle: The Army in Northern Ireland 1969–1984* (London: Methuen, 1985), pp. 60–1.

The lack of overall coherence in British policy meant that the military, at some stages, played the central role in the conflict. Indeed in certain phases it can be argued that the military took advantage of the lack of political coherence to pursue its own line. In 1974, for example, when the Sunningdale Agreement was implemented to promote powersharing in the Province, it was the British military which helped undermine the agreement. The refusal of military leaders to break the strike organized by the Protestants to wreck Sunningdale, raised serious questions about the power of the military in periods of crisis. For example, should the military have been allowed to side with the Protestants, dictating a policy which effectively scuppered the inclusion of Catholics in the political machinery of Northern Ireland? Should or could the military have been overruled? These were and remain serious questions, but on the whole any clash between the civil and military branches in Ireland was avoided because, as Chapter Three demonstrates, the British Government itself was not completely committed to the Sunningdale process. Nevertheless, this instance remains one in which historians are entitled to ask, what would happen to the Sunningdale Agreement had the Army behaved differently? Not least, it raised the issue of whether the Army was effectively siding with the Protestant community against the imposition of powersharing. It was not a new phenomenon in Ireland. The question of the relationship between the British military and the Protestants had suffered criticism throughout the period of military engagement in Ireland, leading at some points to allegations of collusion to keep Unionists within the United Kingdom. This work argues, in Chapter Five, that this was only ever true of certain parts of the military in the contemporary period.

The failure of the Sunningdale Agreement in 1974, if not the military role in it, did however cause a reappraisal in the British side to try to alter radically the security equation in the Province, and if possible reduce the presence of the British troops, in the hope that there would be a concomitant decline in the British involvement in the policing issues of the Province. To this end the strategies of 'policy primacy' or so-called 'normalization' were devised. This meant that, as Chapter Four explains, the Army relinquished its leading role to the RUC and concentrated, in theory at least, on supporting the indigenous forces. From 1977 onwards, the profile of the Army was reduced in the cities, with the RUC adopting a greater role in policing in the cities. Police primacy did not, however, apply to rural areas. Indeed, in the border areas the Army was increased in strength and adopted ruthless counter-insurgency tactics in a bid to defeat finally the PIRA. Far from lowering the profile of the Army, the use of the SAS in the rural campaign provoked a great deal of controversy.[6] The military shift to the border meant a greater attention had to be paid to the views of the southern Irish Government, whose input into the Northern Irish process had since 1969 been marginalized by Westminster.

Despite this, the Government in Dublin had, throughout the period, expressed opinions on the conduct of the British Army in the North. What had particularly soured relations between Dublin and Westminster was the commitment of the southern Government to work towards a unified Republican Ireland. Indeed, even in the late 1970s, with the escalating conflict on the border, the British Government remained adamant that a southern Irish dimension could not be opened up because of this.[7] Yet, on the border, because it provided an escape route for paramilitaries, the southern Irish Government was *de facto* involved in the policing of the Province. There was some cooperation between the Irish police and the RUC, but as Chapter Four illustrates, real agreement on security issues remained problematic for both Governments, and necessarily hinged around the improvement of political relations between Dublin and Westminster. The issue of how far Dublin could be directly involved in the reform of Northern Ireland became one of the central questions of the conflict after 1980.

At the turn of the decade, the British Government remained committed to a strategy of 'police primacy' for the Province, despite what appeared to be successes of the PIRA against the RUC in the late 1970s. The ability of the PIRA, and indeed the other Republican paramilitary organization, the INLA, to score notable successes against the British establishment did cause a wobble, but not a lasting impression on British commitment to the policy. Mrs Thatcher was initially doubtful of the wisdom of allowing the RUC to police the Province, especially after the deaths, in separate incidents, of Lord Mountbatten and thirteen soldiers at Warrenpoint in 1979, but she was persuaded to continue the policy.[8] One issue that appeared particularly vexing

6 See Mark Urban, *Big Boys' Rules: The SAS and the Secret Struggle Against the IRA* (London: Faber & Faber, 1992).

7 See Margaret Thatcher, *The Downing Street Years* (London: HarperCollins, 1993), pp. 397–8.

8 J. Bowyer Bell, *The Irish Troubles: A Generation of Violence 1967–1992* (Dublin: Gill and Macmillan, 1992), p. 574.

was the seeming inability of the British Army and the RUC to share intelligence information and act in a coordinated manner. Attempts to resolve this issue were only ever partly successful, and professional rivalries continued to exist between the forces working in Ireland. This highlights the problem of trying to operate two security forces in a small area.

As Chapters Four and Five point out, the British Government came under increasing pressure at the beginning of the 1980s to restructure its approach to the Province. This was fuelled in part by the continued ability of the PIRA to operate and attract the sympathy of a proportion of the Northern Irish population. Support for the PIRA had grown during the period of police primacy. Partly this was because, alongside the promotion of the RUC, the British Government had also tried to 'depoliticize' the situation in Northern Ireland through a strategy of 'criminalization'. This meant that prisoners convicted of terrorist offences were treated as ordinary 'criminals', without the special privileges and status which had been accorded to them as 'political prisoners'. The reaction of the Republican prisoners and some parts of the Catholic community to this initiative led to one of the critical turning points of the modern conflict. Prisoners in the H-Block staged a series of protests, including a hunger strike. The success of the hunger strikers in attracting international publicity embarrassed the British Government. In the early 1980s pressure from both Europe and North America mounted in criticism of the handling of the 'hunger strike' by the Thatcher administration. One of the lessons of the modern conflict for the British Government was that Northern Ireland was not an area in which controversial strategies could be carried out, as it had in the colonies, without attracting attention. As Chapter Five argues, British leaders were not immune to international pressure. After the hunger strikes, the Thatcher Government did begin to discuss the policing of the Province with the Fitzgerald Government in the south, and the manner in which Dublin might be included in any reform process. All of this indicated a willingness on the British side to redefine the Irish situation. What the Thatcher Government was interested in was a way to decrease tensions, withdraw some, if not all, British troops and reinforce the notion of the conflict as a local one, but also bringing a political settlement closer. As Chapter Five suggests, part of this programme had to include a southern dimension. The Hillsborough Agreement of 1985 was therefore a defining moment for both British and Irish politicians. It not only allowed the southern Irish an institutional role in the affairs of Northern Ireland, but it also redefined the British link to the Province in *conditional* terms. Not surprisingly, this fuelled Unionist fears of a sell-out and the period from 1985–90 was characterized by a growth in sectarian violence and the increased activities of Protestant paramilitary groups[9] which were determined to force Westminster to allow them to stay in the United Kingdom. Despite hopes that after Hillsborough, the conflict in Northern Ireland could be redefined and contained at low levels, the rise in sectarian violence meant that British soldiers once again increased in numbers on the streets of the Province to help a beleaguered RUC. Chapter Six examines the redeployment of additional military resources into Northern Ireland. British troops were once more engaged in containing the PIRA, but were also policing sectarian attacks between the two communities. In the aftermath of the Hillsborough Agreement it appeared that the role of the Army in the Province was so institutionalized that withdrawal was impossible, if further political progress was to be made. By 1990, it appeared as if a stalemate had been reached in the affairs of Northern Ireland. Yet, this impasse sparked enormous efforts after 1990 to resolve the affairs of Ireland. Much of this determination built on the Hillsborough accord and involved a triangular dialogue between Westminster, Dublin and the 'power brokers' in Northern Ireland, namely Sinn Fein and the Ulster Unionists. The decade between 1985 and 1995 marked the move towards the so-called 'peace process' and in particular was characterized by the PIRA's declaration on 31 August 1994 that it had ordered a complete cessation of hostilities. The shift of Sinn Fein into legitimate politics form part of the core of Chapter Six. Sinn Fein leaders became integrally involved in the negotiation of any future settlement. The sight of former para-military prisoners, namely Gerry Adams and Martin McGuinness as central to the peace process was, and is, for many people an odd and uncomfortable one, yet given the development of the conflict, not unexpected. As the book has demonstrated, the British Government has a long track record of negotiating with Irish paramilitaries. Pragmatically, Westminster has recognized that without neutralizing the support for the paramilitary movement, including its leaders, a lasting settlement is impossible. What the peace process of the 1990s does raise in one of those neat but

9 See Bruce, op. cit., pp. 238–9.

ironical twists of Irish history is the prospect that the minority of Ireland will now take its place within the majority of Ireland but create a new minority – the Protestants. Yet, even as the exact parameters of the peace process remain unclear, the Army continues to underpin the process, ready for redeployment if necessary.

The early 1990s were a time of enormous change in world politics. The Cold War ended in 1989 with the collapse of Communism, the enlargement of the European Union seems certain to go ahead and the conflict in Northern Ireland remains one from which many lessons can be derived. In particular, the use of the British Army in Northern Ireland has highlighted the problems of a democratic state using its military forces to counter internal political violence.[10] These have been identified throughout the book. One problem common to such a case is that the commitment of troops into a situation of communal violence can actually make the conflict worse. This is what happened in Northern Ireland. In 1969, both the Protestant and Catholic communities expected the British Army to act on their behalf. When it became apparent that these hopes would not be fulfilled, communal violence dramatically increased, and the Catholics turned against the Army, thus broadening the dimensions of conflict.[11]

A second problem, which has generally been identified in situations of internal security duties is that using troops for such duties in a democratic state fundamentally conflicts with the traditional functions of a military.[12] For example, soldiers are trained to identify and destroy an enemy. However, in situations of internal policing it is often difficult to know who the enemy is. In 1970 in Northern Ireland the military adopted the attitude that the Catholic community was the enemy. Hence, the use of tactics such as internment. This meant that in many ways a self-fulfilling prophecy was set up – the Army targeted the Catholics, who then closed ranks against the Army.

Partly because of these reasons, the British Army found considerable difficulty in adapting to its initial role in Ireland. It was originally committed to what were essentially policing duties

---

10 Paul Wilkinson, *Terrorism and the Liberal State* (London: Macmillan, Second Edition 1986), p. 156.

11 See the Sunday Times Insight Team, *Ulster* (Harmondsworth: Penguin, 1972), p. 141.

12 Wilkinson, op. cit., pp. 156–9.

but without the training of a constabulary. Policemen and women are trained in their primary function, to arrest criminals, soldiers are not. 'Errors of judgement' by the military when they over-reacted to provocations led in turn to violent reactions by local communities. Indeed, one of the problems for the Army in Ireland was that its very presence raised uncomfortable memories of the historic role of the British in 'policing' Ireland. Hostility became a two-way street; Catholics came to resent the military, but equally the soldiers grew to resent not only the hostility of the Catholic community but also the abuse they often encountered while on duty. This was calculated to increase tension.

Yet, the story of British troops in Ireland is not simply of 'an Army' restrained and trying to perform a police function. Parts of the British Army have obviously performed a quite different role from that of 'policing'. Most notably, the use of special forces in Ireland, in particular the SAS, goes far beyond the remit of 'normal policing'. The actions of the SAS in its battle against the PIRA in rural areas was reminiscent of counter-insurgency campaigns in the colonies. Indeed, this explains why, in part, the role of the British Army has provoked so much controversy. In the campaign on the Irish border, soldiers have behaved like soldiers. Action has been taken and questions asked later. None of this should be surprising, but given the constantly maintained view of the British Government that Northern Ireland is not a 'war', the behaviour of the Army arouses comment. Some actions of the Army have been at variance with the publicly held view, maintained since 1973, that this is a controllable civil conflict. The confusion over whether Northern Ireland is 'policed' or 'soldiered' creates for the public concern over whether or not a 'shoot to kill' policy was, or is, operated in the Province. It has also meant for ordinary soldiers confusion over whether their actions are judged by military or civil standards. It is also noted, during this discussion, that with the enlargement of the European Union, Britain cannot now operate in isolation from European judgements; incidents such as the SAS shootings of paramilitary suspects in Gibraltar are shown to have had broader political ramifications. The conflict in Ireland has become a European issue. Chapters Six and Seven argue that some clarification of the role of the military standards by which it can be judged would be helpful.

The paradox of how to categorize the conflict has remained at the heart of the Irish security situation. It is not a war, but the

British have deployed considerable amounts of troops, money and thought in trying to defeat the PIRA.[13] The whole range of emergency legislation has been emplaced to deal with the paramilitaries, not least the 1973 Northern Ireland Emergency Provisions Act which provided the Army with enormous powers. It gave them open-ended permission to enter any premises at any time and to question anybody at any time for up to four hours.[14] Such measures lay uneasily with the notion of a limited conflict, but also with the view that the Province was part and parcel of the United Kingdom. Indeed, the enforcement of emergency legislation meant that it was difficult to achieve a political solution that would include the community – the Catholics – most affected by it. This was the security dilemma of Ireland – how to defeat the PIRA yet reconcile the Catholics and soothe Protestant fears of a 'sell-out'. The Army has had the task of underwriting all three aspects of the conflict.

13 Estimating the full costs to the British Government of its garrison in Ireland is difficult and complex. One estimate is from *Costs of War and Dividends of Peace*, published by West Belfast Economic Forum. It produced a 25-year (1969–94) total cost figure of £18,205 billion. Reproduced in http//wwwvms.utexas.edn/JDAWA/ irehist.html.

14 Charles Townshend, 'The Supreme Law: Public Safety and State Security in Northern Ireland' in Dermot Keogh and Michael H. Haltzel (eds), *Northern Ireland and the Politics of Reconciliation* (Cambridge: Cambridge University Press, 1993), pp. 96–7. See also Gerard Hogan and Clive Walker, *Political Violence and the Law in Northern Ireland* (Manchester: Manchester University Press, 1989).

Postscript

The distinguished historian R. F. Foster had described the politics of Ireland as defined by an absence of peace.[1] There were hopes during 1994–95 that peace could break out – permanently. This did not happen and the question once more for historians and analysts of the island is why has Irish history been so troubled? There are quite literally thousands of books on this subject. Indeed one author has suggested that, in proportion to its size, Northern Ireland has been the most heavily researched area on earth.[2] Despite the scholarship on the subject of the Province, there are few definitive answers to this question. In the 1990s the conflict in Ireland appears at once old fashioned but terribly modern. How – at the end of the twentieth century, an era of unprecedented scientific and economic progress – can men still be killing each other over the destiny of a small piece of land? Yet, given the outbreak of civil wars since the end of the Cold War in 1989, the failure to attain enduring peace in Northern Ireland has had a terrible and familiar resonance for other lands enduring conflict, from Bosnia through to Somalia. The question is a common one; how can peoples with different and conflicting political aspirations live in a small geographic area? When they resort to war, how can they be stopped?

These are big questions that require big answers. Even as this book is finished, in the context of Ireland they seem almost impossible to answer. Men and women on all sides of the Irish

---

1 Roy Foster, 'Defined by the absence of peace' A Review of Thomas Barlett and Keith Jeffery, *A Military History of Ireland* (Cambridge: Cambridge University Press, 1996) in *The Times*, 22 February 1996.

2 John Whyte, *Interpreting Northern Ireland* (Oxford: Clarendon Press, 1990), p. viii.

divide are attempting to find answers to the demands of both communities. But peace in Ireland as always, is fractured by violence. The PIRA have once again reinvigorated their campaign against the British mainland, staging bombings in 1996 in both London and Manchester. PIRA activities have resulted in the exclusion of Sinn Fein from the All Party talks, that it was hoped would set up a new political assembly for the Province. Nationalist paramilitary activity has the capacity to reactivate Loyalist violence and so it seems, the endless spiral of violence continues. Numbers of British troops in the Province are to be increased again.

The book began with an explanation of the roots of the conflict in Ireland during the early parts of this century – the conflict of two nationalisms living (and dying) side by side. The parameters of the struggle remain the same. The Unionists still wish to remain part of the United Kingdom while the nationalists, or the proponents of the more extreme version of it, still do not. Until these two viewpoints – these two Irish nationalisms – are reconciled, the British military will continue its historic role of being both part of the Irish problem and yet central to the underwriting of any solution.

Summer 1996

Select Bibliography

Books

ADAMS, GERRY, *Falls Memoirs* (Dingle: Brandon Books, 1982).

BARTLETT, THOMAS and JEFFREY, KEITH (eds), *A Military History of Ireland* (Cambridge: Cambridge University Press, 1996).

BARZILAY, DAVID, *The British Army in Ulster*, vols 1, 2 and 3 (Belfast: Century Books, 1973–81).

BELL, J. BOWYER, *The Secret Army. A History of the IRA* (Dublin: The Academy Press, 1970).

BELL, J. BOWYER, *A Time of Terror – How Democratic Societies Respond to Revolutionary Violence* (Columbia, NY: Basic Books, 1978).

BELL, J. BOWYER, *A Time of Terror: How Democratic Societies Respond to Revolutionary Violence* (New York: Basic Books, 1981).

BELL, J. BOWYER, *IRA Tactics and Targets* (Dublin: Poolbeg, 1990).

BOYLE, KEVIN, HADDON, TOM, HILLYARD, PADDY, *Ten Years on in Northern Ireland: The Level and Control of Political Violence* (London: The Cobden Trust, 1980).

BOULTAR, ROGER, *Death on the Rock* (London: W.H. Allen, 1990).

BRUCE, STEVE, *God Save Ulster! The Religion and Politics of Paisleyism* (Oxford: Oxford University Press, 1986).

BRUCE, STEVE, *The Red Hand: Protestant Paramilitaries in Northern Ireland* (Oxford: Oxford University Press, 1992).

BURTON, ANTHONY, *Urban Terrorism – Theory, Practice and Response* (London: Leo Cooper, 1975).

CALLAGHAN, JAMES, *A House Divided* (London: Collins, 1973).

CLUTTERBUCK, RICHARD, *The Long War: The Emergency in Malaya 1948–1960* (London: Cassell, 1967).

CLUTTERBUCK, RICHARD, *Protest and the Urban Guerrilla* (London: Cassell, 1973).

COOGAN, TIM PAT, *The IRA* (Glasgow: Fontana, 1980).

COOGAN, TIM PAT, *The Troubles: Ireland's Ordeal 1966–1995 and the Search for Peace* (London: Hutchinson, 1995).

CRONIN, SEAN, *Irish Nationalism: A History of its Roots and Ideology* (Dublin: Academy Press, 1980).

CURTIS, LIZ, *Ireland the Propaganda War* (London: Pluto Press, 1984).

DEVLIN, BERNADETTE, *The Price of My Soul* (London: Pan, 1969).

DEWAR, LIEUTENANT-COLONEL MICHAEL, *The British Army in Northern Ireland* (London: Arms and Armour Press, 1985).

DILLON, MARTIN, *The Enemy Within: The IRA's War Against the British* (London: Doubleday, 1994).

DILLON, MARTIN and LEHANE, DENNIS, *Political Murder in Northern Ireland* (London: Penguin, 1973).

DUNN, JOHN, *Modern Revolutions: An Introduction to the Analysis of a Political Phenomenon* (Cambridge: Cambridge University Press, 1972).

EVELEGH, ROBIN, *Peace-Keeping in a Democratic Society* (London: Hurst and Co., 1978).

FALIGOT, ROGER, *The Kitson Experiment* (London: Zed Press, 1983).

FARRELL, MICHAEL, *Northern Ireland: The Orange State* (London: Pluto Press, 1980).

FARRELL, MICHAEL, *Arming the Protestants. The Formation of the Ulster Special Constabulary and the Royal Ulster Constabulary 1920–1927* (London: Pluto, 1983).

FAULKNER, BRIAN, *Memoirs of a Statesman* (London: Weidenfeld and Nicolson, 1978).

FISK, ROBERT, *The Point of No Return: The Strike Which Broke the British in Ulster* (London: André Deutsch, 1975).

FITZGERALD, GARRETT, *All in a Life* (Dublin: Gill and Macmillan, 1989).

FOSTER, ROY, F., *Modern Ireland 1600–1972* (London: Penguin, 1988).

HAMILL, DESMOND, *Pig in the Middle: The Army in Northern Ireland 1969–1984* (London: Methuen, 1985).

HANNING, HUGH, *Ulster, Brasseys Annual* (June 1971).

HASTINGS, MAX, *Ulster 1969* (London: Gollancz, 1970).
HOPKINSON, MICHAEL, *Green Against Green: The Irish Civil War* (Dublin: Gill and Macmillan, 1988).

KEE, ROBERT, *The Most Distressful Country.* Vol. one of *The Green Flag* (London: Quartet Books, 1976).
KELLY, KEVIN, *The Longest War* (Dublin: Brandon Books, 1982).
KEOGH, DERMOT and HALTZEL, MICHAEL (eds), *Northern Ireland and the Politics of Reconciliation* (Cambridge: Cambridge University Press, 1993).
KITSON, FRANK, *Low-Intensity Operations: Subversion, Insurgency, Peacekeeping* (London: Faber & Faber, 1971).
KITSON, FRANK, *Bunch of Five* (London: Faber & Faber, 1977).

LACQUER, WALTER, *The Terrorism Reader* (London: Wildwood House, 1979).
LAWSON, NIGEL, *The View from No. 11* (London: Bantam, 1982).

MACSTIOFAIN, SEAN, *Memoirs of a Revolutionary* (London: Gordon Cremonesi, 1975).
MANSERGH, NICHOLAS, *The Unresolved Question. The Anglo-Irish Settlement and its Undoing, 1912–1972* (New Haven, CT: Yale University Press, 1991).
MCARDLE, PATSY, *The Secret War* (Dublin: Mercier Press, 1984).
MCGUFFIN, JOHN, *The Guineapigs* (London: Penguin, 1974).
MCGUIRE, MAIRA, *To Take up Arms* (London: Penguin, 1973).
MCKITTERICK, DAVID, Endgame: *The Search for Peace in Northern Ireland* (Belfast: Blackstaff Press, 1994).
MOSS, ROBERT, *Urban Guerrillas* (London: Temple Smith, 1972).
MUENGER, ELIZABETH A., *The British Military Dilemma in Ireland Occupation Politics, 1886–1914* (Kansas/Dublin: University Press of Kansas/Gill and Macmillan, 1991).
MURRAY, R., *The SAS in Ireland* (Cork: Mercier Press, 1990).

NELSON, SARAH, *Ulster's Uncertain Defenders: Protestant Political, Paramilitary and Community Groups and the Northern Ireland Conflict* (Belfast: Appletree Press, 1984).

O'BRIEN, CONOR CRUISE, *States of Ireland* (New York: Pantheon Books, 1972).
O'FARRELL, PATRICK, *Ireland's English Question* (London: Batsford, 1971).

O'MALLEY, PADRAIG, *The Uncivil Wars, Ireland Today* (Belfast: Blackstaff Press, 1983).
O'NEILL, TERENCE, *Ulster at the Cross-roads* (London: Faber, & Faber 1969).

PAGET, ROBERT, *Last Post, Aden* (London: Faber & Faber, 1969).
PIMLOTT, BEN, *Harold Wilson* (London: HarperCollins, 1992).
PURDIE, B., *Politics in the Streets: The Origins of the Civil Rights Movement in Northern Ireland* (Belfast: Blackstaff Press, 1990).

ROSE, RICHARD, *Governing Without Consensus: An Irish Perspective* (Boston, MA: Beacon Press, 1971).

SMITH, M.L.R., *Fighting For Ireland: The Military Strategy of the Irish Republican Movement* (London: Routledge, 1995).
STERLING, CLAIRE, *The Terror Network* (London: Weidenfeld and Nicolson, 1981).
SUNDAY TIMES INSIGHT TEAM, *Ulster* (Harmondsworth: Penguin, 1972).

TABER, ROBERT, *The War of the Flea* (St Albans: Paladin, 1971).
TAYLOR, PETER, *Beating the Terrorists* (London: Penguin, 1980).
TOWNSHEND, CHARLES, *Political Violence in Ireland: Government and Resistance since 1848* (Oxford: Oxford University Press, 1983).
TOWNSHEND, CHARLES, *The British Campaign in Ireland 1919–21: The Development of Political and Military Policies* (Oxford: Clarendon Press, 1975).

URBAN, MARK, *Big Boys' Rules. The SAS and the Secret Struggle Against the IRA* (London: Faber & Faber, 1992).

WALLACE, MARTIN, *Northern Ireland: 50 Years of Self-Government* (Newton Abbott: David and Charles, 1971).
WAPSHOTT, NICHOLAS and BROCK, GEORGE, *Thatcher* (London: Futura, 1983).
WATT, DAVID (ed.), *The Constitution of Northern Ireland: Problems and Prospects* (London: Heinemann, 1981).
WHITELAW, WILLIAM, *Memoirs* (London: Aurum, 1989).
WHYTE, JOHN, *Interpreting Northern Ireland* (Oxford: Clarendon Press, 1990).
WILKINSON, PAUL (ed.), *British Perspectives on Terrorism* (London: Macmillan, 1986).
WILKINSON, PAUL (ed.), *Terrorism and the Liberal State* (London: Macmillan, Second Edition 1986).

Articles

ARCHER, JEFFREY, 'Constitutionalism and Violence: The Case of Ireland', *Journal of Commonwealth and Comparative Politics* 22 (1984), pp. 111–27.

ASCHER, WILLIAM, 'The Moralism of Attitudes Supporting Intergroup Violence', *Political Psychology* 7 (1986), pp. 403–25.

AUGHEY, ARTHUR, 'Between Exclusion and Recognition: The Politics of the Ulster Defence Association', *Conflict Quarterly* 1 (1985), pp. 40–52.

BELL, J. BOWYER, 'The Chronicles of Violence in Northern Ireland: A Tragedy in Endless Acts', *Review of Politics* B8, no. 4 (October 1976), pp. 510–33.

BEW, PAUL and PATTERSON, HENRY, 'The Protestant–Catholic Conflict in Ulster', *Journal of International Affairs* 36 (1982), pp. 223–34.

BOWDEN, T., 'The IRA and the Changing Tactics of Terrorism', *Political Quarterly* xl, vii (1976), pp. 425–37.

CARLTON, CHARLES, 'Judging Without Consensus: The Diplock Courts in Northern Ireland', *Law and Policy Quarterly* 3 (1981), pp. 225–42.

CHALFONT, LORD, 'The Army and the IRA', *New Statesman* (2 April 1971).

CHARTERS, DAVID, 'Intelligence and Psychological Warfare Operations in Northern Ireland', *Journal of the Royal Services Institute for Defence Studies,* September 1977, 122 (1977), pp. 22–7.

COLE, JOHN, 'Security Constraints' in DAVID WATT (ed.), *The Constitution of Northern Ireland* (London: Heinemann, 1981), pp. 140–5.

ENLOE, C.H., 'Police and Military in Ulster: Peace-keeping or Peace Subverting', *Journal of Peace Research* 15, 3 (1978), pp. 243–59.

FIELDS, RONA M., 'Psychological Genocide: The Children of Northern Ireland', *History of Childhood Quarterly* 3 (1975), pp. 201–24.

FINN, JOHN E., 'Public Support for Emergency (Anti-Terrorist) Legislation in Northern Ireland: A Preliminary Analysis', *Terrorism: An International Journal* 10 (1987), pp. 113–24.

FISK, ROBERT, 'The Effect of Violence' in *The British Question Erroneously Called the Irish Question*, The Polytechnic of Wales Environment Group (26 February 1976).

FOLEY, THOMAS P., 'Public Security and Individual Freedom: The Dilemma of Northern Ireland', *The Yale Journal of World Public Order* 8 (1982), pp. 284–324.

FOX, MAJOR K.O., 'Capital Punishment and Terrorist Murder: The Continuing Debate', *Army Quarterly and Defence Journal* 106, (1976), pp. 189–93.

FROMKIN, DAVID, 'The Strategy of Terrorism', *Foreign Affairs* (July 1975), pp. 683–98.

GARRET, B., '10 Years of British Troops in Northern Ireland', *International Security* 4 (1980).

GRAHAM, LIEUTENANT-COLONEL P.W., 'Low Level Civil Military Co-ordination – Belfast 1970–1973', *Royal United Services Institute Defence Study Journal* (September 1974), pp. 80–4.

HALL, R.A., 'Violence and its Effects on the Community', *Medico-Legal Journal* 43 (1975), pp. 89–100.

HANNING, HUGH, 'Ulster', *Brasseys Annual* (June 1971), pp. 147–57.

HILLYARD, PADDY, 'Law and Order in John Darby' in Paddy Hillyard (ed.), *Northern Ireland: The Background to Conflict* (Syracuse, NY: Appletree Press, 1983).

HOLDEN REID, BRIAN, 'The Experience of the British Army in Northern Ireland' in Yonah Alexander and Alan O'Day, *Ireland's Terrorist Dilemma* (Dordrecht: Martinus Nijhoff publishers, 1986), pp. 249–61.

JACKSON, H., 'The Two Irelands, The Problem of the Double Minority – A Duel Study of Inter-group Tension', *The Minority Rights Group Report No. 2* (London: Minority Rights Group, 1972).

JANKE, PETER, 'Return to Direct Rule', *Conflict Studies* 50 (October 1974), pp. 1–7.

JORGENSEN, BIRTHE, 'Defending the Terrorists: Queen's Counsel before the Courts of Northern Ireland', *Journal of Law & Society* 9 (1982), pp. 115–26.

LOWRY, DAVID R., 'Terrorism and Human Rights: Counter-insurgency and Necessity at Common Law', *Notre Dame Lawyer* 53 (1977), pp. 49–89.

MCILHENEY, COLIN P., 'Arbiters of Ulster's Destiny? The Military Role of the Protestant Paramilitaries in Northern Ireland', *Conflict Quarterly* 5 (1985), pp. 33–40.

MOXON-BROWN, E., 'The Water and the Fish: Public Opinion and the Provisional IRA' in Paul Wilkinson (ed.), *British Perspectives on Terrorism* (London: George Allen and Unwin, 1981), pp. 41–73.

MOXON-BROWN, E., 'Alienation: The Case of the Catholics in Northern Ireland', *Journal of Political Science* 14 (1986), pp. 74–88.

MURRAY, RUSSELL, 'Killings of Local Security Forces in Northern Ireland 1969–1981', *Terrorism: An International Journal* 7 (1984), pp. 11–52.

O'DONOGHUE, JOSEPH and O'DONOGHUE, MARY ANN, 'Toward Understanding Group Conflict in Northern Ireland', *International Journal of Group Tensions* 11 (1981), pp. 119–25.

O'KEEFE, TERENCE, 'Alienated in Ulster', *The Tablet* (15 December 1984).

POCKRASS, ROBERT M., 'Terroristic Murder in Northern Ireland: Who is Killed and Why?', *Terrorism: An International Journal* 9.4 (1987), pp. 341–59.

PRICE, D.L., 'Security Attrition Tactics', *Conflict Studies* 50 (October 1974), pp. 7–21.

ROSENHEAD, J., 'Less Lethal Weapons', *New Scientist* (16 December 1976).

SCHELLENBERG, JAMES A., 'Area Variations of Violence in Northern Ireland', *Sociological Focus* 10 (1977), pp. 69–78.

SPJUT, ROBERT J., 'Criminal Statistics and Statistics on Security in Northern Ireland', *British Journal of Criminology* 23 (1983), pp. 358–80.

STONE, J.L. JR, 'Irish Terrorism Investigations', *FBI Law Enforcement Bulletin* (October 1987), pp. 18–23.

TUGWELL, MAJOR-GENERAL MAURICE, 'Revolutionary Prospects and Possible Counter Measures', National Defence College, 1976/77.

WARNER, BRUCE, 'Extradition Law and Practice in the Crucible of Ulster, Ireland and Great Britain: A Metamorphosis?', *Conflict Quarterly* 7 (1987), pp. 57–92.

Newspapers and periodicals

The Economist	*The Listener*
The Guardian	*The Times*
The Irish Times	*The Sunday Observer*

Reports

Amnesty International, UK, *Killings by Security Forces in Northern Ireland* (updated) London, 1990.

Bennett Report on RUC Interrogation Methods, Cmnd 7497, HMSO, London, 1979.

Cameron Report into Disturbances in Northern Ireland, Cmd 532, HMSO, Belfast, 1969.

Diplock Report of Commission on New Legal Procedures to Deal with Suspected Terrorists, Cmnd 5185, HMSO, London, 1972.

Hunt Report on Police in Northern Ireland, Cmd 535, HMSO, Belfast, 1969.

The Parker Report, Cmnd 4901, HMSO, London, 1972.

The Scarman Tribunal, Violence and Civil Disturbances in Northern Ireland in 1969, Cmd 566 (2 vols), HMSO, Belfast, 1972.

Report of the Tribunal Appointed to inquire into the events of Sunday January 30, 1972 which led to the loss of life in Connection with the procession in Londonderry on that day. By the Rt Hon Lord Widgery, OBE. HL 101, HC 220.

Official publications

British Army Land Operations, Vol. 3 Counter Revolutionary Operations (Ministry of Defence) 29 August 1979.

The Future of Northern Ireland. A Paper for Discussion, HMSO, London, 1972.

The Government of Northern Ireland, Proposals for Further Discussion, Cmnd 7950, HMSO, London, 1980.

The Northern Ireland Constitution, Cmnd 5675, HMSO, London, 1974.

House of Commons Parliamentary Debates, 5 series.

House of Commons Parliamentary Debates, 6 series.

Maps

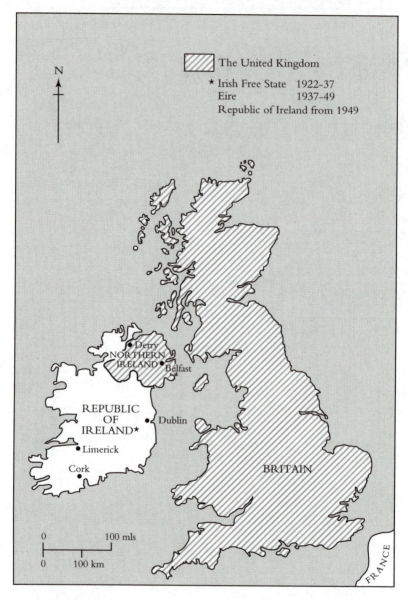

1 *The British Isles*

N

DONEGAL
U L S T E R
LONDONDERRY
ANTRIM
TYRONE
FERMANAGH
DOWN
ARMAGH
MONAGHAN
SLIGO
LEITRIM
MAYO
CAVAN
ROSCOMMON
LOUTH
C O N N A C H T
LONGFORD
MEATH
WESTMEATH
GALWAY
L E I N S T E R
DUBLIN
OFFALY
LEIX
KILDARE
WICKLOW
CLARE
CARLOW
KILKENNY
LIMERICK
M U N S T E R
TIPPERARY
WEXFORD
KERRY
CORK
WATERFORD

0   100 km
0   60 mls

– – – counties
–·–·– administrative provinces
——— boundary between
Northern Ireland and
the Republic of Ireland

2 *Ireland*

3. *Northern Ireland*

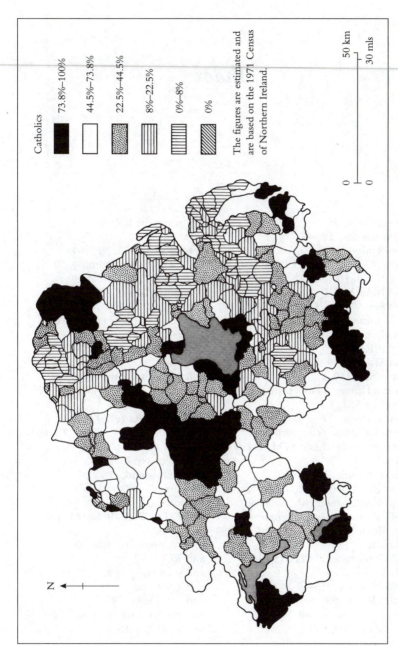

Catholics

■ 73.8%–100%

□ 44.5%–73.8%

▨ 22.5%–44.5%

▥ 8%–22.5%

▤ 0%–8%

▧ 0%

The figures are estimated and are based on the 1971 Census of Northern Ireland.

N ←

50 km
30 mls
0
0

4 *Sectarian population distribution*

Index

Hillsborough Castle, 122
historical factors, 11, 33
Holroyd, Fred, 144
Home Rule, 10, 11, 12, 15
Home Rule Act, 1914, 13
Homeless Citizens League, 40
hot pursuit, 102
House of Lords, 133
house searches, 53, 54
housing, 40, 44, 50
Howes, Robert, 138
Hume, John, 90, 117, 121, 140,
   141, 142, 146, 149, 152, 154, 160
Hume/Adams principles, 154, 157
hunger strikes, 86, 87, 100–1, 107,
   113, 114, 115, 174
Hunt, Sir Peter, 71–2
Hunt Committee, 80
Hunt Report, 50, 51, 80
Hurd, Douglas, 121, 139

identities, 8, 10, 30
identity cards, 66
information sources, 60, 88
informer witness *see* supergrasses
INLA (Irish National Liberation
   Army)
  activities of, 84, 109–10
  and supergrasses, 115
institutions of the Province, 2, 21,
   22
integration policy, 106
intelligence, use of, 65, 67–8
intelligence documents, 145
intelligence operations, 67–8
intelligence sources, 55, 74
international opinion, 107, 111,
   113–14
'internationalization' of the
   conflict, 6
internment, 2, 22, 29, 54–5, 57,
   58–60, 61, 68, 80, 86, 88, 100,
   114, 135, 171
interrogation, 68–9, 88, 114
IRA (Irish Republican Army), viii,
   14, 17, 43–4
  activities by, 20, 28–9, 46, 47
  and Anglo-Irish treaty, 19–20

attitude to Dublin of, 2
attitude of British Government
   to, 16
and Civil Rights movement, 43
conference, 43–4
during WWII, 26
electoral activity of, 108
formation of, 13
internal schism, 30
irregulars, 19–20
and North, 28, 29
Northern parts of, 23
role of, 51–2
under Collins, 16
see also communism; PIRA
Ireland, Republic of, constitution,
   99–100
Irish Army, 117
Irish Broadcasting Act, 108
Irish Committee, 1919, 18
Irish Constitution, 20, 25–6, 28,
   119, 160
Irish Framework Document of
   1995, 166
Irish Free State, 17, 20
Irish Government *see* Dublin
   Government
Irish Independent Party, 140
Irish language, 152
Irish National Liberation Army *see*
   INLA
Irish nationalism *see* nationalism
Irish Parliamentary Party, 13
Irish Rangers, 162
Irish Republican Army *see* IRA
Irish Republican Brotherhood, 13
Irish Special Branch, 43
Irish Supreme Court, 133
Irish War of Independence *see*
   Anglo-Irish war
Israel, 56, 57

James II, king of England, 9
judicial system, 115, 136, 138, 139
judiciary, problems of, 115, 134

Kelly, John, 62
Kilbrandon Committee, 119